the great book of
ARCHAEOLOGY

vmb
PUBLISHERS

the great book of
ARCHAEOLOGY

CONTENTS

Introduction	page 10
EUROPE	page 20
Lascaux (France)	page 28
Carnac (France)	page 34
Stonehenge (Great Britain)	page 36
Knossos (Greece)	page 38
Mycenae (Greece)	page 48
Athens (Greece)	page 56
Paestum (Italy)	page 64
Tarquinia (Italy)	page 74
Pompeii (Italy)	page 78
Rome (Italy)	page 96
Hadrian's Villa (Italy)	page 114
AFRICA	page 120
Saqqara and Giza (Egypt)	page 128
Karnak (Egypt)	page 144
Luxor (Egypt)	page 158
West of Thebes (Egypt)	page 166
The Nubian Temples (Egypt)	page 192
Abu Simbel (Egypt)	page 200
Philae (Egypt)	page 208
Leptis Magna (Lybia)	page 216
ASIA	page 228
Nemruth Dagh (Turkey)	page 236
Ephesus (Turkey)	page 246
Herodion (Israel)	page 256
Masada (Israel)	page 260
Petra (Jordan)	page 266
Palmyra (Syria)	page 278
Babylon (Iraq)	page 288
Ur (Iraq)	page 292
Persepolis (Iran)	page 296
Sanchi (India)	page 312
Mamallipuram (India)	page 320
Ajanta (India)	page 330
Pagan (Burma)	page 340
Borobudur (Indonesia)	page 352
Angkor (Cambodia)	page 362
Xi'an (China)	page 380
The Caves of Longmen (China)	page 394
AMERICAS AND OCEANIA	page 402
Mesa Verde (U.S.A.)	page 410
Teotihuacan (Mexico)	page 416
Monte Albán (Mexico)	page 424
Palenque (Mexico)	page 430
Tikal (Guatemala)	page 442
Uxmal (Mexico)	page 450
Chichén Itzá (Mexico)	page 460
Chan Chan (Peru)	page 470
Cuzco (Peru)	page 476
Ollantaytambo (Peru)	page 482
Macchu Picchu (Peru)	page 488
Tiahuanaco (Bolivia)	page 498
Easter Island (Chile)	page 502
GLOSSARY	page 510
BIBLIOGRAPHY	page 510

Texts
Maria Ausilia Albanese,
Fabio Bourbon,
Guido Massimo Corradi,
Sara Demichelis,
Furio Durando,
Maria Longhena,
Sarah Kochav,
Giuseppina Merchionne,
Desideria Viola,
Francesco Tiradritti

Editors
Valeria Manferto De Fabianis
Fabio Bourbon

English translation editor
Irene Cumming Kleeberg

Translation
C.T.M. Milan

Graphic design
Patrizia Balocco, Anna Galliani,
Paola Piacco, Clara Zanotti

An imprint of White Star S.p.A., Italy

© 2005, 2007 White Star S.p.A.
New integrated edition

© 1998 - SPLENDORS OF
THE LOST CIVILISATIONS
White Star S.p.A.
Via Candido Sassone, 24
13100 Vercelli, Italy
www.whitestar.it

ISBN: 978-88-540-0395-8

1 The work of Phydia, this slab
of Ionian frieze that adorned the
cell of the Parthenon, showing
Poseidon, Apollo and Artemis.

2-3 Portrayed for eternity
in the stone of the temple of Luxor,
Ramses II looks solemnly on at the
unstoppable passage of time.

4-5 The Colosseum is the most
grandiose monument of Ancient
Rome, regarded as the symbol of
the city itself in the course of the
centuries.

6-7 The temple of Zeus rises
majestic in upper Cyrene in Libya.

8 This splendid bas-relief
on the Stupa 1 of Sanchi is
typical of the elaborate and
extremely rich decorative tastes
of India.

9 Discovered in 1860 by a group
of French botanists, Angkor was
the superb capital of the Khmer
empire, in the modern
Kampuchea, between the 9th
and 13th centuries.

INTRODUCTION
Introduction

How many times have we asked ourselves, "What happened to them?" How many times, walking among the ruins brought to light by an archaeological excavation or, more simply, watching a documentary from the comfort of our armchair, or leafing through a magazine with photographs of Pompeii, have we wondered, "How did they live? What were their habits and passions, and their daily problems?" At times like this, we have to go further and ask, "What did they think of their predecessors, what questions did they ask about their own past, these predecessors of ourselves, living in the here and now?" It may seem strange, but it really was like that - the Romans observed the pyramids of Giza and asked themselves about the pharaohs who had built them, just like the Aztecs, as they wandered through the immense remains of Teotihuacan, asked themselves what had happened to the builders of the deserted metropolis. Right from the start of civilisation, when men think about the generations that have passed, they asked themselves these questions, as they are aware that their history, enclosed in a brief period of time, makes sense only because there is nothing definite or concluded about it, it is not an episode with a beginning and an end, but part of an infinite sequence, an effect that generated a cause in an eternal play of movement. Men soon discovered that if they wanted to know themselves well they

would have to find out what had been there before them and at the same time leave behind evidence of themselves to those destined to follow them. And it is precisely for this reason that history has always taken the trouble to clear up the events of the past and understand as far as possible their meaning and the reasons behind them. In this ongoing research, every minimum detail is useful, every piece of evidence could be of inestimable value - inscriptions, parchments, papyrus documents. But also monuments, statues, everyday objects, weapons, cooking utensils and jars. To put it simply, archaeological finds. All these things are useful to history, to produce a more complete picture and clarify our vision, and in this difficult task archaeology is our closest ally. The meaning of this word, deriving from the Greek, is literally "the science of ancient things", which means that archaeology is the discipline that studies the civilisation of the past by seeking out buried evidence. Archaeology takes fabulous cities and the memory of struggles, victories, conquests and defeats from obscurity and makes them re-emerge, but it also deals with knowledge of the daily events of peoples who suffered, rejoiced and loved, just like we do. Archaeology brings to light the more or less grandiose remains of their efforts, aspirations and beliefs, their opinions on life and death. Archaeology gives us back the art of the past and helps us to understand how it was produced. It reconstructs the battlefields and explains what weapons were used by armies reduced to dust many centuries ago. It discovers the *boleuterion* of Pryene and reveals how the Greeks ran their political

affairs. It tears the towering pyramids of Tikal from the green embrace of the jungle and enables us to imagine how the Mayan religious ceremonies were run. It rebuilds the *stupas* of Taxila and discovers how Buddhism evolved. If we look at it in these terms, archaeology is no longer that boring subject that we so often imagine it to be. It is more than just a heap of stones recomposed, or a tedious scattering of shards and fragments, or drawings of the plans of four broken walls. It is the rediscovery of our very essence as human beings, the heady perfume of spices we have never tasted, the passionate discovery of different solutions to the same problems. When we stop thinking of archaeology as a trite jumble of architectural remains, or a succession of glass cases full of precisely catalogued objects, terribly cold for anyone not involved in the work, archaeology is transformed into a magnificent adventure, a living creature able to take us on a trip through time. Archaeology opens windows on scenes we had never imagined, or surprises us by revealing the precious secret

of the little things, of forgotten customs, gestures repeated to infinity in the spiral of the centuries.

Every day, in some part of the world, the archaeologists provide us with the answers to a thousand questions, transforming the past into a living, breathing reality, capable of changing the way we look at our present. The curiosity to know how the Romans ate, how they dressed or decorated their homes, how they entertained themselves or spent their evenings is not a mere exercise of the imagination. The attempt to discover the means of heating and lighting in ancient China is not just an empty gesture.

To find out how the Incas were able to cut immense stone blocks without using metal tools is as concrete an activity as learning to use a computer. Answering these questions helps us to understand a little more about ourselves. To discover that Roman matrons used umbrellas or carried handbags, that Egyptian women used anti-wrinkle creams and dyed their hair is not just an entertaining pastime, but teaches us that desires and aspirations, as well as the solutions to contingent problems, remain the same throughout time and place, and that it is exactly this that makes us belong to *homo sapiens*. It is impossible to think about our world in the here and now without imagining a past, and we cannot

10-11 A crossroads of different cultures, Petra was the capital of the Nabatians. In its rock monuments - here we see the "Convent" - the styles of Syrian art can be seen alongside those imported from the Greek-Roman world.

11 below Even the greats of history had their weaknesses. This great colossus of Amenophi III, in front of the passageway that leads from the first courtyard to the great colonnade in the temple of Luxor, was usurped by Ramses II.

think of this world of the past in any other way than as something similar to our own, with the needs, habits and ways of life which have always been imposed on man from the very condition of his being. Archaeology, to paraphrase Thucydides, is a "*ktèma es aièï*", a possession for eternity, as it offers us the keys to universal understanding, with which we can face up to the future, knowing that at any time we might find ourselves faced with identical or similar realities to those that have already existed. Even more, archaeology is above the ethical, political and religious models, as it expresses no assessments or judgements, but merely testifies to what has been in every time and place. From this great ocean of information and data, it is up to us to distil a comprehension that is truly and literally universal.

Archaeology tells us, in fact, that in different times and places men worshipped different gods in identical ways, fought different wars for the same ideals and build different types of structures to affirm the same dominance over the elements. It tells us that some civilisations have emerged and others fallen, that at every latitude men have built bridges

to cross rivers, at every longitude they have built roofs to protect themselves and offer shelter to their descendants. Archaeology tries to respond to our initial "What happened to them?" to provide an answer to a much more difficult question: "What is going to happen to us?"

It also tells us what mistakes have been made and how many times. It is a warning and at the same time a source of hope, as it explains that after every defeat there comes a rebirth. Overall, archaeology allows us to understand - and this is its great teaching - that beyond religion, language and the colour of the skin, man is simply the "naked ape" described by the great English ethnologist Desmond Morris, a monkey who came down from the trees over a million years ago and is still struggling to trace out his route on this planet.

Often we find ourselves saying, "How times have changed!" Is it true, though?
Let's leaf through the pages of this book, observing temples and fortresses. Everything has been built to respond to the same needs, in the forests of Kampuchea, as on the high plains of Peru. The washing facilities in the palace of Masada, on the Dead Sea, are surprisingly similar to those we use every day, the Etruscans poured out the same wine that delights our palates today, the monks of Borobudur sent the same prayers upwards to the heavens as those recited every day by the disciples of the Dalai Lama.

Certainly, a single book is not enough to explain the wonders of archaeology and - in a broader sense - the wonders of the ancient civilisations. However, this book, which offers an overall and updated view of archaeological research in the five

continents, enables us to go back to the past of man in an engrossing way, thanks to the remarkable photographs and drawings, and the texts that give a brief but comprehensive illustration of the main centres of development of the most important cultures of the entire world. In this way, the original appearance of these places and the lifestyle of their inhabitants re-emerge, from the day-to-day customs of Ancient Rome to the religious ceremonies performed at the foot of the Mayan pyramids of Palenque, from the immense efforts made in the building of the temples of Abu Simbel to the luxury of the Khmer court at Angkor Thom.

In conclusion, the selection of the sites to be included and those to leave out was by no means easy, and may to a certain extent seem subjective. We would just like to say that, considering the non-technical nature of the book, we have given preference to the sites that best represent the various civilisations in terms of their visual appearance.

Fabio Bourbon

12-13 Dancers, saints, princes and courtesans populate the temple of Borobudur, showing how life was lived in Java between the 8th and 9th centuries. In archaeology, books are frequently made of stone.

12 top left The enigmatic eyes of one of the colossal statues of Nemrut Dagh, in Turkey, seem to allude to the infinite secrets that archaeology has yet to reveal.

12 top right Another expression loaded with mystery can be seen in this jadeite mask found in Xochicalco, in Mexico.

12 bottom The moai of Easter Island represent the quintessence of the unknown.

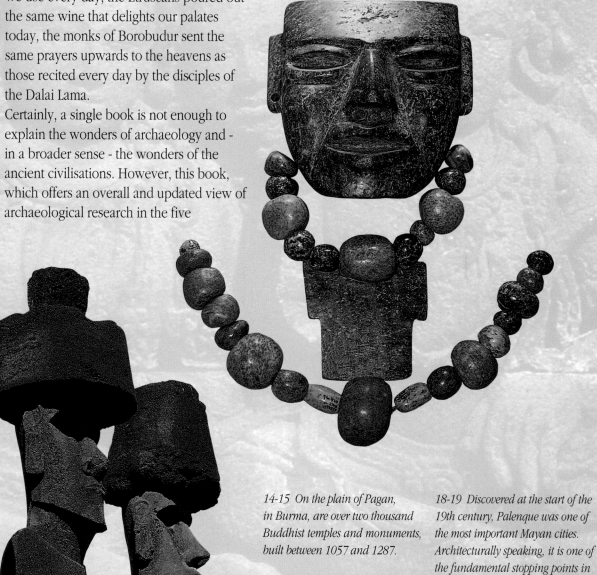

14-15 On the plain of Pagan, in Burma, are over two thousand Buddhist temples and monuments, built between 1057 and 1287.

16-17 The temples of Khajuraho in India are decorated with innumerable statues.

18-19 Discovered at the start of the 19th century, Palenque was one of the most important Mayan cities. Architecturally speaking, it is one of the fundamental stopping points in the history of this ancient civilisation, and yet some of its monuments have still to be unearthed.

EUROPE
Introduction

Europe, the ancient mother of western civilization, has a history dating back thousands of years, a history that can only be told through the marvels of the famous archaeological sites that reveal the past which we would otherwise never know. While the well-known places continue to justify their fame, there are other places, less well-known, which almost take us by surprise with their revelations about the history of this area of the world. And these treasures are not only to be found in archaeological sites. Many of the elements of the past can be found, rightly or wrongly, in museums not only in Europe but throughout the world.

Consider this section of this book, then, as an introduction to what can be seen in Europe, what can be learned. For those who are just beginning to view archaeology as an accessible field of knowledge the well-beaten tracks to Carnac and Stonehenge, Mycenae and Athens, Rome and Pompeii can be seen here. And even those who have already visited these sites will find new information about these places. Furthermore, these examples can inspire visits to other destinations, less well known, in the future. Those wishing to go further should consider the Viking fort of Fyrkat in Denmark, the Greek houses of Ampurias in Spain, the remains of the Gallic Masada, the green Alesia in France, or the Roman remains of Aosta and Aquileia, Carsulae and Herdoniae, Piazza Armerina and Venosa, in Italy, the rock-salt mines of the Celts in Hallein and Hallstatt, in Austria, Diocletian's palace in Split, Croatia, or the solitary Kassope in Epyrus. Every discovery is worth the trip.

The history of ancient Europe is full, rich and fascinating. The little known history before Greek and Rome made their civilizations felt is especially interesting.

No one is sure when man first appeared, although some scholars believe that paleontological finds in France and Spain date back to one and one-half or two million years ago. The first humans who definitely lived on the continent are believed to be Homo Erectus who was apparently present in Spain, France, Germany and Italy between 300,000 and a million years ago during the Early Paleolithic Age, an extremely long period of alternating ice and thaw. These early humans lived in small groups of individuals who knew how to make rudimentary stone tools, and ate vegetables and the remains of prey left behind by larger predators. They began to hunt themselves only in the Middle Paleolithic Age (300,000-30,000 years ago), in communities of the most primitive form of Homo Sapiens, also known as Neanderthal Man, in Germany. They organized the production of more advanced and varied stone tools and found out how to butcher their often enormous prey.

It is at this time that we find the first traces of religion.

The gradual stabilization of the climate after this long ice age led to the start of the short but culturally fascinating Late Paleolithic Age (30,000-13,000 years ago) with the appearance of modern man, *Homo sapiens sapiens*, in a large part of the continent and with significant cultural differences from one region to another. Stone tools reached high levels to back up well-organized hunting, fishing and gathering operations. The evolution of the Late Paleolithic cultures is clear in the production of primitive works of art, based on nature and magical themes, with wall paintings in the caves, etchings and sculptures in horn, bone, ivory from mammoths and stone. Here, too, can be seen the development of more complex rituals and customs.

The end of the ice age about 11,000 BC, followed by the emergence of a very favorable climate throughout Europe led to more abundant and accessible resources with the transformation of the Paleolithic cultures into Mesolithic. The introduction of more refined hunting techniques, such as the invention of the bow and arrow, the uses of fire, the production of small flint tools with a great variety of uses combined with the widespread gathering of food in abundance including legumes, land and sea mollusks, freshwater fish and wild berries to change life further. From Portugal to the Volga and Scandinavia to Trentino, the Iron Gates to the Appenines, a number of communities tried out the first forms of semi-sedentary living. The revolution of the Neolithic Age, with the domestication of wild animals and the cultivation of cereals and legumes, herding and settlement, reached Europe from the

Near East in the 7th millennium BC. The first villages of European Neolithic shepherds and farmers date back to 6,800 BC, and were located on Crete and in Thessaly, in Greece. The Neolithic age emerged shortly afterward in the Balkans. Rudimentary building developed in this period to house communities whose economy, for the first time in history, aimed at the production of food surpluses. Archaeological finds point to the development of the culture of the time. Tools made of polished stone and obsidian, an extremely sharp volcanic glass, indicate wide-spread trade by both land and sea, while pottery shows the need to hold stores of food in the villages, many of which have defensive walls around them of one type or another. Important cultures were scattered throughout Europe in the Early, Middle and late Neolithic Ages. In these we can see the presence of social and economic hierarchies, possible matriarchal descent, developed forms of religion and works of art that indicate the existence of abstract ideas. This period is the period of the first monumental expressions in European architecture. Between the 5th and 3rd millennia BC, and with rare but important examples in the Bronze Age, these appeared in Brittany and the British Isles as well as in the Iberian Peninsula, Scandinavia, Puglia and Sardinia in the form of stunning megalithic complexes which were both sanctuaries and funeral shrines.

A second revolution superimposed itself on that of the Neolithic age with the gradual adoption of copper in Europe in the same areas where the first agricultural and pastoral cultures had sprung up, at times with the appearance of gold and silver. This was the

start of the Copper Age which, after a long experimental phase, brought about deep economic and social changes in the communities. The control of the sources of the metal, the techniques and finished products created deep gulfs between those who could make use of metal tools and those who had to continue using stone tools or objects made from bone, horn or wood. From Greece to the Balkans, as far as Central Europe and the Alps, rich in resources, and the Mediterranean shores, two cultural groups emerged, distinguished on the basis of the fossil-guide of pottery. Communities which were involved in transformation activities developed into communities which were able to exchange a wide range of products, from textiles to metal objects. The long period of the Bronze Age also opened in Greece and the Balkans, with the extremely rapid development of new technologies for the forging of objects in metal alloys which were much more resistant than those of pure copper. This period saw the first true population boom in Europe, the first and probably vast migrations of people, and the explosion of trade. This was also the time when types of settlements began to evolve. In the Greece of the 3rd millennium BC, for instance, we can see architecture first beginning to hint at the grandiose designs of the millennium to come. This was also the age of the Europe of Stonehenge in Britain and Tarxien in Malta, of the last, enormous megaliths, of myriad cultures that meet and at times clash, especially at the end of the 3rd and the start of the 2nd millennium BC as the cultures travel throughout the continent by land, following the paths beaten out by herds of animals, and sea.

The 2nd millennium, during which copper metallurgy spread throughout the continent, saw the first stage in the migration of Indo-European people, a migration which continued for several centuries. Here we see the definition of cultural types that we can often recognize as the predecessors of historic civilizations, such as the proto-Celtic and Mycenean civilizations, and the broadening of the cultures as a result of the interaction of cultures and races. This is also the period when the Mediterranean basin was systematically used as a trading route

and the first maritime powers emerged. The Aegean was ahead of the times, with the development of the Cycladic, Minoan and Mycenean civilizations, due to a highly developed economy based on the vast circulation of goods well beyond the limits of the settlements of these people. The introduction of primitive systems of writing in Crete and Mycenae, the spread of trade exchanges and the emergence of a geographical and economic panorama in which east and west are involved are just as important as the flourishing mining cultures of the Alps and central and west Europe, from the Celts of the Hallstatt area to the Sardinians and the various cultural layers of the Bronze Age in the Iberian Peninsula.

The Europe of the historic civilizations emerged from the crisis that marked the end of the millennium. From the 10th-9th centuries BC on, in fact, after a brief but traumatic series of events, the characters of the peoples of Europe began to define themselves as Greeks, Etruscans, Romans, Italics, Gauls, Germans, Iberians, Illyrians, Dacians and the ethnic minorities from the east (the Phoenicians and the Carthaginians in the western Mediterranean). This is the history we know best, the history of the dreams of the universal empire, the philosophies and ideologies, the history of Greece and Rome.

Furio Durando

CONTENTS

LASCAUX   page 28
CARNAC   page 34
STONEHENGE   page 36
text by Fabio Bourbon

KNOSSOS   page 38
MYCENAE   page 48
ATHENS   page 56
PAESTUM   page 64
TARQUINIA   page 74
text by Furio Durando

POMPEII   page 78
ROME   page 96
HADRIAN'S VILLA   page 114
text by Fabio Bourbon

CHRONOLOGY

Upper Paleolithic
and Mesolithic
(ca. 45,000-6,800 BC)

Rock paintings of Lascaux
(ca. 17,000-16,000 BC)

Rock paintings of Altamira
(ca. 12,000 BC)

Neolithic and the first spread
of copper
(ca. 6800-3500 BC)

First megalithic alignments at
Carnac
(3000 BC)

Protohistory
(ca. 2800-1220 BC)

Formation of the Minoan
civilization
(ca. 2800-2000 BC)

First Minoan city-palaces
(ca. 1700-1450 BC)

Foundation of the megalithic
sanctuary
of Stonehenge
(ca. 1800 BC)

Destruction and
reconstruction of the Minoan
city-palaces
Achaean invasion
of Greece, Flourishing
of Mycenae
(ca. 1700-1450 BC)

Collapse of the Minoan
civilization
(ca. 1450 BC)

Mycenean domination of
trade in the Mediterranean
(ca. 1450-1250 BC)

Trojan war
(ca. 1250-1220 BC)

Indo-European invasions and
end of the Mycenean
civilization
(1220-1120 BC)

Foundation of the first urban
centers in Greece
(1100-900 BC)

The Etruscans settle within
the boundaries of the modern
Tuscany and Latium
(ca. 800 BC)

Foundation of Rome
(753 BC)

Royal period in Rome
(753-509 BC)

Foundation of the Olympic
Games
(776 BC)

Foundation of the first Greek
colonies in southern Italy
(770-708 BC)

First "constitutions"
in Athens and Sparta
(ca. 754-753 BC)

Other Greek colonies
founded in southern Italy
(688-648 BC)

First Etruscan burial
paintings
(600 BC)

Fire at the sanctuary
of Apollo in Delphi
(548 BC)

Banishment of Tarquin the
Proud and foundation
of the Republic in Rome
(509 BC)

Struggles between
Patricians and Plebeians in
Rome
(509-343 BC)

Democratic constitution
in Athens
(508-507 BC)

The "Temple of Neptune"
built in Paestum
(ca. 500 BC)

First revolt against the
Persians in Ionia
(499-494 BC)

The Romans defeat the
Latins in the battle of Lake
Regillus
(496 BC)

The tribunes of the people
created in Rome
(494 BC)

First Persian War
(490 BC)

Second Persian War
Battle of Imera between
Greeks and Carthaginians
(480 BC)

STONEHENGE

CARNAC

LASCAUX

TARQUINIA

ROME   HADRIAN'S VILLA

POMPEII   PAESTUM

ATHENS

MYCENAE

KNOSSOS

Second revolt against
the Persians in Ionia
(479 BC)

Establishment of the
Delian-Attic League
(478 BC)

Naval battle of Cuma
between Greeks and
Etruscans
(474 BC)

War of Athens against
Aegina and Corinth
(464-455 BC)

The laws of the 12 Tables
are issued in Rome
(451 BC)

Peace treaty between
Greeks
and Persians
(449 BC)

Hegemony of Pericles in
Athens
(449-429 BC)

Ichtynos, Callicrates and
Phydia rebuild the
Parthenon in the form
we see it today
(448-438 BC)

Peloponnesian War
(431-404 BC)

The temple of Athena Nike
built on the Acropolis
of Athens
(430-410 BC)

Wars between Greeks
and Carthaginians in Sicily
(409-392 BC)

Spartan rule of Greece
(404-379 BC)

Rome destroys the city
of Veii and cancels out the
Etruscan threat
(396 BC)

The Gauls burn Rome
(390 BC)

The plebeians are admitted
to the consulship in Rome
(367 BC)

Greece submits to Philip II
of Macedonia
(356-338 BC)

Philip II makes Macedonia
the first power of Greece
(359-336 BC)

The Romans fight the
Sannite wars
(343-290 BC)

Reign of Alexander III
the Great
(336-323 BC)

Division of the empire
of Alexander the Great
and formation of the
Hellenic kingdoms
(322-281 BC)

The Romans defeat
Pyrrhus
(285 BC)

Macedonian absolute
monarchy in Greece
(276-239 BC)

First Punic War between
Romans and Carthaginians
(264-241 BC)

The Romans occupy
Cisalpine Gaul
(222 BC)

Second Punic War between
Romans and Carthaginians
(218-201 BC)

Rome liberates the Greeks
from Macedonian rule
(200-196 BC)

The Romans establish
the Hispanic provinces
(197 BC)

The Basilica Emilia is built
in the Roman Forum
(179 BC)

Third Punic War and
destruction of Carthage
by Rome
(149-146 BC)

Seige and destruction
of Corinth. Rome reduces
Macedonia and Greece
to provinces
(147-146 BC)

Caius Gracchus
assassinated in Rome
(121 BC)

Rome conquers southern
Gaul
(121-125 BC)

Marius defeats the Teutons
and Cimbers
(102-101 BC)

The Social War rages in
Italy
(91-88 BC)

Dictatorship of Silla in
Rome
(82-78 BC)

Consulship of Pompey
and Crassus
(70 BC)

The plot of Catiline
(63 BC)

First triumvirate
(60 BC)

Caesar conquers Gaul
(58-51 BC)

Start of the Civil War
(49 BC)

Battle of Pharsalus
and death of Pompey
(48 BC)

Caesar defeats the
supporters of Pompey at
Munda
(45 BC)

Assassination of Caesar
(44 BC)

Second triumvirate
(43 BC)

Octavian defeats Antony
in the battle of Actium
(31 BC)

Octavian receives the title
of Augustus
(27 BC)

The Augustan Forum
inaugurated in Rome
(2 AD)

Death of Augustus
(14 AD)

Empire of Tiberius
(14-37)

Empire of Caligula
(37-41)

Empire of Claudius
(41-54)

The Romans occupy
Britannia
(44)

Empire of Nero
(54-68)

Empire of Vespasian
(69-79)

The Colosseum built
in Rome
(75-80)

Empire of Titus
(79-81)

Eruption of Vesuvius and
destruction of Pompeii
(79)

Empire of Trajan
(98-117)

Trajan conquers Dacia
(101-106)

The Trajan Forum
inaugurated in Rome
(112)

Empire of Hadrian
(117-138)

The Pantheon rebuilt
in Rome
(118-128)

Empire of Antoninus Pius
(138-161)

Empire of Marcus Aurelius
(161-180)

Empire of Septimus
Severus
(193-211)

Empire of Caracalla
(211-217)

The baths of Caracalla built
in Rome
(216)

Empire of Alexander Severus
(222-235)

Aurelian rebuilds the walls
of Rome
(271)

Empire of Diocletian
(284-305)

Diocletian sets up
the tetrarchy
(293)

Crisis of the tetrarchy
(306)

Constantine defeats
Massensius in the battle
of Ponte Milvius
(312)

Constantine unites the East
and West
(324)

Constantinople becomes the
capital of the Roman Empire
(330)

Death of Constantine and
division of the empire
(337)

Constance II reunites
the empire
(353-361)

Valens defeated
at Hadrianopolis
(378)

Empire of Theodosius
(379-395)

Alaricus sacks Rome
(410)

Attila comes down into Italy
(452)

Fall of the Western Roman
Empire
(476)

Europe

Europe

English Channel

Paris •

France

LASCAUX •

Mediterranean Sea

LASCAUX
PREHISTORY'S SISTINE CHAPEL

A Room of
  the Felines
B Nave
C Apse
D Trench
E Passageway
F Axial
  gallery
G Rotunda
H Entrance

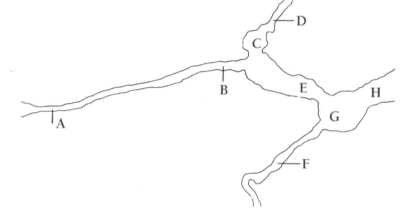

28 left In Lascaux the animals figures were drawn with surprising skill and attention to anatomical detail. Note the muzzle of a cow shown here.

28 top center Galloping horses shown on the cave walls all have disproportionate bodies when they are compared to the length of the legs of the horses.

28 bottom center It is believed Paleolithic man performed magical rites to guarantee abundant game. For this reason some experts say they painted the animals they would meet when hunting.

28 top right The cattle painted on the walls of the so-called Hall of the Bulls have truly impressive dimensions. Some examples are as long as 15 feet.

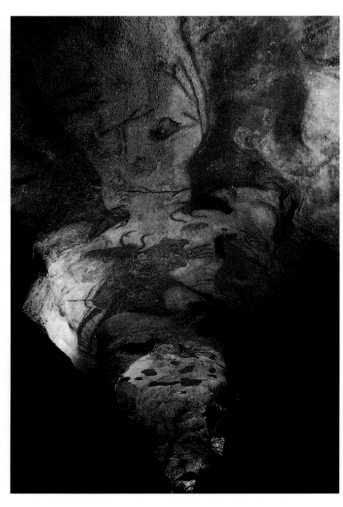

Despite its reputation as an academic discipline archaeology has often proved to be one in which the most spectacular finds have been revealed almost, or actually, by chance. In many cases discoveries which have changed the entire way in which the past is viewed have been made by amateurs. These amateurs can be divided into two groups. There are those who, through an interest in the past, pursued their beliefs and found lost civilizations, and there are those who literally stumbled upon a lost and forgotten site.

The chief of the amateurs who pursued their own theories is undoubtedly Heinrich Schliemann, whose refusal to be discouraged by experts led to the discovery of the location of ancient Troy. There have been many other examples. One of the most astonishing of the accidental examples is that of the caves discovered by four young men from Montignac, near Lascaux, France. On September 8, 1940, these young men, out walking in the forest, came across a deep hole. They made a brief exploration and on September 12 the 17 year old Marcel Ravidat, an apprentice mechanic, returned with three other friends, and went down into a dark hole several feet deep and into a huge natural cavity where he was joined by his friends. Since they only had a box of matches with them they couldn't see very much nor explore very far, so the next day they came back again, this time with an oil lamp.

Using the lamp, they discovered that the main grotto was a room about one hundred feet long, at the end of which there was a natural hallway, narrow but high enough so they could walk in it upright. Here they first discovered a number of designs drawn on its walls in various colors. A few steps further, and by the light of the lamp they made out a number of strange animals of all sizes drawn with some skill.

They realized at once what they had

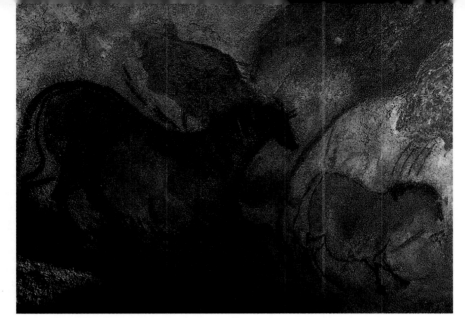

28-29 *Near the figures of many of the painted animals we can see geometric designs which so far defy interpretation. In some cases they may be arrows, in others magical symbols.*

29 top *The extraordinary wall paintings at Lascaux were produced using charcoal black and a number of colored earths with tremendous skill, reproducing the shades of the animals' coats with outstanding realism.*

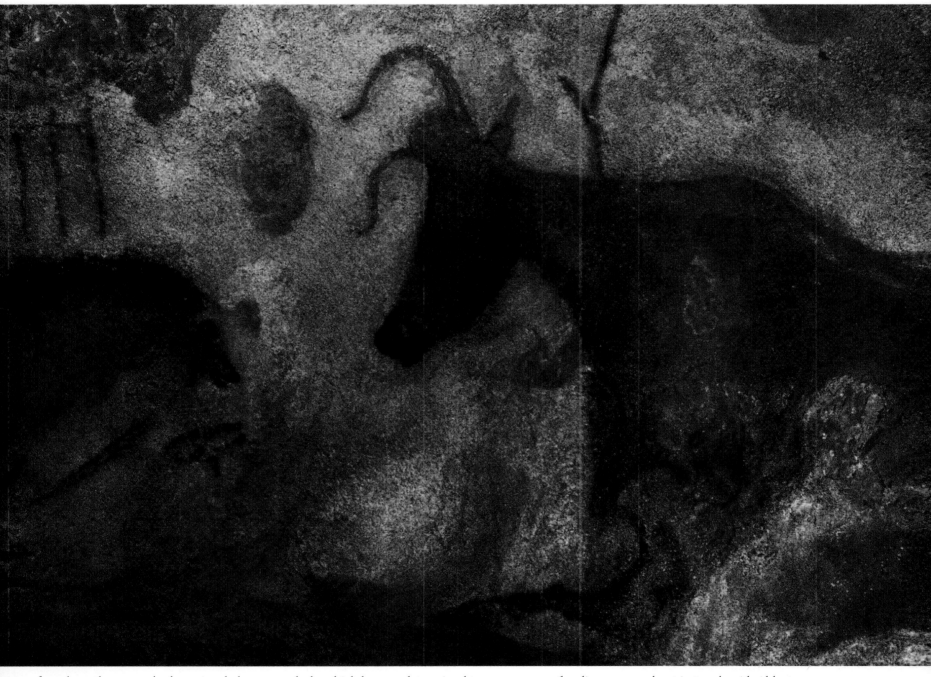

found as other caves had previously been found in the Dordogne area, decorated with wall paintings which had received wide publicity, and they knew they had found caves which had been inhabited by prehistoric men. They explored every angle of the caves, shouting each time they came across a new drawing. It was only when the oil for the lamp grew low that they decided to return to the outside. The next day they returned to the site, each with a good lamp, and continued to make discoveries. At the bottom of what was to become known as The Well, a steep dank

hole which he was determined to explore, Ravidat found a picture of a wounded bison, charging a man with outstretched arms, at the end, while on the right a rhinoceros seemed to be walking away. This is an unusually realistic drawing which is one of the rare scenic drawings in Paleolithic art. Over the days that followed hordes of young people visited the caves until Ravidat was able to convince the schoolmaster, Leon Laval, to visit by showing him sketches of the drawings in the caves.
Laval immediately realized the value of

the discovery and got in touch with Abbot Henri Breuil, one of the great experts of that time on cave drawings who, after inspecting the site, told the academic world, calling the site "The Sistine Chapel of Prehistory."
Four years later, a film was made about Lascaux and following World War II ever-increasing numbers of tourists began to come to visit the caves. By the 1950s it was clear that the presence of thousands of people was leading to the deterioration of the pigments in the drawings. In 1960 a green algae began to spread over the cave

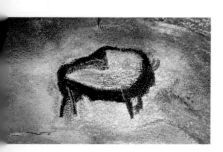

30 top The wall paintings in Lascaux show several bisons, animals which were once common on the European plains. During archaeological excavations on the floor of the cave remnants of animals, pigments used for paints, and a number of lamps, probably filled with oil or animal fat, were unearthed. With these lamps the people of Lascaux were able to eliminate the darkness of the cave and produce their works.

walls with devastating effects, an algae which took ten years to remove so the colors could be restored.

The caves were closed to the public in 1963 and later, permanently sealed. Today, visitors can see a replica of the caves, dug out a short distance from the original and painted faithfully to replicate the original. This same solution has also been put into effect at the caves in Altamira in Spain.

Lascaux owes its fame to the extraordinary quality of the paintings which date from the Upper Paleolithic Age, between sixteen and seventeen thousand years ago.

The caves have an overall area of less than one hundred twenty square yards. One of the most interesting features is the uniformity of the paintings which seem to have been executed within a brief period of time by the same group of artists. The so-called round room, nearest the entrance, shows a group of bison, horses and deer, traced with remarkable realism in charcoal and ochre. The side gallery

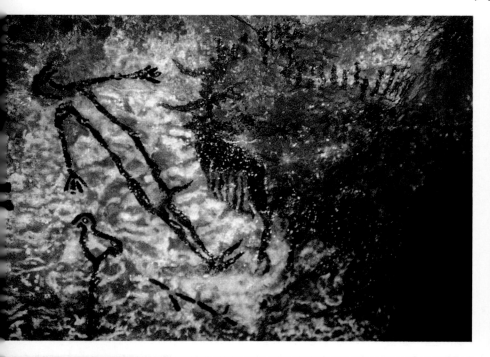

30 center On one of the walls is a painting in black charcoal which some experts say shows a man with open arms being killed by a bison. The animal has been wounded and its inner organs are spilling out of it.
Not all scholars agree on this interpretation. Some say it shows a victorious hunter with the prey he has just killed. In any case, the highly realistic scene is unusual in Paleolithic art.

30 bottom Deer were also shown on the walls of the cave. This splendid one shows an imposing display of antlers.

30-31 and 32-33 The extraordinary wall paintings of Lascaux belong to the period of prehistory known as "Magdalenian", from the name of the French area, La Madeleine, where prehistoric art showed considerable development.

shows deer, horses and cattle, while in the passage and nave we can see, although these pictures are drawn with less accuracy, bulls, cows, ibex and deer. The Room of the Felines has pictures of felines, of course, as well as drawings of countless other animals, including rhinoceroses. The only reindeer drawn at Lascaux is in the area called the apse which is covered with many unfinished drawings. The well we have already described. Throughout the caves, the animal figures are shown together with abstract signs including lines, squares, and rectangles which are not yet interpreted. Some scholars believe that the paintings indicate that Paleolithic man performed magical rites and ritual dances in front of them, including, possibly, sacrifices to the gods, in return for successful results during hunting expeditions.

This would mean that the caves were an ancient center of worship. If this is indeed the case, it is perhaps only fitting that the caves should be once again hidden from curious mankind.

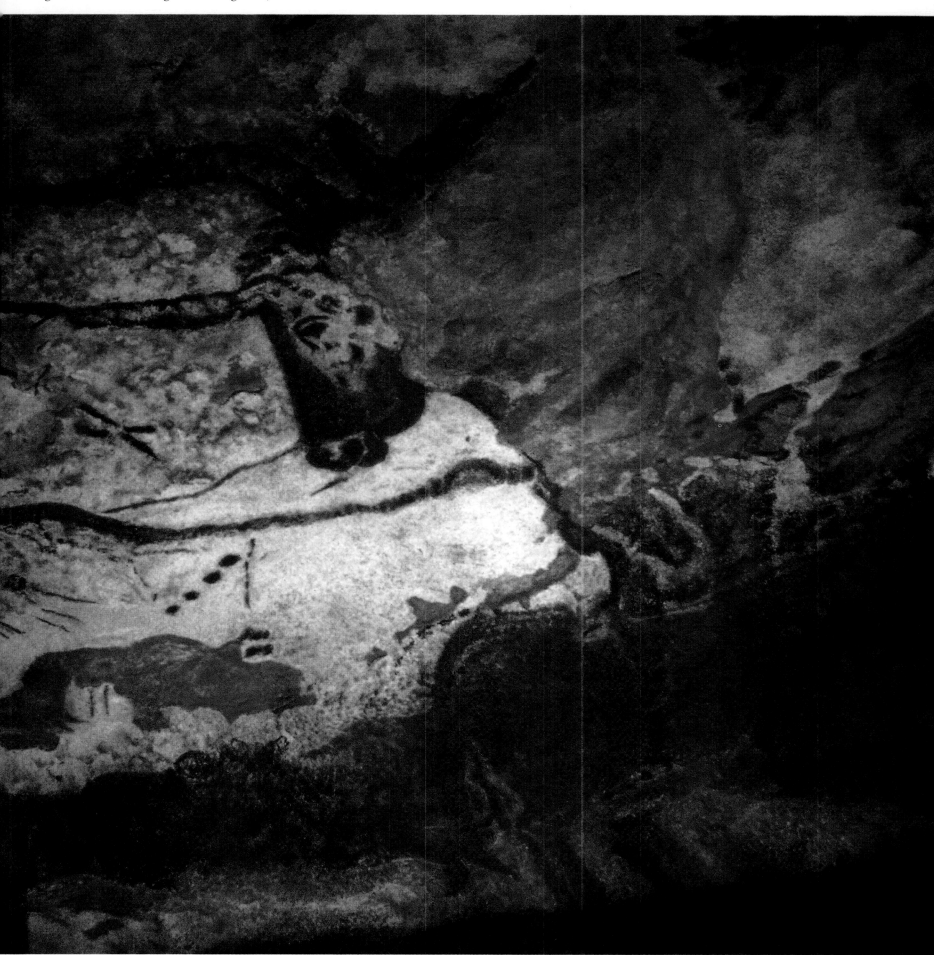

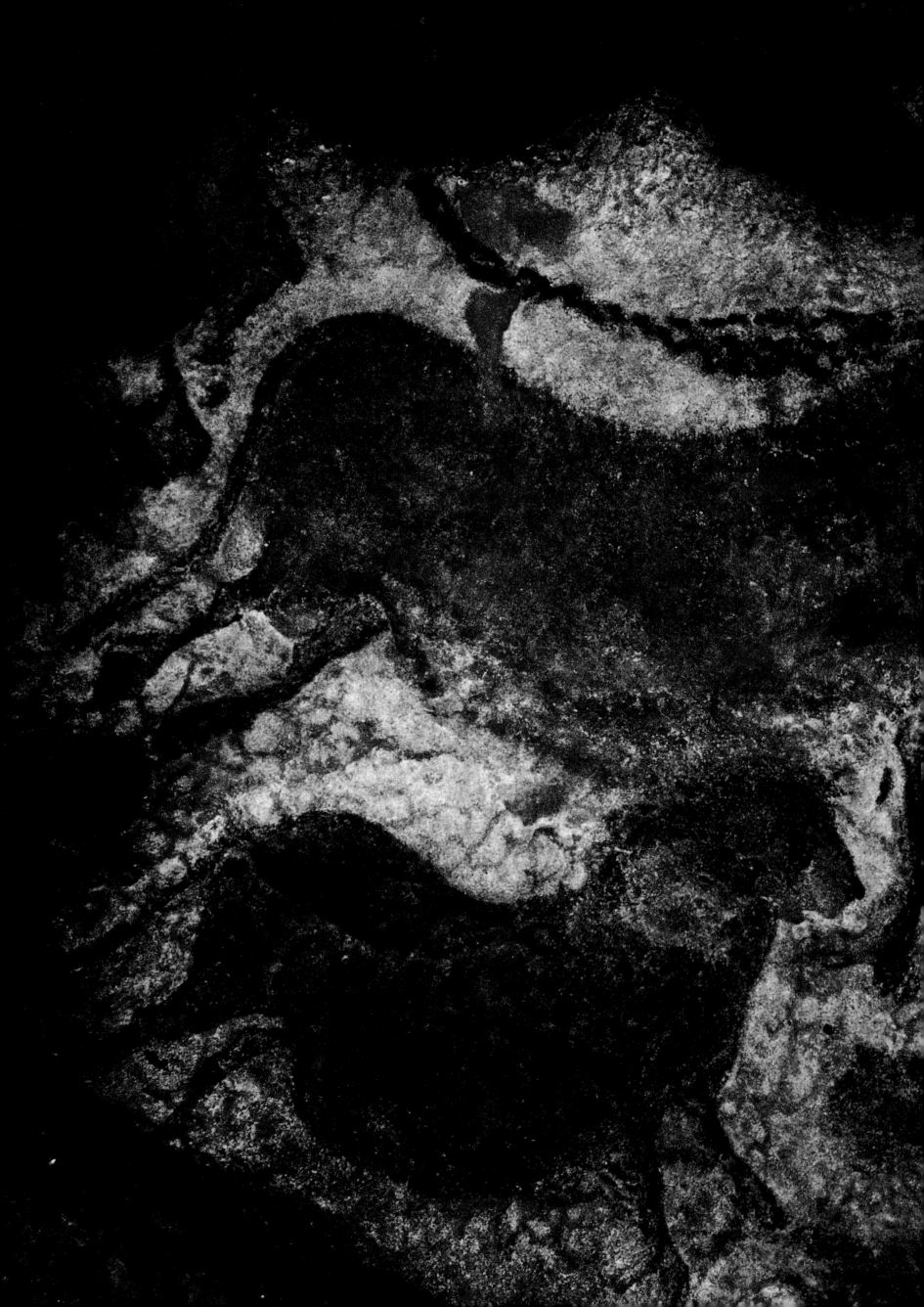

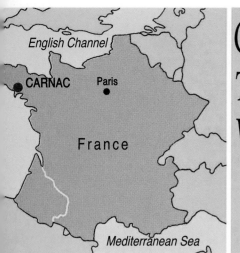

English Channel

CARNAC

Paris

France

Mediterranean Sea

CARNAC, THE MENHIR VILLAGE

34 left The name "Mane Kerioned" of one of the dolmen comes from the Kérions, powerful elves who were said to have lived among the monoliths at Carnac.

34 right Throughout the Carnac region there are many isolated menhirs, such as this one photographed in Morbihan.

35 Eleven separate rows of monoliths can be counted in the western section of the alignment of Mernec.

During Neolithic times, when man began to use tools made from shaped stones, the so-called megalithic civilization grew and spread outward. Many traces of this civilization remain in the form of burial sites and major monuments formed by enormous stone blocks and slabs with relatively simple decorations.

Most typical of this age are *dolmens* and *menhirs*. Both words are from the Celtic and mean table and standing stone, respectively. The tables are individual or communal tombs, formed by vertical stone columns set in the ground and supporting a huge horizontal slab, while the menhirs are single monoliths, usually elongated and set vertically in the ground. They are usually found in isolated positions or, more rarely, in rows or circles. In that case they are usually referred to as *cromlechs*. These sometimes are connected with burial sites in which case they act as grave markers, but otherwise they are difficult to both interpret and date. There are also doubts about the meanings of these megalithic stone circles. Some believe they were boundary markers for primitive areas of worship, meeting areas or, as in the case of Stonehenge, astronomical observatories, although these too are generally believed to be linked with religious ceremonies. Throughout Europe there are several hundred monuments of this kind in the British Isles, Scandinavia, France, Spain, Italy and Malta. The most famous is,

probably, England's Stonehenge, described elsewhere in this book, but the most impressive in the world in terms of size is undoubtedly at Carnac, a village on the south coast of Brittany in France.

The main megaliths at Carnac are arranged in three groups known as Menec, Karmario and Kerlescan. There are 1,099 menhirs in 11 rows, with a total length of over 3,000 feet in the first of these sites, 1,029 menhirs in 10 rows with a length of over 3,000 feet in the second, and the third, with 594 menhirs in 13 rows, about 2,700 feet long. There are smaller groups, somewhat damaged, at Petit-Menec, Kerzhero and Sainte'Barbe, and isolated stones throughout the area. At Kermario there is also a dolmen, while the Kerlescan group is closed by a cromlech with 39 elements, still relatively intact. Near Locmariaquer, about 10 miles or so from the main village, is Table des Marchands, an enormous dolmen with traces of sculpture and remains of what is called the "Fairy's Stone", the largest menhir known, originally over 60 feet high. As a comparison, the obelisk in front of the temple of Luxor in Egypt is almost 70 feet high but that was built by Ramses II in the 13th century BC when the great stones at Carnac were already over 1200 years old. These figures speak for themselves. The average weight of the stones is one to two tons, but many are much bulkier. Unfortunately, much of what we see today is only the remains of what must have been an extremely dramatic sight. Many of the monoliths were taken away in past centuries and used as building materials. The Belle-Ile lighthouse, for instance, contains menhirs from Petit-Menec. Down through the centuries there was a great deal of speculation over the methods by which the Carnac menhirs were carried and placed, but a few years ago a group of about 200 volunteers demonstrated with relative ease how a block weighing 32 tons could be moved. If we consider that a menhir 12 feet high weighs between 10 and 12 tons, we should also consider that the number of

laborers used to create these monuments may not have been as large as sometimes imagined.

The tools that seem to have been most necessary for Neolithic man to create these monuments were stout ropes and good quality wood for slides, rollers and levers. By using inclined surfaces, it is theorized that even the most massive menhirs could have been placed in position.

The blocks are either bare of all decoration or only have the most rudimentary designs. The stones are from the area. It is believed that the construction of these complexes must have taken place during periods of the year devoted to major religious gatherings, so that the work was carried out over a number of decades, with the work supervised by priests and experienced foremen who were able to maintain the original goals of the work. Although we believe we now understand how the stones were built, we have yet to understand their meaning. Through the middle of the 19th century the ruins were believed to be of Celtic or Druidical orign and connected with some form of ancestor worship.

A few of these widely circulated ideas include that they were landing places for spaceships, pentagrams with menhirs indicating the symbols, or, indeed, enormous writing yet to be deciphered, setting out the laws of a lost society. Thanks to modern methods of dating, we now know these spectacular megalithic monuments were built around 4500 years ago and it is believed by most scholars that a religious meaning was central.

There are some who have attempted to provide an astronomical significance to this site (as to others, as discussed elsewhere in this book) but the incomplete nature of the rows of stones and the cromlechs that close them at the ends have made it impossible to prove. Perhaps, it has been jokingly suggested, the best answer is the ancient popular legend that the rows of menhirs were built by a powerful group of "little people" who once ruled the Earth before the dawn of civilization.

STONEHENGE, MEGALITHS OF THE GIANTS

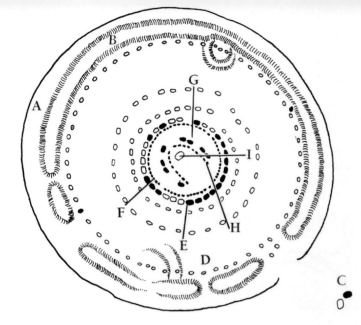

36 A tremendous effort was needed to build Stonehenge, especially since when the monument was begun wheeled carts did not exist. The stone blocks were probably taken to the site using sledges hauled by hundreds of people, then put into position using rollers, tree trunks, levers and wooden beamed structures.

A Ditch
B Earthworks
C Heel stone
D Round holes
E Stone circle
F Blue stone circle

G Triliths
H Blue stones
I Altar stone

The stones still standing are marked in black

Stonehenge, a few miles from Salisbury in the English county of Wiltshire, is a megalithic stone complex that dates back to the period between the Neolithic and the Bronze Ages. Despite its imposing appearance and its fame throughout the world only a limited part of the structure still stands. This consists of a gigantic *cromlech*, the name given to flat stones resting horizontally on upright similar stones, and a number of other monoliths, large single stones. This monument has always fascinated visitors and in the past was actually feared. There remain many doubts as to its origins and purpose and many fantastic explanations have been developed.

The first time that Stonehenge is mentioned is in a history of the kings of Britain which was written by Godfrey of Monmouth around 1136. Unfortunately, his account is both unsatisfactory and improbable as he says it was built by giants in the far distant past in Ireland and subsequently brought to Stonehenge by Merlin, the magician of the King Arthur legend, using his magical powers to move the enormous stone blocks. Godfrey also said the stones had miraculous healing abilities and could cure many illnesses.

This superstition that Stonehenge has healing power is still found in some groups today. In the past, the Church was forced to face the magic of Stonehenge, with Pope Gregory I ordering in 601 AD that this temple of the ancient Britons not be destroyed, but sanctified with holy water.

As time passed, the theory that the stones were the remains of a temple came to be more and more accepted, but no one seemed able to solve the bigger question which was who were the people who built it? One theory, not very logical, was that the construction was Roman and the elementary shapes were deliberately designed, almost as an insult, for the unsophisticated inhabitants of the British Isles. Another theory was that the builders were invaders from Scandinavia, and still others said it was the work of the Druids.

The first scholar who realized its functional importance, if not its origins, was John Smith who worked out its significance as a calendar in 1771, based on a number of fairly elementary astronomical observations. In the middle of the 19th century, as a result of some archaeological discoveries in Greece,

there was tremendous enthusiasm for the theory that the great stone circle had been erected by the Myceneans, who were believed to have the technical knowledge needed to move and put into place such huge blocks of stone. Scholars considered the possibility that it was built by the Greek conquerors while poets and painters, including Lord Byron and John Constable, attracted not so much by the scientific discussions as by the romantic appearance of the ruins in the obscure green Wiltshire fields, were also fascinated by it.

It wasn't until the end of the 19th century that the construction of the megalithic circle was accepted as being the work of ancient native peoples. With the development of modern dating techniques it was possible to reach a conclusion about the age of the monument. Carbon 14 dating showed that the monoliths were raised four or five hundred years before the Mycenean monuments, eliminating that theory. During the 1950s, work carried out by R.J.C. Atkinson demonstrated that the complex had been built over a number of different stages.

Originally it was thought that there had been three distinct phases, but today it is generally believed that there were four. During the first stage, in the second half of the 3rd millennium BC, the site was made up of a circular ditch 110 yards wide, with a mound of earth on either side. The entrance to the sacred circle was marked by two monoliths, while a third, which is still on the site and known as the Heel Stone, was outside the enclosed area. Later, fifty-six holes were dug along the inner edge of the earth mound. There is still controversy over the purpose of these holes although the discovery of remains of bones suggests they may have been cremation sites. During the third stage, which

was between the end of the third millennium and the beginning of the second BC, eighty blue stones, which had been formed by volcanic activity and brought from quarries hundred of miles away, were built in a horseshoe shape in two rows.

The most spectacular stage in the construction of the monument is believed to have taken place in the 16th or 15th century BC when the blue stones were removed and thirty large monoliths made of local sandstone took their place. These were arranged in a circle and united by enormous crossbeams of the same sandstone. Approximately forty blue stones were used to form a second circle within the first, and in the midst of these five huge triliths (two monoliths with a third on top), each over twenty feet high, were raised in a horseshoe formation. The focal point of the structure

was occupied by a single flat stone block, called the altar stone, which was separated from the triliths by another horseshoe of blue stones. The astronomer Fred Hoyle discovered that the entire structure had been built as a kind of instrument for forecasting eclipses. This could possibly have been used to give power to religious leaders who, by showing their ability to predict such exceptional events could achieve both prestige and power. Today, although many of the mysteries of Stonehenge have been revealed, we are still unable to explain how the great monoliths, some of which weighed fifty tons, were moved into their positions, although the work at Carnac in France (see that section in this book) may offer a suggestion. In any case, archaeologists are able to confirm that the men of the period had the technology necessary to perform this task.

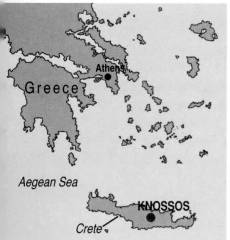

KNOSSOS
AND THE THRONE OF MINOS

38 top This magnificent rhyton, a vase used in religious ceremonies, featuring a bull's head profile with gilded horns, is made of soap stone, hard stone and mother-of-pearl. An exceptional find, it dates back to 1500 BC.

A Theatre
B North entrance
C Colonnaded hall
D Warehouses
E Throne room
F Central courtyard
G Great stairway
H Megaron of the king
I Southern portico
J High priest's house (southern house)
K South eastern house

In the 16th century BC Knossos lay between the northern coast of Crete where today the capital, Heraklion, lies and the hills to the south where the river called Katsabà, known as Kairatos to the ancients, runs. It is believed that at this time the landscape was an orderly one with isolated white houses, small rural villages and large farms. About seven miles from the Aegean, on a gentle, rolling hill, was what is believed to be the most fascinating architectural complex in the western world of the 2nd millennium BC, the enormous "city palace" known as Knossos with nearby residences of aristocrats and rich merchants and a network of paved roads. It is believed that at least eighty thousand, and perhaps as many as one hundred thousand, people inhabited this city with at least ten thousand living in the palace alone.

38 center This view of the residential area of the southern section of Knossos shows us the remains of the restored Southern House. In the center of the image is a decorative motif that recurs in the architecture of the biggest and most famous Minoan city-palace. This is a huge pair of stylized bull's horns, perhaps one of the symbols of power.

38 bottom These large terra-cotta jars, called pithoi, are still in their original place where they were used to store foodstuffs in the palace warehouses.

38-39 The Corridor of Processions started from the western entrance to the city-palace of Knossos and was lined with friezes. Today we can see what these looked like in excellent copies that have been placed on the walls of the restored porticoes.

39 bottom This detail from the group of frescoes along the walls of the Corridor of Processions shows the strong sense of nature, the vibrant colors, and the fine details that are typical of Minoan art.

This city combined agriculture with stone quarrying and metal work of all kinds and also sent forth a large merchant fleet to the rest of the world.

Knossos is known not only through the archaeological research that has been made on its site but also through the Greek mythology in which it plays such a major role. Minos, for instance, the cruel sovereign who forced King Aegus of Athens to pay annual tribute with young lives, Daedalus, inventor of the Labyrinth (the "city palace" itself, some experts believe), Theseus and Ariadne who fought against the Minotaur, the monster of the Labyrinth, are all figures who were based in Knossos.

Crete itself is rich in archaeological sites, but Knossos is the most outstanding of them all. A great deal of the credit for our present knowledge of Knossos should go to a determined Englishman named Arthur J. Evans, who over many decades excavated every site he could find that belonged to the same period in the "city palaces" in other areas of the island, thus establishing a basic record of the splendid flourishing of this important Mediterranean island during the Bronze Age.

In addition, his work supplied the chronological base for the study of the development of Cretan civilization unknown until that point, which Evans himself called "Minoan" after King Minos. Restoration and conservation work began as a result of his discoveries but unfortunately this was carried out in an arbitrary and unscholarly way that is typical, perhaps, of early archaeological work.

40-41 The remains, carefully restored, of a portico decorated with frescoes from the Neo-Palatial period can be found down from the northern entrance to Knossos. The shape of the columns, originally made of wood, is typical of Minoa. The downward tapered cylindrical column rested on a low plinth and held up the entablature by a simple swollen ring capital. The colors used in the restoration are identical to the original ones.

The so-called "city palace" was a structure extending for tens of thousands of square miles with over a thousand rooms and connections running through two, three or four floors, built around a central courtyard as large as a soccer field.

Crete's history began toward the end of the 3rd millennium BC. At this time it became commercially dominant over the flourishing islands of the Cyclades, sailing through the Aegean and eastern Mediterranean seas with a large merchant fleet and carrying its power toward mainland Greece and the Peloponnese as is indicated by several myths.

had places of worship, administrative areas and space for warehousing and shops belonging to craftsmen and merchants. It is believed that they were an expression of the power and prestige of absolute sovereigns who, some scholars believe, had privileges and power similar to that of the Egyptian pharaohs. It has been suggested that the name Minos actually referred to this type of ruler rather than to an actual individual halfway between history and legend. This suggestion makes a good deal of sense. There are many experts who believe that this kind of ruler provided the drive toward the transformation of Crete, an island that was rich in many resources, into the first true Mediterranean maritime power. The safety under which the Cretans lived and worked appears to have been total, as there is a lack of defensive structures around the palace complexes. It is not so clear as to how Cretan society was stratified.

At a fairly early date, the dominant role of a number of centers on the island was established. These centers went on to divide the control of the territory and to handle the profits from the production and trading operations, based on the exchange of foodstuffs and items made by skilled craftsmen including potters, ebony carvers,

In this time, it laid the foundation for what was to be recognized even in ancient times as the first "thalassocracy" through its activity as a maritime power that by constant development earned both respect and admiration through the centuries and established trading bonds even with such distant nations as the Egypt of the pharaohs and the Middle Eastern kingdoms.

At the start of the Bronze Age, between 2000 and 1750 BC, the first city-palaces emerged in Mallia, Phaestos and Knossos. These vast royal residences, in which hundreds and sometimes thousands of people lived also

41

metalworkers and goldsmiths who worked and sold their goods in the shops in the city-palaces. Between 1750 and 1700 BC an early form of hieroglyphic script, which may have been used primarily for religious purposes, was abandoned and replaced by the still undeciphered Linear A script which, one theory goes, may have been used mainly for accounting purposes in the city-palaces. Around 1700 BC, however, for reasons that are not entirely clear although most experts consider a series of catastrophic earthquakes the most likely, the city-palaces were destroyed and then rebuilt in even more extended and luxurious forms.

It is from these later complexes, which mark the beginning of what is called the neo-palatial phase of Middle Minoan III, that the typical features of the city-palaces such as the one in Knossos have been defined. It was at this point that they were ornamented with elaborate porticoed antechambers and corridors with stepped open spaces which are usually viewed as the prototypes for open-air theaters, although it is not clear whether they were meant for religious rites or theatrical performances. At this time we can also see the creation of a variety of residential models, including lesser palaces that were perhaps owned by aristocrats or rich merchants, farm-villas in the country (the finest remaining one is considered to be that of Haghia Triada, near Phaestos), and rural centers that show a demographic

42-43 In the throne room of Knossos we can still see the well-preserved chairs along the walls of this room at right angles to the simple but dignified alabaster throne. The room is at the level of the great central courtyard. Exact copies of the frescoes from the Neo-Palatial period, showing griffins crouching among high stems of flowers, fragments of which were found during the excavations, help reproduce the elegant atmosphere of this room. The dominant color is the red of the background, perfectly suited to the dignified setting.

42 bottom This famous fresco showing a school of dolphins and shoals of fish leaping among the waves, together with lively floral friezes, decorates the walls of the Queen's Apartment, a comfortable residential complex with a large private bathroom.

43 top right These frescoes date from the same period as those shown above. The motifs show two-lobed shields in bull's skin and are somewhat reminiscent of the custom of hanging shields and banners from the walls of aristocratic residences.

43 bottom right The different floors of the city-palace at Knossos were connected by broad, monumental stone stairways such as the one in this photograph of the stairway that used to lead from the central courtyard to the level above the nearby throne room.

development without equal in the western world of the period.

Dwellings and tombs were often decorated with imported luxury goods, including royal gifts from the East and Egypt. Paved roads, as in Knossos, connected the smaller towns to the city-palaces and complexes of religious or funerary importance.

The Minoan influence extended to the southern Cyclades. In Thira, called Santorini today, the site of Akrotyri contained a flourishing town with houses of up to four floors in height, decorated with frescoes and other signs of wealth all of which were only to be wiped out by a terrible catastrophe. Some time between the first half of the 16th century and the middle of the 15th century BC the active volcano which had formed the island exploded and covered Thira in the way Pompeii was later, burying it in a layer of over fifty yards of ashes. The inhabitants were, apparently, able to abandon the island in time, as up to now no bodies have been

found, but several archaeologists believe that the decline of the Cretan civilization was one of the side effects of this terrible event. In addition to the showers of ash there were earthquakes and tidal waves and a frightening darkening of the skies, similar to what happened on the Caribbean island of Montserrat in 1997, which may have led to significant changes in climate.

It was, therefore, a weakened Crete which was subjected between 1450 and 1400 to the increasing expansion of Mycenae in the Aegean and the invasion which ended the independence of the political entities that centered on the city-palaces. When we study the structure of the palace of Knossos we see a surprising ability to design and plan a colossal complex of over a thousand rooms, built on two, three or four floors, with staircases, porticoed corridors and ramps for carts. The residential structures were built around open courtyards which not only introduced light into them but also provided

good ventilation. There was, in addition, a huge, almost perfectly rectangular courtyard at the center of the entire complex. This indicates a building that was planned from the start and completely unfortified. There was definite logic in the distribution of the functions throughout the various wings of the city-palace. This is illustrated by the position of the warehouses and shops to the west, the extremely formal position of the throne room at courtyard level with the alabaster throne of the sovereign and the benches at the side for councilors still intact today, and the location of what are called the servants' quarters alongside the royal chambers. These royal chambers have bathing facilities which are both efficient and sumptuous.

The restoration work we referred to above includes reproductions of parts of the complex of Knossos in plaster painted in what are believed to be the original colors. In the load bearing structure, these emphasize the practical and effective combination of stone blocks and shards with a very solid wooden framework supported by widespread use of what is considered the typically Minoan wooden column. This column, which tapers strongly toward the base and is fitted with a low collar-shaped top and stone base, supported airy porticoes and bright open courtyards in the most frequented and spectacular public areas. These were decorated with many magnificent frescoes which are now in the Archaeological Museum of Heraklion. They have been replaced on the original site with faithful copies.

It seems apparent that this was a civilization that delighted in the spectacular as can be seen by the sinuous but not casual routes taken by the corridors. These corridors were apparently used for processions as were the connecting ramps between the floors and wings of the city-palace. These were not only panoramic but also seem to have been designed to break up the compact nature of the architecture by introducing variations in the surrounding landscape, looking both out from and in toward the city-palace. It is here that we see the triumph of the refined architectural decoration of this civilization and the Cretans' great love of bright colors. Here we can walk along the so-called royal road, which is completely paved, from the flat area of the theater's terraces, which are

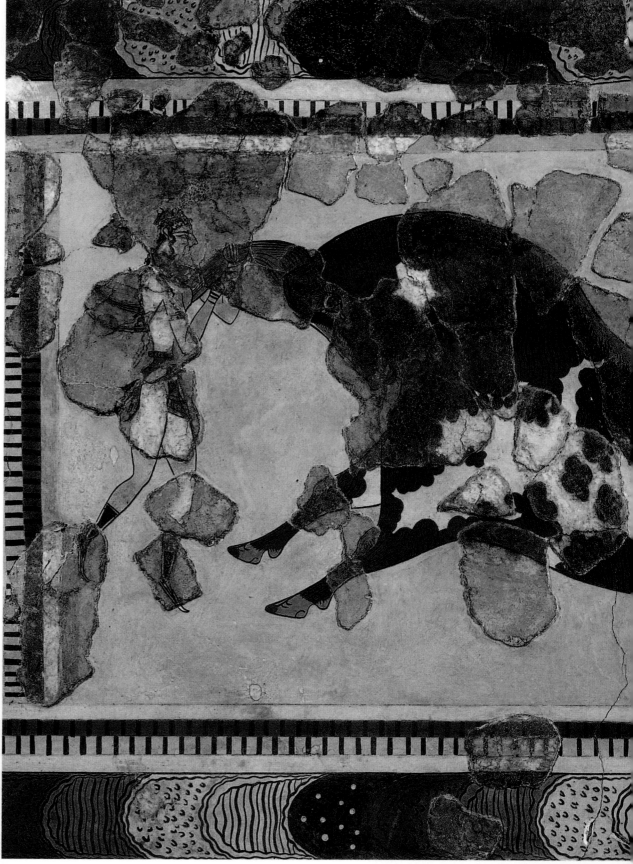

actually more suited for standing than seated spectators, and a structure called the "royal stage" toward the monumental western gate. Here what is called the Corridor of Processions begins. It is decorated with copies of the frescoes, including the Prince of Lilies, a masterpiece of Minoan painting. Although there are many rooms in the city-palace whose purpose has yet to be defined, there are two which cause no such problems. These complexes face each other. One is a construction that Evans believed was a mortuary chapel, and the other is the

luxurious royal apartment, which has elegant service and accessory areas and is decorated with a number of famous frescoes including the so-called Frieze of the Dolphins.

Although it is difficult to actually visit the residential complexes excavated by Evans and his successors, we can see them around the city-palace and they have contributed to scholars' understanding of residential models in the Middle and Recent Minoan Periods as well as when they are viewed in relation to the burial areas of Gypsades, Zafer Papoura, Kephala, Isopata and those near Heraklion.

44 bottom The elegant, famous outline of the "Prince of the Lilies" walks in a solemn procession. Originally, this probably showed a sacrificial victim being led by a rope.

44-45 This is without doubt the most famous fresco in Knossos. It shows a certain sensitivity to three dimensions and is of three young men playing a dangerous game of agility on the back of a powerful bull. The bull's profile has been deliberately exaggerated to further stress the youths' bravery.

45 bottom On the left complex hairstyles and extravagant costumes combine with grace and fascination in these frescoes of two high-caste women from the palace of Knossos. On the right, an admirable naturalism is seen in this figure of a young man walking while carrying a heavy vase in his hands.

46-47 This procession of women appears in a fresco from the Minoan age.

MYCENAE AGAMEMNON'S GOLDEN ROCK

A Gate of the Lions   E Megaron
B Burial circle   F North gate
C Temple   G House of columns
D Palace of the Atrides   H South gate

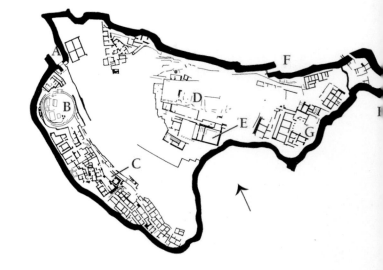

48 left One of the finest examples of Mycenean painting is this fragment showing the so-called "Dame of the Court". It is believed to date from the 13th century BC.

48-49 In this aerial view of the excavation at Mycenae we can clearly see at the top of the arcopolis the huge area occupied by the royal palace of the Atrides.

49 top In this detail from Burial Circle A, we can see the outer corridor and the tombs which were excavated by the amateur archaeologist Heinrich Schliemann in 1876.

The road to Mycenae is marked by an uneven row of eucalyptus trees and citrus groves. As we near Mycenae the walls of the acropolis inside which the Atrides ruled are hard to distinguish from the virgin rock of the hill from which the enormous blocks used to build them were quarried. The walls are dominated by two bare summits of this rock. In August 1876, Heinrich Schliemann, the amateur explorer who was famous for the discovery of Troy and the Mycenean civilization, thrilled to the same sight when he returned to Mycenae to begin his first excavations after his 1868 journey and comments on the excavations of 1874. He followed the route Pausanias, the Spartan general, took toward the middle of the 2nd century. This route was illustrated in his book on Greece which acted as the main guide book and essential reading for the cultured tourists who came to visit the Greek antiquities in the 18th and 19th centuries. Sixty workers in three teams each had brought to light the partially buried, colossal walls, the superb Lions' Gate and the royal tombs. With this work, Mycenae Polychrysos, the "rich in gold" city referred to by Homer began to

49 bottom The long artificial gallery dug out of the northern side of the hill of Mycenae to reach the water reserves of the Spring of Persela is one of the finest examples of Myceanean architecture between the 14th and 13th centuries BC. It is especially impressive because of its large overlapping stone blocks using the false arch technique. A long series of low stairways drops down for almost 400 feet to the spring, making it impossible to capture the city by cutting off its water supply.

emerge from the past and with the city the records of a people Schliemann called Myceneans. These people were Indo-Europeans who came and settled in Greece between the 20th and 16th centuries BC. They spoke a language very similar to the future Greek dialect which was found on texts drawn on clay tablets and called Linear B. Linear B was a distant archetype of later alphabets. Mycenean civilization flourished from the 16th to the end of the 13th century BC. From the Peloponnese to Phthiotis and Crete as well as in Argolis and Laconia small settlements were founded on natural farm areas near fertile plains or valleys, usually close to good natural harbors. These expanded under the guidance of rulers called Wanakes, who were the top rank of a social hierarchy kept stable through the possession of land and weapons. The key to the widespread and high levels of success of this developing civilization was the combination of an agricultural and pastoral economy with the

50 top left Funerary Circle A (sixteenth century BC) was incorporated within the site by the last defensive wall.

50 center left The entrance to the greatest Mycenean tholos tomb, known as the Treasure of Atreon, opens up at the end of a long access road.

50 bottom left The road leading

to the tomb of Egistes was dug out from the rocky terrain of the hill.

50 right We can clearly see the Minoan origins of Mycenean painting in this fresco showing a young woman (14th century BC).

51 An unusual aerial view of the main entrance to Mycenae, with the ramp passing over the Gate of the Lions.

52-53 Mycenae's Gate of the Lions takes its name from the huge monolithic block over the crossbeam of the main entrance to the fortified citadel which dates back to the 13th century BC. Two lionesses face each other with their forelegs on the plinth of a Minoan column, symbol of the palace of Atrides.

transformation of raw materials, both precious and non-precious, into sought-after finished products including highly refined ceramics and superb gold, silver, and bronze objects. Thanks to an enterprising merchant navy these products were spread from the Iberian Peninsula to the valley of the Po, from central and southern Italy to the coasts of Syria and Palestine and the island of Cyprus, from the Balkans to Egypt and the kingdom of the Hittites. This distribution was, of course, of supreme importance in establishing Mycenae.

In viewing Mycenae the deep ideological, technical, structural and decorative differences between the typical Mycenean "city fortress" and the Minoan "city palaces" can be clearly seen. James G. Frazer, in his book Pausanias and Other Greek Sketches (1900) compared Mycenae to the "gloomy stronghold of some old brigand, a lord of Skye or Lochaber."

It can also be said that there is a similarity between the austere walls and towers of the Mycenean palaces, which are much less extensive than those of the Cretans, and a number of Italian medieval villages which grew up around the castle of a feudal lord. Mycenae owes a great deal of the preservation of its ruins to the crisis and rapid decay that took place in the 12th century BC, during the Doric invasion. Although the acropolis shows signs of continued inhabitation up to 468 BC, the year of destruction by Argos, and there are some modest Hellenic remains, the Doric invasion did not lead to later cities or quarters being built on the area as has happened in so many other ancient cities.

The sturdy triangle of walls surrounding the acropolis was built between the middle of the 14th and the end of the 13th century BC, using almost regular rows of blocks of stone without mortar. The final stage of development also included the so-called Burial Circle A inside the walls. This was an artificial circular platform, reinforced by a high wall made of small stones. This is where Schliemann and the Greek archaeologist Stamatakis found, almost intact, six chambered tombs containing gold, silver and bronze burial treasure and ceramics. Schliemann attributed this treasure to Agamemnon and other figures from the saga of

Mycenae

the Atrides immortalized by the Oresteia of Aeschylus. Actually, it is now believed that the dating of the tombs should have been much earlier than the presumed reign of Agamemnon, during the period when Mycenae first flourished, in the 16th century BC.

The access route to the city was the same then as that still used today, the Lions' Gate, which was given its name from the relief which was sculpted on the ten foot high triangular block over the entrance. This shows two lionesses, facing each other in heraldic fashion, at the sides of a column whose origins are clearly Minoan.

The secondary access was through the North Gate. Both gates were placed at the end of long narrow passages between the main walls and an outer wall, thereby forcing any aggressors to be exposed to defensive forces on the parapets. A small doorway remains in the north eastern corner of the walls. As in the case of the nearby artificial gallery, which was built to guarantee access to the water supply and the Gate of Perseus even if there were a siege, this doorway is placed much lower down than the acropolis and was created using the "false arch" technique. Large blocks of stone were placed from a height of six feet upwards with a progressive ledge to the point where the two top parts touched and discharged their counter-thrusts to the underlying elements at each side down to ground level.

The Lions' Gate is a good example of a typical Mycenean technical-structural architectural solution, the so-called "discharge triangle." Above the large gates, whether they had single stone direct bearings or block posts, the architects left an empty triangular space at the segment of the monolithic architrave above the gate opening. The heavy blocks, carved as necessary and placed in a progressive ledge formation, discharged their weight to the ends of the architrave, thus providing the necessary stability to the structure.

The royal palace dominated the residential quarters which were found along the slopes of the acropolis and outside the walls. This was a complex of buildings, partially terraced, built over a primitive citadel from the 17th-15th centuries BC. There are a number of private and service rooms around the basic Bronze Age residential model. The remains show the horizontal design of this model with its double-columned portico, vestibule and great hall with stucco floor, Minoan style wall frescoes and a large central hearth in the middle of four columns.

Mycenae also offers what are probably the best examples of burial architecture from this civilization. The trench tombs in Circle A are from the 16th century BC. These are underground chambers lined with small blocks or slabs of stone, covered by slabs resting on wooden beams and earth used as

55 *The funeral mask of Agamemnon (16th century BC), given the incorrect name by which it is still known today by Schliemann, shows a stylized portrait of an old Mycenean prince, buried in the rich tomb V of Burial Circle A.*

a seal. From the 15th century BC onward, the tholoi, or "false cupola," tombs appeared in Mycenae in the form of huge circular chambers beneath a tumulus of earth, which may be based on a Cretan archetype. The most famous of these is the so-called Treasure of Atreum, dated around 1330 BC. A corridor, measuring over 100 feet long and 18 feet wide runs between steep walls made from huge rectangular blocks. The blocks are in even rows leading to the wide façade where there is a gate which is 15 feet high by 10 feet wide. The discharge triangle is above the broad architrave.

From the entrance, we reach the huge circular hall. This is over 90 feet high and has a diameter of 45 feet. Thirty-three rings of blocks which have been shaped and stuccoed take on a perfectly concave shape. They are placed on top a continuous ledge all the way to the top of the structure, where all the thrusts of the system are blocked and discharged downward to the base.
A small burial chamber dug directly from the rock is at the right of the entrance. The inside of the great tholos was probably decorated by bronze wall decorations. Just as interesting, although they are smaller and in

poor condition, are nearby tholoi which some believe may be those of Clytemnestra, Agamemnon's unfaithful wife, and Aegestes. The excavation at Mycenae resulted in the discovery of many treasures from Circle A, including the death masks found by Schliemann on the faces of the bodies buried there, the golden crockery, the jewels and ornate daggers, the fine ceramics that were known to have been exported by the Myceneans throughout the Mediterranean as well as interesting examples of cult and votive objects and fragments of the frescoes that decorated the palace.

ATHENS, WHERE PERFECTION WAS THE GOAL

56-57 Symbol of the ancient city and the splendors of the age of Pericles, the acropolis of Athens stands out against the intensely blue sky of Attica, dramatically emphasizing the imposing, elegant profile of the Parthenon, the finest temple of the ancient world, a masterpiece by the architects Callicrates and Ichthynus and the sculptor Phydia. At the foot of the southern side of the hill is the temple of Herod Atticus and the sanctuary complex of the god Dionysus, with the famous theater where Aeschylus, Sophocles, Euripides, Aristophanes and other great dramatists presented their plays. In the background on the right is the hill of Likavitos, one of the best places from which to view Athens.

A Acropolis
B Parthenon
C Theatre of Dionysus
D Odeon Hereos Atticus
E Porticoes
F Olympieion
G Pnice
H Efesteion
I Market place
J Stoà of Attalos
K Library of Hadrian
L Roman market place

57 top left This bronze head of a goddess with its sweet expression is typical of Attic art between the end of the 5th and the middle of the 4th century BC. It can be found in the National Archaeological Museum in Athens.

Beneath the very modern sky of Athens, with its atmospheric pollution typical of crowded cities, there remain museums and archaeological sites that have been rescued and continue to display many of the most important remnants we have telling of the history of this symbol of Greece and Greek culture.

The famous Acropolis is almost 500 feet high and surrounded by bare rocks. This space was inhabited from Neolithic times, dedicated to Athena. It was the religious heart of the city from the 10th century BC although almost no trace remains of the Doric temples of Athene Polyades, the "protector of the city", the first of which was built around 565 BC and measured 100 Attic feet long. A few painted statues from the gable still remain. The second of these temples, which had a double row of columns and elegant Ionian proportions, was built under the tyrannical reign of Hypia and Hyparchos. A few of the marble figures from the gable of this temple remain. Following the sack of the Acropolis by the Persians in 480 BC, the ruins of these and other lesser religious buildings and works of art which had given Athens its reputation as a living museum of the faith were buried in the trenches of the so-called Persian Fill. The amazing heritage that had been concealed in this way was found in excavations on the site that took place from 1886-1887.

What we see today is the extraordinary result of the Athenian civilization of the 5th century BC when the city, at the height of its democratic government, devoted its efforts under the leadership of Pericles, who

headed the government, to the construction of a society which aimed for a learned perfection of philosophy utilizing mathematics and the sciences which finally synthesized into an artistic creation.

In the period between 449 and 447 BC Pericles continued, in a more elaborate manner, a building project which had been set up during the government of Kymon. He drew up the ideological and material guidelines for this, arranged for the financing

57 top right The great temple of Herod Atticus, built during the reign of Hadrian, rests against the southern slopes of the acropolis in sight of the hill of Pnika and the port of Piraeus.

57 center right The elegant temple of Athena Nike, which dates from around 430-420 BC, is almost intact. It was designed by the architect Callicrates in Ionian style with a front colonnaded plan.

57 bottom The monumental porticoes of the acropolis in Athens, designed by the architect Mnesicles (437-433 BC) are a grand prelude to the dramatic sight of the Parthenon.

58 top This section from the Ionian frieze that adorned the inner section of the Parthenon enables us to see the superb artistic levels reached by the skilled sculptor Phydia. Notice how the impetuous rhythm with which the young horsemen launch themselves into the race or, possibly, parade in honor of Athena has been realistically transferred to the beautiful white marble from the quarries of Mount Pentelis, a few miles from Athens.

58-59 In this impressive view of the Parthenon from the western side we can see its proportional and aesthetic elegance. This side leads to the Ionian colonnaded hall which contained an extremely old cult image of Athena. On the front is shown the myth of Cecrops and the dispute between Poseidon and Athena for the protection of the city.

required and turned the supervision of the site and of many of the plans over to the man considered the greatest artist of the ancient world, the Athenian Phydia. Phydia hired the services of architects, sculptors and leading painters as well as a great number of obscure craftsman. All were equally proud to be considered worthy of belonging to the group of both known and unknown contributors to the masterpieces of the Acropolis.

The Parthenon (built between 447 and 432 BC) and dedicated to Athene Parthenia (parthenia means virgin in Greek), was the work of Callicrates, who had been responsible for the Kymon project, and Ichthynos, who used a good deal of the platform already prepared on the southern side of the Acropolis and the large quantities of architectural materials that were available. The result is a splendid Doric eight-column temple. The measurements are such that each element and space is part of a system producing perfect harmonic proportions. This building not only satisfied the requirements of the religion and enhanced the building as an example of absolute

entrance portico we see the building at an angle which places its profile on the southern side of the hill, toward Piraeus and the sea. There are also several optical adjustments which were made by the designers of this building which cancel the effects of the imperfect view that the human eye can manage. The slightly convex shape of the pedestal avoids the illusion of concavity, while the impression of spatial expansion is eliminated by the special placing of the columns with respect to their axis.

The sculptures in the temple were

beauty but also had a philosophical role as an expression of the understanding of being itself. As an example, in the peristasis, denser and closer to the walls of the inner part of the temple, the ratio between the lower diameter of the column and the interaxis is 4:9 as between the façade and its height up to the horizontal cornice of the gable. Studies have shown that there seems to have been a base module of 10 Attic dactyls (around 23 inches) long. All the proportional ratios between the parts and between the parts and the whole are based on this module. This immense edifice also contained the colossal gold and ivory statue of Athene Parthenia, the work of Phydia, which was in the central section of the temple. Unfortunately, we only know about it from contemporary descriptions and through a number of small scale copies such as the Athene of Varvakion or part models, such as the Medusa Rondanini. The location itself of the Parthenon helps to accent its perfect harmony of measurements and proportions. As soon as we cross the

59 top This fragment from the Ionian frieze of the Parthenon shows the figures of Poseidon, Apollo and Artemis seated on the acropolis, to which the Pan-Athenian festival, honoring Athena, is headed. This is yet another example of the unequaled quality of Phydia's art.

59 bottom An impressive collection of Greek inscriptions from the 6th century BC up to the Roman period was found in the acropolis of Athens. All of these describe public and private monumental building work, administrative deeds and religious acts, although they are often only fragments.

masterpieces made by Phydia and his assistant. On the gables are told the tale of two myths of great importance to the city. These are the birth of Athene from the head of Zeus and the dispute between the goddess and Poseidon over the possession of Attica. Some groups of marble figures remain, showing the very high level both of idealization and freedom in showing human figures which was achieved by Phydia. The square spaces of the Doric frieze of the peristasis, which has been the subject of a great deal of discussion by scholars concerning its proto-classical style and the number of artists who were believed to have worked on it, showed the eternal struggle between good and evil, civilization and barbarism, justice and injustice through myth and epic, including the Killing of the Giant on the east, the Destruction of Troy on the north, the Killing of the Amazons on the west, and the stories of Erechtheus and Theseus (including the Killing of the Centaur) to the south. The long Ionian frieze of the inner part of the temple is a splendid example of the stylistic perfection of Phydia. It describes the Games and the Great Procession of the four yearly Panathenian Festival, when all the aspects of the religion,

60 top From this impressive picture showing the western and southern sides of the Erecteon the complexity of the building is clear. It was built at the northern edge of the acropolis toward the end of the 5th century BC and was mainly dedicated to Poseidon. An olive tree grows today at the same point where one given to the city by Athena was venerated.

60 center The eastern face of the Erecteon stands in full dignity, its six Ionian columns testifying to the skill of Greek architecture. On the right is the northern portico. Legend says that the mark of Poseidon's trident was concealed in the rock.

60 bottom The Caryatids of the lodge on the southern side of the Erecteon wear elegant Ionic clothing. There is something almost casual in the way they stand, forming a harmonic contrast to the grandiose dignity of the nearby Parthenon.

60-61 This spectacular view of the Erecteon from its western side shows how complex this unusual building is. It had at least two floors, and possibly more, with details on them showing religions of various different extremely ancient origins. The entire scene is united by the Ionian architecture, with its slender columns and the remaining friezes of the entablature.

politics and ideology of the Athenian community were celebrated and enhanced. Between 437 and 433 BC the architect Mnesicles built the Propiles, a monumental entrance to the Acropolis of elegant and dignified proportions. A six-column Doric entrance precedes an extended vestibule which is divided into three aisles by rows of Ionian columns and closed by a wall with five doors, crossed by four low steps and a central ramp for vehicles and animals. On the eastern side is the symmetrical counter-pronaos, an ideal place for viewing the

Phydian bronze statue of Athene Promachus, now lost but known to have been over 20 feet high, and the Parthenon. On the northwestern side of the Propiles we can still see the small porticoed wing that was by the art gallery, well-known for its collection of paintings. The gracious, four-columned marble Ionian temple of Athene Nike, based on an old design by Callicrates which dates back to around 450 BC, was built on the southwestern bastion of the Acropolis to celebrate the ephemeral victories of Athens during the first stages of the Peloponnesian War.

61 bottom This detail of the sixth column from the left of the eastern portico of the Erecteon gives us the chance to admire the fine styling of the Ionian capital in this building. The scrolls graphically underline the profile and the abacus has a pearl motif, while the top of the stem is adorned with plant decorations. All these touches enrich the column as an example of the chiseller's art rather than as a load-bearing element.

The final building that was built on the Acropolis, known as the Erecteon, was built before 400 on an ancient meeting place which had been used by different and very ancient religions dating back to before Athene was recognized as a multifaceted divinity. This building was apparently designed by Callicrates, Mnesicles or Philocles and, from its T-shaped plan, it appears that it followed ritual demands and ancient models. The six-columned Ionian pronaos on the east is older than the cult religious center part in which the ancient xoanon of Athene Polyades was placed. On the northern side, a high, six-columned Ionian portico was dedicated to one of the prodigies of Poseidon during the dispute with Athene while, on the west, an olive tree donated by the goddess was venerated. At the southern side is the Lodge of the Caryatids, which tradition says is the tomb of the mythical King Cecrops. Watching over the site are six statues of elegantly dressed young women replacing the original ones and an excellent example of a post-Phydian interpretation of a typically Ionian ornamental element, the Caryatid. The famous theater of Dionysus, the protector of the dramatic games of the Great Dionysian festivals, is on the south of the Acropolis.

62 left Two views of the Theseion complex, a six-columned Doric temple dedicated to Ephestus, the Greek god of fire. It was built at the same time as the Parthenon and has elements in common with it. This complex is set in a gently sloping area set back from the marketplace.

62 bottom left There are three hills to the southwest of the acropolis, Mousion, Pnika and Nymphon. One of the most interesting remains of Roman Athens, the monument to Julius Antiochus Philopappus, Roman consul and citizen of Attica is on the first of these three hills. This monument, built between 114 and 116 AD, is an excellent example of the classic style in Hadrian's time.

62 bottom right Near the Roman marketplace is a very well-preserved octagon called the "Tower of the Winds" after the figures on the upper frieze. Actually, it is a large hydraulic clock made by Andronikos Kyistes in the 1st century BC.

62-63 Here are seen the terraces, orchestra pit and stage of the famous theater of Dionysus on the southern slopes of the acropolis, still showing some of its marble covering and sumptuous shapes which date from the time of Alexander the Great. Although this was not the biggest theater in Greece, it was definitely the greatest in terms of the works staged in it.

The visible structures in this sacred enclosure date back to 330 BC but were rebuilt during the Roman period. Here immortal masterpieces of classical Greek theater were performed. The imposing theater of Attic Herod, from the imperial Roman age, is still used for theatrical performances today. Across the hill of Areopagos is the agora, the great market place and the administrative and economic center of the city. Among the remains that can be dated from the days of the tyranny to the late Roman period are the modern reworking of the great portico of Attalos II of Pergamon (2nd century BC), the site of the Museum of the Agora and, almost opposite, the six-column Doric temple of Ephestos, still intact. This is of the same date as the Parthenon and was built in marble by an architect who had obviously carefully

studied the Acropolis, as can be seen by the dimensions and proportional ratios. The building was placed in an area that had housed bronze sculptors and pot makers, and perhaps was built for their use. The area that was occupied by the potters (Kerameikos) is an archaeological area of unusual interest as it is connected to a huge burial area, the Dipylon. Spectacular remains from both the Hellenic and, above all, Roman, periods can be found on the hills to the southwest of the Acropolis (for instance, the monument of Philopappos), in the area of the Roman square with the Tower of the Winds by Andronikos Kyrriste and, to the south of the acropolis, where the emperor Hadrian ordered the completion of the enormous double-columned Corinthian temple of Zeus Olympio.

63 bottom left This chair, set in a prominent position in the theater of Dionysus, was reserved for the priests devoted to this god during events staged during the great Dionysian festivals.

63 bottom right The many works of art that speak of the god Dionysus and his story reveal to us, living today, the importance that this god had in the past. We can still see these works in his theater.

PAESTUM,
GODS AND HEROES

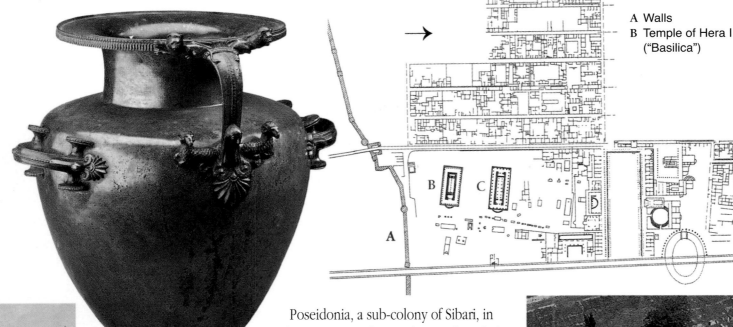

A Walls
B Temple of Hera I ("Basilica")
C Temple of Hera II ("Temple of Poseidon the God")
D Underground temple
E Temple of Athena ("Temple of Ceres")

64-65 and 66-67 Although called the Temple of Poseidon the God, this building was actually dedicated to Hera around the middle of the 5th century BC. It is the most elegant sacred building in ancient Poseidonia. Its shape, which is based on Doric styles of architecture, also shows the influence of the proto-classical period.

64 bottom left Ancient Greek painting is reflected in the various figures, some very plain and others quite sophisticated, with which the inhabitants of Paestum decorated the tombs of their dead during the classical period.

64 bottom right This fine aerial photograph shows the perfect alignment, apparently for ritualistic reasons, of the two Temples of Hera in Paestum, the Basilica and the Temple of Poseidon the God. All were built within a century of each other from the middle of the 6th to the middle of the 5th century BC in the Doric style. They are extremely well preserved.

Poseidonia, a sub-colony of Sibari, in what is now southern Italy, was founded on the plain of Sele near the Tyrrhenian Sea in the first half of the 7th century BC. It flourished for over two centuries before falling into the hands of the Lucani. It acquired its better known name, Paestum, in 273 BC, when it became a Roman colony. Today, it is considered by many to be one of the most fascinating archaeological sites of the Greek, Italic and Roman worlds, not only due to its three well-preserved temples but also because of an exceptional fairly recent discovery.

It was on the late afternoon of June 3, 1968, during an archaeological dig carried out by Mario Napoli in the northern necropolis, that the Tomb of the Diver, a work which has become a symbol of Paestum, was brought to light and thereby gave us the oldest known record of Greek mural painting and one of only a very few examples which have survived over the centuries.

Mario Napoli described the discovery with these words. "Right from the start it was clear that the discovery was something exceptional. From the outside, the tomb appeared to be well looked after and we observed that the joints were very precise and adjusted and perfected with stucco work that guaranteed perfect holding. . . The tomb faced in the normal direction, east to west.

65 top left This magnificent bronze hydria, a masterpiece of Greek metal work dated 510 BC, was found along with other precious works of art in the treasure of the Heroon, a colonnaded sanctuary of a type common in the Greek world and used to venerate heroes from the mythical past of the city.

65 right Another two views of the temple of Hera II (also known as the Temple of Poseidon the God). These give us the chance to notice the vigorous harmony of the structure and the division of the central religious areas into three naves with a double row of columns. A similar plan was used at the end of the 6th century BC in Aegina, on the Gulf of Saronika.

TARQUINIA, THE AFTERWORLD PAINTED ON THE ROCK

A The city today B The Etruscan city C Etruscan tombs

Tarquinia, the city of the mythical Tarcontes and considered one of the stars of the southern Italian area of Etruria imposed its rulers, Tarquinius Priscus and Tarquinius Superbus on Rome. Still mainly buried in the enormous plain known as the Plan di Civita and surrounded by its huge necropolis it is in a perfect setting for its steep profile of medieval towers and bell towers, with the River Marta descending through sheer volcanic rock toward the sea over the arid ancient Etruscan landscape. The city has inspired enthusiastic writing about it. G.W. Dennis, in a book called *Cities and Cemeteries of Etruria* published in 1848 reported himself to be thrilled by it. D.H. Lawrence also wrote about it, but unfortunately with little regard for accuracy.

The city was founded in the distant past, perhaps in the 10th but certainly in the 9th century BC. It was one of the cradles of the culture known as Villanovan, the first phase of the Etruscan civilization (10th to 8th century BC) and was marked by many burials performed by incineration inside molded double-cone clay urns that were decorated with etched or printed geometric motifs. Its position between the sea, which meant it was able to have traffic with the Greeks and Phoenicians, and the mineral deposits of central Tyrrhenian Italy, as well as rich soil and excellent defenses at the site made it one of the most dynamic centers in the area, both ready to receive and to transform the cultural and economic changes taking place in the surrounding Mediterranean and Italic areas to its own advantage. Tarquinia was one of the first Etruscan cities to abandon the Villanovan model and to accept and develop the forms of the Middle Eastern phase in Mediterranean civilization. This was linked to an increasing consolidation of power in the hands of certain aristocratic families during the 7th century BC. In the 6th century BC, the city seems to have played a major role in the creation of a balance of

74 top This splendid fragment of pottery with its pair of winged horses dates to the 4th century BC. It was a decoration on the wooden entablature of the huge temple known as the Queen's Plow, probably actually dedicated to Juno.

74 bottom The wall paintings in what is called the Baron's Tomb (510-500 BC), with their pictures of ornamental trees, show the farewell to the dead noble.

power with an Etruscan-Punic axis against the Greeks and in the establishment of the Etruscans as the major Tyrrhenian Sea power. In addition, it was in a flourishing trade area and was able to attract people with both economic and cultural skills, including artists. During this period the city grew enormously and became known both then and in the following centuries as unique in Italy for the incredible number of underground chambered tombs it had. These are covered in multicolored mural paintings and were basic to the passing on of knowledge for the development of ancient painting which was introduced and cultivated here, probably primarily by either Greek or Greek-trained artists.

The crisis that followed the Greek victory at Cuma in 474 BC, the end of the Tyrrhenian dominance and the loss of power to the ascendant Rome led to a period of comparative decadence, during which the entrepreneurial, commercial and craft economy that had characterized this civilization gradually gave way to an agrarian-pastoral economy which was based on land ownership and the concentration of power in the hands of the aristocracy. Later wars with Rome (4th century BC) followed by the city itself becoming part of the Roman Republic made it a major center among the Roman allies, so that it kept a reasonable level of splendor to the start of the 1st century BC, after which Etruscan

civilization was completely absorbed by the Romans.

Visiting Tarquinia today means, first of all, discovering the exceptional heritage of its painted tombs. A few of these deserve special mention due to the excellent state of preservation of their wall paintings. The Tomb of the Auguries is especially famous. Its name comes from the Etruscan priests whose job it was to foresee the future by interpreting the flight of birds. It consists of a single chamber, dating to 520 BC. A sumptuous wall design by a painter who may be Greek-Ionian, possibly from Phokeios, or Etruscan-Ionian shows a sequence of athletic contests, spectacles and ceremonies in honor of the deceased noble, all celebrated under the guidance of the auguries. Wrestling scenes alternate with scenes of mourning and with the not entirely understood bloody game of Phersu which may be a gladiatorial battle honoring the deceased.

The Tomb of the Baron is slightly more recent, dating from between 510 and 500 BC. This is the work of a Greek-Ionian artist, a composed and well-balanced scene that we can view as the deceased leaving for the after-world, if we consider this to be symbolized by the stamping horses which are held back with reins. Here again is evident the strong, lively coloring of Etruscan painting and the tendency to fill in the figures although

without suggesting a third dimension. Etruscan tombs, which are considered a residence for the hereafter, at times show decorations that underline the architectural structures of a house, thus providing us with precious information on the history of residential building. This is the case, for instance, with the ceiling of the Bartoccini Tomb (520 BC) and the Tomb of the Chariots (490 BC) which has walls showing a splendid banquet below a frieze of athletic and equestrian contests. Another of the city's most famous tombs, called the Tomb of Hunting and Fishing, dates to around 510 BC It takes its name from the well-known and unique hunting and fishing scenes with their animated figures and their strong sense of the relationship between the figures and the landscape. This tomb may have been created for a wealthy aristocratic customer involved in both maritime trading and the typical leisure pursuits of his class.

The Tomb of the Bulls perhaps dates back to 550 BC. The back wall of the main chamber shows a rare epic scene of Greek derivation, perhaps with some funereal significance. The scene shows the ambush by Achilles of the young Trojan prince Troilus. Troilus had rashly gone into the sacred wood of Apollo Thymbaios to reach a fountain where the Thessalian hero had hidden himself. The landscape is highly stylized and the scene shows the moment just prior to the tragedy. This scene is clearly understandable. Another, on the other hand, showing various figures in extremely realistic erotic positions is not so easily explained.

The 4th and 3rd century BC paintings from the Tombs of the Ogre I, II, and III are part of the classical and Hellenistic phase of Etruscan art. These tombs belonged to the very important Velcha and Spurina families. The first tomb shows the scene of an aristocratic banquet with newlyweds in beautiful clothes. Here, the melancholy, fascinating profile of Velia Velcha is considered particularly beautiful. On another wall, the horrible figure of the underground demon Charun, known as Charon by the Greeks and Romans, is a reminder of death and, in a sense, of the Etruscan decline itself. The stylistic refinement of the metalworking suggests it was produced by someone under the influence of the Greek world, perhaps Taranto.

The Tomb of the Ogre III shows an unusual scene, with strong colors and a certain naiveté which is, however, interesting for its attempts at realism. It shows the blinding of Polyphemus by Ulysses and his companions, as explained in captions above the figures of Cuclu (Cyklops) and Uthusie (Odysseus).

One of the last painted tombs of Tarquinia is the aristocratic one of Typhone (200-150 BC), which belonged to the Pumpu family. This rectangular tomb has a sequence of graded steps and a sturdy central pillar. From this protrude the poorly preserved remains of naked winged demon figures with expressions as of beings seeing an hallucination and with hats in the form of serpents. The plastic nature of the bodies and the extreme expressions are reminiscent of the baroque of Pergamon.

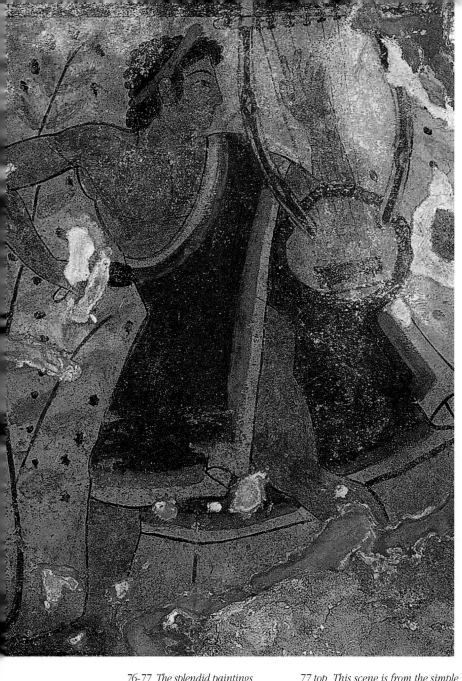

77 center *The Tomb of Hunting and Fish (late 6th century BC) has vivid paintings which tell strong stories. In this detail of the scene which gave its name to this burial complex in Tarquinia the dynamic figures are outstanding against the contrast of the heavy background.*

77 bottom *This superb marble sarcophagus, now in the National Archaeological Museum of Tarquinia, is from the last quarter of the 4th century BC.*
It is the tomb of an aristocrat, whose body is shown on the cover. The coffin shows a relief illustrating the battle of the Amazons.

76-77 *The splendid paintings from the Tomb of the Leopards date from 480-470 BC and are among the most important found in Tarquinia. Here is shown a celebration of some kind in which a guest at a banquet is entertained by two musicians. One plays a double flute, the other a barbiton, a stringed instrument with the soundbox made from a turtle shell.*

77 top *This scene is from the simple but famous Tomb of the Augurs (520 BC). It shows the custom, clearly of aristocratic Greek origin, of holding sporting contests in honor of the deceased.*
Two naked wrestlers face each other while on the left a soothsayer follows the flight of the birds from the right to interpret what their passage portends.

Italy

Rome
POMPEII

Tyrrhenian Sea

Mediterranean Sea

POMPEII, *A CITY REBORN*

78 left This aerial view of Pompeii shows how the Temple of Jupiter was flanked by two tiled honorary arches, originally covered in marble. One was dedicated to Tiberius and the other to Germanicus.

78 top right The Forum, seen here facing the side with the public building, consisted of three large adjacent spaces which housed the main courtrooms and was the center around which the political, economic and religious life of Pompeii revolved. Around the square was a continuous portico supported by Doric columns, partly surmounted by a second colonnade in Ionian style.

78 bottom right The Temple of Jupiter, which occupied the southern side of the Forum area, was a large building in Corinthian style built on a high podium.

One August morning, during the first year of the reign of the Roman Emperor Titus, Pacuius Proculus was suddenly awakened by a deep, resounding tremor, a type of boom that he had felt once before in his life, as a boy. He was annoyed by the tremor, but gave it no further thought. Vesuvius had been misbehaving for some days and a few similar minor tremors had already alarmed his servants. In fact, he wasn't worried in the least. Occurrences of this kind were fairly frequent in Campania, in what was later to become Italy. Anyway, it would be ridiculous to neglect his work for something so trivial. Seventeen years earlier, under Nero, the situation had been different. That had been a real earthquake. Then the columns of the temples had collapsed, the roofs had opened up, and the statues of the family gods had crashed to the ground. This morning it was only when his wife, normally such a calm woman, begged him to follow her to the inner courtyard of the house to see for himself that Pacuius felt

A Temple of Apollo
B Temple of Jupiter
C Forum
D Building of Eumachia
E House of the Vettii
F Triangular forum
G Central Baths
H Gladiators' barracks
I Theatre
J Odeon
K House of Centenary
L House of Paquius Proculus
M Great Gymnasium
N Amphitheatre

82 The Temple of Apollo, dating to the 2nd century BC, is located near the Forum, in the center of a 48-columned courtyard. In front of the portico, on one of the long sides, was a bronze statue of Apollo with a bow, now replaced by a copy.

83 top left The sanctuary dedicated to Apollo was being restored following the earthquake of 62 AD. The columns, originally Ionian, were changed to Corinthian and the bare architrave was covered with a layer of plaster and decorated with a frieze of griffins and festoons. These changes have almost disappeared today, so the complex has a more ancient appearance.

83 bottom left The remains of the Basilica, dating from the end of the 2nd century BC, are in the western corner of the Forum. This is one of the oldest remaining examples of this type of building. It was used as a courtroom and for business, evolving over the centuries until it became the first form of Christian architecture.

nervous in spite of himself. A huge cloud was rising from Vesuvius, a vast column of dense black smoke moving skyward and then expanding so that it took on a profile similar to that of a pine tree.

However, always the businessman, he felt there was no time to lose looking at Vesuvius. Business called and this spectacular sight was no excuse for making a late start. He left his wife alone in the house with the servants, trying to remain calm even as the earth continued to tremble and, gradually, a fine shower of ash, initially light and hardly visible, began to cover the flower beds. She was slightly comforted by the unexpected return of her husband Pacuius, but then her worst fears were confirmed when a terrible noise drowned out every other sound. The ornaments in the house jingled and the flames of the oil lamps in front of the household gods flickered. The whole house shook as if ready to break up at any moment. Howls and screams could be heard from the street. The sky had suddenly gone dark and the air was heavy and dense with a strong smell of sulfur that seemed to suck out both breath and strength. Pacuius went as pale as death itself. His wife understood then that it was all true: the gods had turned their backs on

Pompeii! At that moment she knew that if they wanted to go on living they would have to take flight immediately, leaving all their possessions behind and without looking back.

We'll never know whether Pacuius and his wife, whose famous portrait was found in Pompeii, were really in Pompeii on that terrible day to witness the horrendous catastrophe, or if they were able to save themselves, unlike many other inhabitants of the town, whose bodies, contorted in their death throes, were gradually discovered by archaeologists and filled with plaster to show how they appeared in death.

One thing that we do know is that many of the inhabitants of Pompeii were never aware of the appalling fate the volcano held in store for their town. They didn't want to abandon their houses immediately. Indeed, many of them were still repairing the damage caused by the earthquake of 62 AD. They died in the hundreds, suffocated by the death-dealing clouds from the cracks that opened along Vesuvius, trampled underfoot by terrified horses, or killed by falling masonry.

We know many of the details of these frightening events due to Pliny the Younger

83 top right Together with the Via Nola, the Street of Abundance was one of the two main east-west roads in the city, crossing the entire street network. This important road linked many central points in the city and was heavily traveled. It not only had private houses but also shops of every kind, inns, eating houses, brothels and private clubs. On the top floor of the house of Popidius Montanus, the club of the latruncularians, chess players of the time, was found.

83 bottom right The bath complex near the Forum was the smallest but also the most elegant in Pompeii. It was decorated with multicolored stucco, marble and mosaics. In spite of its small size it contained everything for the complete bathing ritual (dressing rooms and rooms for cold, lukewarm and hot baths), divided into separate areas for men and women. The photograph shows a view of the caldarium, the hottest room, with its great marble bath.

86-87 In the rooms to the side of a shrine in the gardens of the House of the Golden Bracelet, a number of magnificent frescoes in the Third Style were found, showing gardens in bloom and many different types of birds.

86 bottom This painting, which shows two theatrical masks, was part of the very rich wall decorations found in the House of the Golden Bracelet. The house is in the western section of Pompeii, next to the city walls.

technology so that experts can identify even the types of trees and shrubs grown in the gardens of Pompeii. Amedeo Maiuri, director of the excavations from 1924 until his death in 1961, not only worked to free the buildings from the solidified ash but also stressed the importance of taking every possible step to protect the finds as they were unearthed.

Although about a fifth of the site is still unexplored, Pompeii is probably the most famous archaeological site in the world. It tells of a culture and lifestyle of a major city whose existence was snuffed out almost in a moment, a city that was fossilized without the gradual abandonment and decay typical of other urban centers during Roman times. Today, we know that Pompeii was founded on the outer southern reaches of Vesuvius at the end of the 8th century BC by a group known as the Oscan people. They were followed by the Etruscans and later by the Greeks. Toward the end of the 5th century the city was taken by the Samnites who held it until 310 BC when they became allied with Rome.

It was during the Samnite period that those centers essential to public life, including the forum, the so-called Triangular Forum complex, the Basilica, the Gymnasium, the Spa Complex of Stabia, as well as the houses with their atriums and the imposing fortifications were built. Over time, the old and new inhabitants intermarried and both Latin and Oscan became official languages of the colony. Later, the city was promoted to municipal status and the inhabitants had all the privileges of Roman citizenship. In 80 BC, after the Civil War, it became a colony with the name Cornelia Veneria Pompeianorum and, thanks to the patronage of the Silla political party,

87 *The two details shown on this page are also from decorations found in the House of the Golden Bracelet. They were produced with the finest fresco technique with the color spread on plaster while it was still wet. The wall paintings of Pompeii have shown a resistance to wear and tear over the centuries that surpasses even those from the Renaissance. The true nature of the technique for the application of colors and the exceptional quality of the Roman paintings have yet to be fully explained although there does seem to be little doubt that the calcium carbonate film that formed over the color as the lime in the plaster reacted with the air played a basic role. The materials used to obtain the different pigments are, however, known, from Spanish cinnabar for bright red to copper oxides for the greens and resinous carbon for black. Two paint factories have been found in Pompeii.*

underwent a period of major renovation. It was during this time that a number of major public buildings were erected, including the baths, the odeon, a building for musical performances, the capitolium of the forum and the amphitheater, which held 20,000 spectators. It was at this time that the streets were paved with stone.

From 27 BC on, an intense period of Romanization took place and it was during this time that new artistic and architectural models were introduced that reflected the official Roman culture. During the Julian-Claudian period the gymnasium was built alongside the amphitheater, as well as the market, the Eumachia Building, the temple of Fortuna Augusta and the so-called temple of Vespasian, but the basic layout of the city remained more or less the same.

As in Rome, Pompeii was organized in quarters, or insulae, and Larian shrines were

placed at the crossroads. The names of these quarters can often be found on the electioneering messages painted on the outside walls of the houses.

More than 40 fountains have been discovered along the streets, usually placed about 80 or so yards apart. The water supply came from a number of deep wells dug from the base of lava and volcanic rock on which the city was built as well as on the aqueduct built during the time of Emperor Augustus. The water entered the city near the Gate of Vesuvius, where a large collection tank, known as the *castellum aquae* was placed which distributed it through the main city pipes. The pipes were

made of lead and ran underneath the roads. From these pipes the water was channeled into private houses.

Pompeii's daily water consumption must have been enormous, as was the case in all Roman cities. Only the poorest people had no running water, but they had access to the public fountains.

Pompeii had two forums which were the centers of city life. In these places people gathered to listen to speeches by politicians, to discuss business and, of course, simply to chat. The first of these forums, which was surrounded by a Doric colonnade with an Ionian portico, has its buildings laid out in a logical way although they were built around

it at different times. The capitolium and courthouse were at the shorter sides, and the courtyard was surrounded by the temples, the basilica, the covered market, two memorial arches and the Eumachia building, which was dedicated to Eumachia, priestess of Venus, and patroness of the corporation of weavers and dyers, the city's major industry. The second forum, which was in a cramped triangular space, was also used as a theater. Its oldest section dated back to the 2nd century BC and also contained the odeon, which was a small covered theater. The remaining public buildings included gymnasiums and bathhouses.

88 top In the lower part of the House of the Vettii, one of the most luxurious residences in Pompeii, is an elegant frieze with a black background showing cupids involved in various activities. Here they are preparing perfumes.

88 bottom This fresco painting, showing Hercules as a child strangling the serpents sent by Hera, decorates a room in the House of the Vettii, which belonged to two rich merchants of excellent taste.

88-89 and 89 bottom These superb wall paintings are also from the House of the Vettii.

90-91 The exedra in the House of the Vettii has richly frescoed walls.

92-93 The atrium of the House of Marcus Lucretius Frontone was decorated with marbles and fine paintings.

Pompeii, however, is famous most of all for its private buildings. There is no other place, with the possible exception of Herculaneum and Ostia, where we can find such a complete understanding of the Roman house with all its features, from its basic structures to its decoration and even its household ornaments. The evolution of the domus, the most common type of residence in Pompeii, began in the 4th century BC with Samnite construction with Tuscan entrance halls and enormous façades and moves on to the houses of the Republic, which reflected the Greek influence, with elegant inner courtyards, plaster walls and decorated façades.

By the time of the Empire, the houses had complex, extensive plans, finely painted walls, balconies and elaborate ornamental gardens. The wall paintings, many of which have been preserved, also reflect the development of Roman taste and especially of decorative taste. The so-called First Style, which was dominant between 200 and 80 BC, was influenced by the Greeks and was a colored plaster imitation in relief designed to look like square blocks of marble. In the 1st century BC the Second Style was dominant. This was based on perspective, with architectural or landscape decorations. The Third Style, fashionable until around 40 AD, was ornamental, flat, and more schematic. The Fourth Style, which was in vogue following the earthquake of 62 AD, was almost fantastic in its conception and rich in optical illusions. The local aristocracy lived in elegant, enormous houses which often had colored marble or mosaic floors. Some of these houses included shops opening onto the street which were rented out to freed slaves or run by slaves for selling their masters' products, such as foodstuffs, to the public. Trade was a major part of life in Pompeii, especially along what is now called the Via dell'Abbondanza or Street of Abundance, one of the main streets. Buildings included workshops, dye works, taverns serving drinks, inns and brothels and gaming houses.

The elegant preservation of the furniture, silverware, pots and pans, lamps, glassware and tools in general is extraordinary in both the houses and the shops.

Another fascinating feature of Pompeii are the many inscriptions, the painted signs, the election posters and graffiti which can still be seen on the walls of the city, giving us further insight into the life of this lively town until the moment when, on the 5th of February in 62 AD, a disastrous earthquake struck the town and other nearby cities, including Herculaneum.

The reliefs which are part of the household shrine of Lucius Cecilius Jocundus in Pompeii show several buildings in the town as the wave of the earthquake was felt. The damage was so severe that, over fifteen years later, reconstruction and repair was still going on.

Prior to this earthquake the population had been around twenty thousand. After the earthquake the population was cut in half. Trade, which had been the major activity of Pompeii, was replaced with construction and an accompanying speculation in property. There was no lack of money. The city became almost one enormous building site. But it was all to no purpose. With the terrible eruption of Vesuvius on that dreadful day in August of 79 AD the city was literally annihilated, bombarded without stop for four days by a combination of stones and ash which reached several feet. Many people, overcome by toxic gases, fell to the ground in a variety of positions and were buried under the volcanic materials. The prints in the rocks left by their bodies are the most dramatic testimony to the tragedy of Pompeii.

At least two thousand people, perhaps more, were unable to save themselves and died here. We can see them today as anonymous, reconstructed plaster statues, lying in the way and where they died. Whether or not a citizen such as Pacuius Proculus and his wife are among them we can never know.

94-95 *The Villa of Mysteries was built in the middle of the 3rd century BC and then extended and enriched over the years. It owes its name to the famous frieze showing the most important stages in a rite of initiation into the Dyonisian mysteries.*

This extraordinary fresco, with 29 life-size figures, was painted by an artist from Camania in the 1st century BC. It covers the walls of a room entered through a single door. Since the rites themselves are not known, interpretation of the scenes is difficult. Although the

paintings in Pompeii have been conserved in excellent condition, they no longer have the brilliance that made them shine like mirrors, a brilliance written about by writers of the period. We do not know how this brilliance was achieved.

Italy

●ROME

Thyrrhenian Sea

ROME, A UNIVERSAL CAPITAL

A Tomb of Hadrian
B Tomb of Augustus
C Field of Martis
D Stadium of Nero
E Pantheon
F Theatre of Pompey
G Portico of Octavia
H Theatre of Marcellus
I Temple of Capitoline Jupiter
J Arx

K Trajan's Forum
L Baths of Constantine
M Baths of Diocletian
N Castra Praetoria
O Baths of Trajan

P Colosseum
Q Temple of Venus and Rome
R Palatine
S Circus Maximus
T Baths of Caracalla
U Porticus Aemilia

Symbol of a metropolis, a huge, complex city with buildings zooming upward to the sky in a seemingly infinite number of styles. A melting pot of races and nationalities, a maze of streets alive with bustling activity, never-ending traffic and an almost neurotic feeling. The constant movement of businessmen and women, children, housewives, noisy workers on building sites, beautiful women, handsome men, rich and poor. In short, a tremendous confusion of noise and color, a cacophony of languages and variety of customs, fashionable shops and humble grocery stores, trendy night clubs and sleazy bars, all set in a dramatic architectural backdrop which almost demands extravagance. New York? No.

This is Rome. The Big Apple of the ancient world, the first true megalopolis in human history. It was a city with everything anyone could imagine. It was a city with

the best bathhouses in the empire, the best libraries, theatrical performances by the best companies, shops supplied with the best merchandise every day, excellent doctors, learned lawyers. There was something for everyone in Rome. During the imperial period, which was when most of the monuments admired today were built, the Eternal City must have been a truly amazing sight. It was a city constantly growing, with over a million inhabitants in the 4th century AD, not including slaves and recent immigrants. Architects were forced by this increasing population to build ever upward, with some buildings reaching six, seven or more floors. The numerous shops, called *tabernae*, made the city seem almost like a giant bazaar with officially licensed traveling peddlers, moving through the crowds shouting out their wares, adding to the impression that anything anyone wanted could be bought in Rome.

96 bottom and 98-99 The
Column of Marcus Aurelius,
standing in front of Palazzo
Chigi, was erected between 176
and 193 to celebrate the
emperor's victories against the
Germans and the Sarmathians.
About 60 feet high, it has spiral
decorations showing the events of
the military campaigns.

96-97 The Roman Forum, in the
valley at the foot of the Palatine
Hill, was the heart of the public
life of Rome for centuries.
Temples, basilicas, triumphal
arches and votive columns were
added over the centuries.

97 right This circular bas-relief is
part of the rich decoration of the
Arch of Constantine, taken from
buildings dating back to the times
of Trajan, Hadrian and Marcus
Aurelius and put together with
considerable balance.

97 bottom This marble relief,
showing a dramatic view of
ancient Rome, is of exceptional
documentary interest.

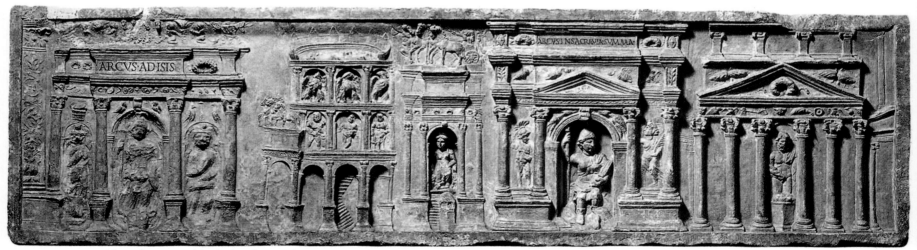

The tabernae sold a little of everything, from groceries to fabrics, cushions to crockery, jewelry to books. There were also many services available, including laundries, dyeworks, tanneries, bakeries and workshops of blacksmiths, shoemakers, potters, carpenters, glassmakers, carvers and knifemakers. In the *tabernae argentariae* exchange of foreign currency could be arranged. These banks also offered deposit services and loans at interest, as well as the opportunity to make investments in businesses. Those who were involved in legal action or had important business to discuss had a choice of various spots in the city to go to for just that purpose. Rome was packed with public works of every kind, including those for extravaganzas and special shows. Leisure was just as central to the life of ancient Rome as it is to us today. There were almost innumerable choices of ways in which to spend leisure time for all classes. They could wander through the forums and various places of business or drink and gamble in forerunners of the modern bar. The working day finished early, afternoons tended to be long, and the evenings were not considered safe times to be out after dark.

100 top The arch of Septimus Severus was built in the Roman Forum to celebrate the victories of the emperor in the east.

100 center Among the most impressive monuments in the Roman Forum is the House of the Vestals, the convent of the priestesses who guarded the fire sacred to Vesta, goddess of the hearth. This burned in the nearby circular white marble temple.

100 bottom Constantine's arch was completed in 315 to celebrate the emperor's victory over Massensius in the battle of Ponte Milvius. The arch has three openings, about 80 feet high, and is in an isolated position near the Colosseum. Many of the parts of this arch were taken from older buildings. A few reliefs made specifically for it were clearly done in something of a hurry.

One popular way of spending the time between work and dinner was the bathhouse, which can still be seen in the modern city, two of which, those built by Caracalla and Diocletian are outstanding. Going to the baths was an everyday habit for both rich and poor, young and old, men and women. During the imperial period entrance was free or at least much less than the cost of a loaf of bread. The rooms were arranged in accordance with the order of the operations. First came the dressing room or *apodyterium*, followed by the hot bath or *calidarium*, then an intermediate room with lukewarm temperatures, called the *tepidarium*, and finally the cold bath or *frigidarium*. The pool, called the *natatio*, was usually outside.

All around the main rooms were smaller ones, used as saunas, for the application of oils and ointments, massage, and hair removal. The gymnasiums, which were usually part of the bathhouse structure, were also important and these complexes included libraries, reading and meeting rooms and snack bars. These very popular public health facilities were not just about health and fitness but also social centers, where people got together for pleasure, to talk about politics, sport and business. Other major attractions for the Roman population were the circus and amphitheaters. Public spectacle in Rome was always used for political and electoral propaganda so that it was one of the most valuable tools in keeping absolute imperial power. As these shows became more important in this role, they became more and more frequent with a growing number of public holidays to which they were linked.

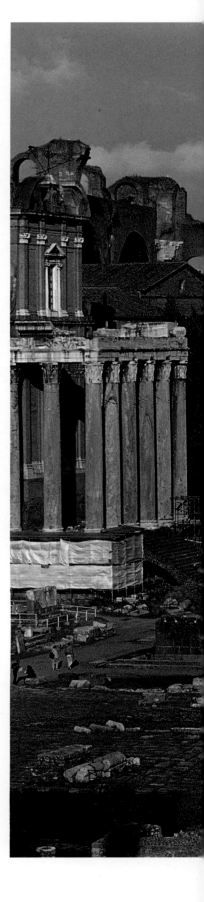

Rome

100-101 The Roman Forum was not only a place to celebrate the personal victories of the leaders but also for political and business discussions, religious ceremonies and a marketplace. In the photograph, to the left of the Temple of Antonius and Faustina, we can see the rebuilt section of the Temple of Vesta in the center and the three remaining columns of the Temple of Discuros on the right. Behind this is the Arch of Titus, built in 81 to celebrate the victories of Vespasian and his son over the Judeans.

101 bottom In the circles of Hadrian which decorate Constantine's Arch, two of which are shown here, the head of the emperor was replaced with that of the new leader, who became the ruler of Rome after defeating and killing his rival Massensius. The honorary arch built to celebrate an important figure is one of the most typical architectural features of Roman civilization. Arches can also be of religious significance or a means of marking the boundaries of a city.

102 top This marble relief adorned one of the finest palaces on Rome's Palatine hill.

102 bottom According to tradition, Romulus founded the city of Rome on the Palatine hill where the emperors later built their palaces. In the foregrounds are the remains of the Domus Augustana, built by Augustus. The long structure in the center is the Domitian stadium.

102-103 The last of the Forums built in Rome, the one built by Trajan in 112 with booty from the Dacian wars, was also the most grandiose. It was built by Apollodorus of Damascus who introduced the transverse position of the Ulpian Basilica in relation to the rest of the complex and the great semi-circle of the Trajan Markets, a group of tabernas arranged on six floors.

They could last for hours, even a whole day, as was the case with the gladiatorial combats. Although these events usually took place during the day they were sometimes held by night using torches for lighting.

The games in the circus were the most ancient and took place in the Circus Maximus which could hold 250,000 spectators on wood scaffolding and stone terraces. Among the most popular events were the chariot races, in which special, lightweight vehicles drawn by two, three or four horses raced in a counter-clockwise way at great speed, skimming the central platform and doubling at the two ends of the track where three conical pillars stood. What rules there were were made to be broken and there was a definite attempt to force the competing chariots off the track and overturn them.

Events in the amphitheater were viewed even more passionately. This building, named the Flavian Amphitheater and known today as the Colosseum was worthy of a city as grand as Rome. It was opened in 80 AD, elliptical in shape with a circumference of 1700 feet and a height of just about 150 feet. It could hold 50,000 to 70,000 spectators. Underneath the arena, which was paved with a wooden platform covered in sand, were the underground passageways used for the various services needed for the different events, including machinery needed to change scenery. Spectators were protected from the sun by large sheets of canvas, raised and lowered by special squads from the navy. This stadium was used for the famous hunting of wild animals from all over the empire and for gladiatorial contests, in which trained fighters fought for their lives. The games were considered a great social occasion, and the audience dressed to express the importance of the event.

103 bottom The Trajan Forum contains a column built to celebrate the victory of the emperor over the Dacians. It is 100 feet high. The stem is decorated with a continuous spiral covered with reliefs containing about 2,500 figures which were originally multicolored and show the main episodes of the military campaign in great detail. The column was originally topped by a statue of Trajan but now it bears a statue of Saint Peter which was placed there in 1587. The cubic podium, 30 feet high and covered with friezes, contains the funerary remains of the emperor.

108 top Built in 309 outside the city walls, the Circus of Massensius is one of the best conserved in the Roman world. It is over 550 yards long.

108 center The Circus Maximus dates back to the royal period in Rome and was rebuilt several times. It was the biggest building for public performance in Rome. During Trajan times It was 660 yards long. Although experts disagree, most believe it could hold 250,000 spectators and, on special occasions, up to 320,000.

108 bottom left The Theater of Marcellus was completed in 13 BC on the orders of Augustus, who dedicated it to his nephew and original heir, who had died two years before. This theater, it is believed, could hold between 15,000 and 20,000 spectators.

and ponds as well as other water-based activities. The most advanced sewage system in the ancient world effectively removed filthy water.

The problem of overcrowding was not, however, limited to traffic and the water supply. During the time of Cicero (106 BC-43 AD) Rome looked as if it were suspended in air, someone said, due to the height of its buildings. Under Augustus they went higher still. The state did occasionally intervene to control building but more often than not with relatively little effect. Augustus himself, who said he had been given a city of bricks and left it made of marble, was unable to solve the general situation of overcrowding and congestion in the poorer quarters.

Fires and building collapses were among the most common incidents. The upper floors of the buildings were often based on wooden frameworks supporting lightweight masonry structures which were both quick and cheap to build but also very fragile and highly inflammable. It was, strangely perhaps in view of his generally bad reputation, Nero who deserves the credit for stopping this state of affairs and partially renovating the city.

The terrible fire of 64 AD which destroyed so much of the city led to the issuing of strict laws against unauthorized building. Property owners were forced to ensure that specific safety regulations were followed. Buildings could be no taller than twice the width of the road, wood ceilings were forbidden, broad porticoes had to be built at the front and the houses had to be separated from each other. Rome was never a planned city. During the imperial age, although it was the greatest city of the ancient world, the first true world capital, it was both chaotic and shapeless in form. The inhabitants were crowded into what little space was left free after the imperial palaces, markets, gardens and countless public buildings were built. In the 4th century AD it is estimated there were about 1,800 private houses in the city and another 44,000 apartment houses. These huge apartment houses were the most common type of housing in Rome.

They were built of brick with a tile covering and usually had shops on the ground floor

109 bottom The aerial photograph shows the imposing remains of the Baths of Diocletian, the largest in the Roman world. This enormous complex was built entirely of tiles between 298 and 306. It could be used by 3,000 people at once. In 1566 Michelangelo transformed the frigidarium, about 95 yards long and 90 feet high, into the church of Saint Mary of the Angels.

108 bottom right Among the many works of art in the Baths of Caracalla, the marble group of the Farnese Bull is outstanding. This is a precious copy from the Antonine period of a Greek original by Apollonius of Thralles.

108-109 The Baths of Caracalla were begun in 212 by Septimus Severus in 212 and opened four years later by his son, for whom they are named. These baths were among the most luxurious in Rome. They stretched over an enormous area and could hold 1,600 people.

112 top In front of Hadrian's tomb, today known as Castel Sant' Angelo, the River Tiber flows under the elegant Ponte Elio, built by Hadrian to link his tomb to the field of Martius.

112 center The Fabricio Bridge connects the island of Tiberina to the left bank of the Tiber. The oldest bridge in Rome, it was built in 62 BC and measures 200 feet long.

112 bottom The marble pyramid of Caius Cestius, alongside the Porta San Paolo, is the original tomb of this praetor and tribune who died in 12 BC. The building, inspired by models that became fashionable after the conquest of Egypt, is covered with marble squares and is over 115 feet high. It was incorporated within the Aurelian walls nearly three centuries after being built.

112-113 The enormous mausoleum Hadrian built for himself and his successors was changed over the centuries into what is now known as Castel Sant' Angelo. The great cylindrical structure, which was on a huge four-sided base topped with a mound of earth planted with cypresses, was topped by a high podium, on which there may have been a group of statues or a bronze equestrian statue.

This, then, is the side of Ancient Rome that we should keep in mind along with the history, the battles the writing and the drama. It was also a major urban center and, as such, it speaks to us today in a language we understand as clearly as if it were our own. As we have said, the problems of Ancient Rome are the problems we face today. The overcrowding in the poorer centers of our cities that contrasts so dramatically with the wealthy areas was visible in Rome, too. In many of our urban centers wealth and poverty live almost side by side. We, like Rome, face problems of ensuring sound healthy water supplies and we, like Rome, luxuriate in the creation of more and more places where we can indulge our bodies' desires for cleanliness and health. But it is, perhaps, in the homes of the ordinary people, in the apartment houses rising above the skyline of Ancient Rome and reflected everywhere in the world today, that we can see ourselves most clearly. Throughout the world people live in multistoried buildings, neighbor next to and above and below neighbor in this way which we tend to think unique to our age but which the Romans knew, too. They, too, suffered from noise at night but contrasted it with the stimulation of life in a large city. We have seen how the Romans loved, enjoyed, almost demanded entertainment and there, too, we have an echo in our own lives. Despite the fact that we have television and radio to entertain us we go to see sports ourselves. Our stadiums are filled, our children wear caps supporting their favorite teams. We cheer for one side or one individual over another. How is this different from Rome? The theater is a rich part of our lives, whether it is the theater as represented by the movies or the live stage. We, too, like the Romans have a choice of either spoken or musical performances. And, although many of us pride ourselves on our level of appreciation for high culture, often that is not the most successful at the box office. Rome was then and now is now and yet, as we have stressed throughout this book, we can see ourselves today in the life of the past.

Rome

113 top The tomb of Cecilia Metella, daughter-in-law of the triumvir Crassus, is the most famous monument on the Appian Way. This tomb dates to the last decade of the republican period and was turned into a fortress in medieval times.

113 bottom left Originally, the two arches of the Porta Maggiore were not part of the Aurelian Walls but of the aqueduct built in 52 AD under Claudius. Lead water pipes ran along the top.

113 bottom right With a single opening flanked by towers, the Gate of Saint Sebastian opens onto the Aurelian Walls, which ran around the city for almost 12 miles. The walls, begun in 271 under Aurelian, were completed by Probus.

Italy

Rome
HADRIAN'S VILLA

Thyrrhenian Sea

HADRIAN'S
SUMPTUOUS VILLA

A Theater
B Circular temple
C Triclinii
D Hospitalia
E Courtyard of the
  Libraries
F Maritime theatre

G Peristilium
H Room of the Doric pillars
I Golden Square
J Guards' barracks
K Pecile
L Aquarium
M Nympheon

N Building with
  three exedras
O Small rooms
P Small bath-house
Q Great bath-house
R Vestibule
S Canopy

Hadrian was one of the great historical figures of all time. Roman emperor, he was born in 76 AD in Italica in Spain, and was still very young when he held his first public offices which were granted to him because of his strength of character and military bravery.

A versatile man, he was a restless, romantic spirit, a deep thinker, a poet, and a refined admirer of Greek civilization.

Appointed successor to Trajan, the man who had carried Rome to its furthest frontiers, he was appointed emperor in 117 AD when he was governor of Syria, when he was just over 40 years old.

He returned to Rome where he embarked on a complex program for consolidating the political and military system of the empire. He visited Germany, France and Britain, where he arranged for the building of the

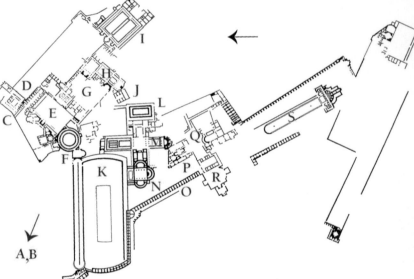

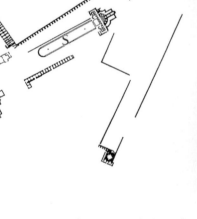

famous "Hadrian's Wall", as well as Spain, Africa, and the East.

He was back in Rome in 134 AD and from that time until his sudden death in 138 he devoted his energies to the administrative reform of Italy and fiscal reorganization of the provinces. The place he loved most was Tivoli, where he went to escape from the stress of his office.

Ancient Tibur, the city founded originally by the Latins to the southeast of Rome, became during the time of Augustus one of the most fashionable resorts for wealthy Romans. Among those who stayed in Tivoli were Cassius, Horace, Catullus, Augustus, and Hadrian.

As well as the pleasant nature of the area, visitors were also attracted by a famous statue of Hercules, the Oracle of Sybil and

the sulfur springs, believed to have healing powers, nearby.

Today, of course, Tivoli is famous above all for its grandiose Hadrian's Villa, placed in a spacious plain among the slopes of the Tiburtine Hills to the southwest of the town. The huge complex of buildings fills an enormous area and is one of the most impressive archaeological parks in all Italy, a country noted for its historical remains. Built on the site previously occupied by a villa from the Republican period, Hadrian's Villa blends harmoniously into the surrounding landscape in such a way that it looks almost as if it grew there naturally.

It was, however, quite deliberately planned. It has been described by B. Cunliffe as "a studied architectural landscape".

Building work on the villa began in 118 and

114 left In his luxurious villa near Tivoli, Hadrian wanted reminders of the monuments he had seen during his long travels to the four corners of the empire, especially Egypt and Greece. The Pecilis, here seen from above, is named after a great porticoed square in Athens.

114 right Hadrian was a genius with many talents including those of an architect. In his elaborate residential complex he experimented with advanced building techniques, making wide use of cupolas and semi-cupolas such as those in the Small Bath House (center) and the Great Bath House (below).

114-115 The aerial photograph shows the huge size of the residential complex built by Hadrian. In the foreground are the remains of the square portico with the so-called aquarium. To the left is the Small Bath House, to the right the Guards' Barracks and the circular structure of the Maritime Theater. In the background is the great pool of Pecilis.

115 bottom This delicate mosaic from Hadrian's Villa was produced using extremely small chips of glass-like material. It is the copy of a work by Sosos of Pergamon. Hadrian, who is said to have spoken Greek perfectly, was a great admirer of ancient Hellenic culture.

116-117 Some experts believe that the Maritime Theater, surrounded by a portico and moat, was actually the small villa where Hadrian went to meditate alone, away from the rest of the world. It is probable that the residence of Augustus on the Palatine Hill and, even earlier, the palace of Dionysius the Elder in Syracuse were used for similar purposes. However, a fairly recent theory by the Swiss scholar Henri Stierlin is that the structure was actually a complex cosmic symbol at the center of which was the wooden dome of a planetarium.

117 top This red marble faun, a precious copy of a bronze Hellenic original, was found in Hadrian's Villa. It is now in Rome's Capitoline Museum. Hadrian was a highly cultured man and in his luxurious residence he built up an extraordinary art collection, most of which was lost during the Renaissance. In the middle of the 16th century, for example, Cardinal Ippolito d'Este financed major excavations at the site of the villa with a view to finding as many sculptures and other works as possible to decorate his own elegant villa near Tivoli.

went on for over ten years, while Hadrian was traveling and inspecting the various provinces of the empire.

The villa can almost be interpreted as representing an anthology of memories of these travels and a symbol of the immense territory unified by the emperor.

Hadrian, a great lover of both art and Greek tradition, took his inspiration from famous objects of the past, freely imitating the places and monuments that he remembered best. This explains the great variety of the structures flanking the residential part of the complex which is quite unusual in Roman architecture. Originally, the work consisted of simply restructuring and extending the existing buildings to which a spa and gymnasium complex and an official banqueting hall were added.

All the rest, including warehouses, porticoes, swimming pools and theater were built as the site took on its final, monumental dimensions, completed in 133 AD.

The entire area had a system of underground passages, some of which were suitable for wheeled traffic. This was apparently a kind of independent service network, designed to avoid disturbing events going on above.

The main entrance to the villa was from the north, by a side road from the Tiburtine Way, running alongside the Vale of Tempe, named because of its similarity to a place of the same name in Thessaly. This was the site of the dormitory for the Praetorian guards who watched the entrance.

Nearby were two rooms which are known as libraries although they actually were summer dining rooms. They are part of the oldest section of the building. At the rear of one of these are the remains of the Maritime Theater, one of the most impressive parts of the entire complex. This is formed by a curved wall with porticoes on the inner side which separate the structure from the rest of the villa and a space which marks off a circular island, once linked by two small bridges. On this artificial island there is a miniature villa for rest and relaxation built around a courtyard with a fountain and complete with a small bathhouse complex. This is believed to be copied from the residence of Augustus on the Palatine Hill which was influenced by the palace of Dionysius the Elder in Syracuse.

It is important to know that Hadrian's Villa was originally designed as a government building with all the facilities necessary so that it could back up or even replace the imperial palace in Rome.

This sumptuous residence could not only house all the public functions of the emperor but it also guaranteed privacy, keeping Hadrian away from the court that surrounded him in Rome and from the control of the senate.

Here he was also able to put his own architectural ideas into practice, ideas which at times seem to combine classics with an almost Baroque richness along with eager use of new building methods.

Hadrian's villa

117 bottom Shown is a view of the circular portico that surrounds the Maritime Theater, whose name is due to an imaginative interpretation by 19th century archaeologists. According to the contemporary archaeologist Henri Stierlin, however, the island represents the Earth, the channel at its edge is the Ocean, known to the Greeks as Chronos, god of time and father of Zeus. In the hall at the center of the structure which was covered by the wooden dome of the planetarium, Hadrian went from time to time to carry out his studies in astronomy and meteorology, practice divination and make horoscopes.

The villa is famous for its use of curved surfaces and the variety of domes of all types, including semi-spherical, segmented, and pointed in combination with design details that carefully play with light and shade.

The central part of the villa extends beyond the Maritime Theater.

It includes the courtyard of the libraries, the palace, the Nymphs' Shrine, the hall of the Doric pillars with the guards' barracks off to the side, and finally the Golden Square which is surrounded by a large peristyle and double naved portico.

The hall of the Doric pillars leads to the area known as the Throne Room, probably a kind of assembly room for the formal

world, occupying a narrow valley and consisting of a long hall with its short, convex side decorated with a colonnade and highly decorated architrave.

Other colonnades flank the long sides of the valley and were originally decorated with imitations of famous Greek statues. The valley is closed off by a great semi-circular hall covered by a segmented, flat and concave semi-cupola. This was a refined, imposing summer dining area.

The plan seems to take its inspiration from those of the Egyptian temples and fits in well with the adjacent stretch of water. In ancient times, Alexandria had been linked to the city of Canopus and its famous temple of Serapis by a canal. The canal and

the city were famous for their celebrations and banquets, an echo of which we can also find in the famous Nilotic mosaic of Palestrina.

Antinous, the handsome favorite of the emperor, was drowned in the Nile in Canopus, an event that plunged Hadrian into a deep depression.

This may explain why the finest statues of the young man were found here, alongside the faithful imitations of the Caryatids of Erechtheus.

Many other copies of famous sculptures, such as the imitation of Venus of Knidos by Praxiteles, were in various sections of the villa, reflecting the emperor's great love of collecting.

The richness of these finds and the ease of access to the ruins made Hadrian's Villa a favorite destination for scholars and antiquarians during the Renaissance. Unfortunately, this means that a great deal of the fine heritage from this villa is now scattered throughout Europe in museums and private collections.

This continued until 1873 when the first Italian government-sponsored excavations began. Today, Hadrian's Villa is visited by thousands of tourists every year and continues to be studied by scholars. It is a fitting memorial to a complex and extraordinary man.

sittings of the imperial court.

The northern side of the Golden Square consists of an eight-sided vestibule covered by one of the most famous examples of a segmented cupola. To the south, the large, complex, semi-circular Nymphs' Shrine is found, perhaps a summer dining area for the emperor.

Against the western wall of the Philosophers' Hall, at the Maritime Theater, is one of the short sides of the Peciles, a spacious square surrounded by porticoes which forms a Greek-inspired area designed specifically for walking and learned conversation.

Toward the east is another series of buildings, the most famous of which are the stadium and summer banqueting hall for official occasions.

Other areas include the small and great bathhouses, the vestibule and, finally, the Canopus. This is one of the most famous architectural complexes of the ancient

118 top Along the edge of the basin occupying the central part of what is called the Canopy is an elegant colonnade of copies of famous Greek statues.

118 bottom Several statues of Antinous, Hadrian's favorite who drowned in the Nile during a voyage to Egypt with the emperor, were found near the Canopy.

119 Hadrian's skill as an rchitect is clear in the elaborate layout of the Canopy, which occupies an artificial valley to the south of the residential complex. In this monument the emperor intended to copy the Temple of Serapides at Canopus in Egypt and the canal that linked that town with Alexandria. In the foreground the great semi-cupola of the Serapeon stands out.

AFRICA
Introduction

The Sahara divides North Africa like an immense sea of sand. Like an ocean, it can only be crossed with method and great knowledge. Even today, a journey in the vast expanse of dunes that is the Sahara is an adventure in every sense.

In the distant past, the emergence of the desert meant the separation of the African peoples who occupied the territories along the Mediterranean shores from those who lived in the interior of the continent. North and south began to develop independently of each other, giving rise to ways of life and culture that went on as time passed to differ irreversibly from each other.

Between the Mediterranean and the rest of Africa, however, there remained one point of contact to the east. The fast flowing Nile runs between the rocks of the high desert plains of the Sahara for hundreds of miles, creating a corridor of fertile land that links Lake Victoria with the Mediterranean. The good living conditions created by the annual flooding of the river were at the basis of the development along its banks of one of the most ancient civilizations on earth.

People, probably coming from the southern edges of the Sahara, settled near the fertile land along the Nile around 6,000-7,000 years ago. They then moved up along the river, gradually changing from a mainly semi-nomadic lifestyle in which they survived by hunting, fishing and the fruit and vegetables they were able to pick to a sedentary one which enabled them to develop an economy based on agriculture and the breeding of animals. The trading relationships with the Mesopotamian regions led to fast technological and cultural development. Between the middle and the end of the 4th millennium the people living between the First Cataract on the Nile and the shores of the Mediterranean grouped into a single state. And, scholars believe, Egyptian civilization showed from the beginning the features that were to distinguish it in the almost three thousand years of its history.

This civilization also built the earliest cities on the African continent. The foundation of the first capital of a unified Egypt was considered such an important event that it has become a legend. According to this legend, Memphis was attributed to Menes, the first man to put himself in the place of the gods as leader of Egypt. For this reason, the city always retained a role of primary importance throughout the history of the Pharaohs.

The desert not far from the town was chosen as the site of the rulers' tombs. These imposing funerary complexes were built in various locations, including an area stretching for about 40 miles. With the founding of the Ancient Kingdom, these were transformed into that most spectacular of monuments, the pyramid, so unique and extraordinary that it has become the symbol of the entire Egyptian culture.

Today, Cairo, overcrowded and suffering from a severe housing shortage, has spread out to touch the high plain on which the pyramids of Cheops, Chefren and Mycerine stand. Giza is no longer the name of just this historic site, but also a densely populated area of the capital of modern Egypt, with concrete houses stretching far out along earth roads. The road that leads to the archaeological site is flanked by bars and taverns where frantic nightlife goes on in this metropolis full of contradictions which is in constant balance between east and west, old and new.

Nevertheless, the first sight of the pyramids at Giza is always unforgettable. Their imposing structure and sacred aura cancel out everything around them. Overwhelmed by their amazing presence in the desert, there is no space in the viewer's eye for anything else.

Memphis, the capital of Egypt for centuries, later lost this role to Thebes, called by the Egyptians Uaset or "the powerful" and corresponding to modern Luxor. It was from this city that the rulers of the XI dynasty came (2150-1050 BC) who united Egypt again after a period of territorial division and internal disputes between bordering mini-states.

120-121 The rock temple of Abu Simbel, in Lower Nubia, is not only the most famous monument of Ancient Egypt after the pyramids, but was also a personal triumph for the most powerful of the pharaohs, Ramses II. Dug entirely from sandstone around 1260 BC, the sanctuary is 125 feet wide and reaches over 100 feet in height.

The funerary complex built by Mentuhotep
II at the base of the natural amphitheater of
Deir el-Bahri dates back to the beginning of
this period. The remains of sacred buildings
at Karnak, site of the temple dedicated to
Amon, god of the city, date to roughly the
same time. With the ascent of the Theban
dynasty to the throne of Egypt, the cult of
Amon spread throughout the country, with
the result that the temple of Karnak
expanded over time as each ruler added
something to what his predecessors had
already built.

Today, Karnak is a monument without
equals. As one walks through it one moves
backward in time. From the Ptolemaic
pylon we reach the buildings of Thutmose
III through 300 yards of halls, columns,
obelisks, statues and walls covered in
painted scenes and inscriptions, attesting to
nearly fifteen hundred years of human
history.

Thebes had its period of maximum
splendor when the Pharaohs were at their
most powerful, during the New Kingdom.
Many monuments were built by the rulers
of the 18th, 19th and 20th dynasties in this
opulent capital that governed a vast
territory. The mountain overlooking Luxor
was chosen as the burial place of the rulers,
whose final resting place was dug out from
deep in the rocky banks of a gorge where a
roaring river flowed during the rainy
season. It was here, in 1922, that the intact
tomb of Tutankhamen was found, together
with the most splendid burial treasure ever
discovered. On the eastern bank of Thebes
are the ruins of the temple of Luxor, once
connected to Karnak by an avenue lined
with sphinxes, five miles long. The greatest
building expansion took place under
Ramses II, who had scenes of the battle he
had fought against the Hittites in Qadesh
painted on the outer walls of the first pylon.
The same scenes and inscriptions can also
be found on the walls of the first columned
room in the Greater Temple at Abu Simbel,
dug out of the rock over 300 miles south of
Luxor. Here Ramses II celebrated his
greatness, deifying himself while still alive,
and enhancing his own glory with symbols
and allusions which
become more and more
explicit as we approach the
inner part of the temple. The
smaller rock sanctuary,
dedicated to his wife, simply
repeats the message of the
greatness and divinity of
Ramses II.

Abu Simbel is in the region
known as Nubia, whose
northern boundary is marked by
the modern town of Aswan. Not
far from here, the history of the
Egypt of the Pharaohs came to an
end. The temple complex dedicated
to Isis, once standing on the island of
Phylo and now on Agilkia, where it was
moved during the 1970s to prevent its
being flooded as part of the amazing
engineering work involved in building the
Aswan Dam, is one of the most important
centers of worship in the Egypt of the later
period. On its walls, among the many
inscriptions referring to the devotion of
Egyptian, Greek, Roman and Merotic
pilgrims to the wife of Osiris, there is one
from the August 24, 394 BC, believed to be
the most recent hieroglyphic ever found.
Although Egypt dominates African
archaeology, with its wealth of famous
monuments, there are other regions that
show signs of a more recent but equally
glorious past. The coasts of North Africa
enjoyed a period of extraordinary vitality
from the start of the first millennium BC
and reached their maximum splendor in
the beginning of the first millennium AD.
At this time they were provinces of the
Roman Empire, lively, dynamic centers of
culture and birthplaces of many figures
who made important contributions to the
growth and development of Roman
civilization. One of these cities is Leptis
Magna in Libya. The ruins of this city may
be said to testify more than those of any
other city to the coast of North Africa at the
dawn of our age as one of the most crucial
meeting points in human history.

Francesco Tiradritti

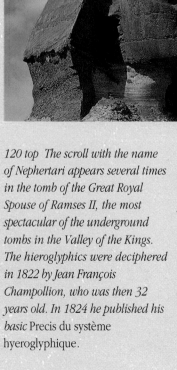

Leptis Magna

CHRONOLOGY

Paleolithic and Neolithic period
(60000-3000 BC)

Pre-dynastic Period in Egypt
(3300-2920 BC)

Proto-dynastic Period
(2920 -2670 BC)

I Dynasty
(ca. 2920-2770 BC)

II Dynasty
(ca. 2770-2670 BC)

Ancient Kingdom
(2670-2150 BC)

III Dynasty
(ca. 2670-2570 BC) Main
rulers: Sanakht, Djoser,
Sekhemkhet.

IV Dynasty
(ca. 2570-2450 BC)
Main rulers: Snefru,
Cheope, Chefren,
Mycerene.

V Dynasty
(ca. 2450-2300 BC)
Main rulers: Userkaf,
Sahura, Neferirkara,
Neuserra, Unas.

VI Dynasty
(ca. 2300-2150)
Main rulers: Teti,
Pepi I, Merenra, Pepi II.

1st Intermediate Period
(2150-2100 BC)

Middle Kingdom
(2100-1750 BC)

XI Dynasty
(ca. 2100-1955 BC)

XII Dynasty
(ca. 1955-1750)

2nd Intermediate Period
(1750-1640 BC)

Period of Hyksos
domination
(1640-1550 BC)

XIII-XVII Dynasties
(ca. 1750-1550 BC)

New Kingdom
(1550-1076 BC)

XVIII Dynasty
(ca. 1550-1295 BC)
Main rulers:
Thutmose I, Thutmose III,
Hatshepsut, Amenophi II,
Thutmose IV, Amenophi III,
Amenophi IV/Ekhnaton,
Tutankhamen, Horemheb.

XIX Dynasty
(ca. 1295-1188 BC)
Main rulers:
Ramses I, Sethi I,
Ramses II, Merneptah.

XX Dynasty
(ca. 1188-1076 BC)
Main rulers:
Ramses III, Ramses IV,
Ramses IX, Ramses X,
Ramses XI.

XXI Dynasty
(ca. 1076-945 BC)

XXII Dynasty
(ca. 945-828 BC)

XXIII Dynasty
(ca. 828-742 BC)

XXIV Dynasty (Saitic)
(ca. 742-712 BC)

XXV Dynasty
(ca. 712-664 BC)
Main rulers: Shabaka,
Taharqa.

XXVI Dynasty
(ca. 664-525 BC)
Main rulers:
Psammetico I, Psammetico
II, Amasi.

1st Persian Period
(ca. 525-405 BC)

XXVII Dynasty (Persian)
(ca. 525-405 BC)

XXVIII Dynasty
(ca. 405-399 BC)

XXVIX Dynasty
(ca. 399-380 BC)

XXX Dynasty
(ca. 380-343 BC)
Main rulers:
Nectanebo I, Nectanebo II.

2nd Persian Period
(343-332 BC)

Macedonian Dynasty
(ca. 332-304)
Main rulers
Alexander the Great,
Philippus Arrideus,
Alexander IV.

Ptolemaic Dynasty
(ca. 304-30 BC)

Destruction of Carthage and
start of Roman rule in Africa
(146 BC)

Cyrenaica becomes a
Roman province
(74 BC)

Caesar annexes the
province of Numidia
(46 BC)

Egypt becomes a Roman
province
(30 BC)

Mauretania becomes a
Roman province
(40 AD)

Vespasian proclaimed
emperor at Alexandria
(69)

Septimus Severus born in
Leptis Magna
(146)

The army of Queen Zenobia
occupies Lower Egypt, but
is pushed back
(268-270)

Under Constantine, Egypt
becomes a diocese
(324-337)

Egypt becomes part of the
Byzantine empire
(395)

Egypt is occupied by the
Arabs
(640)

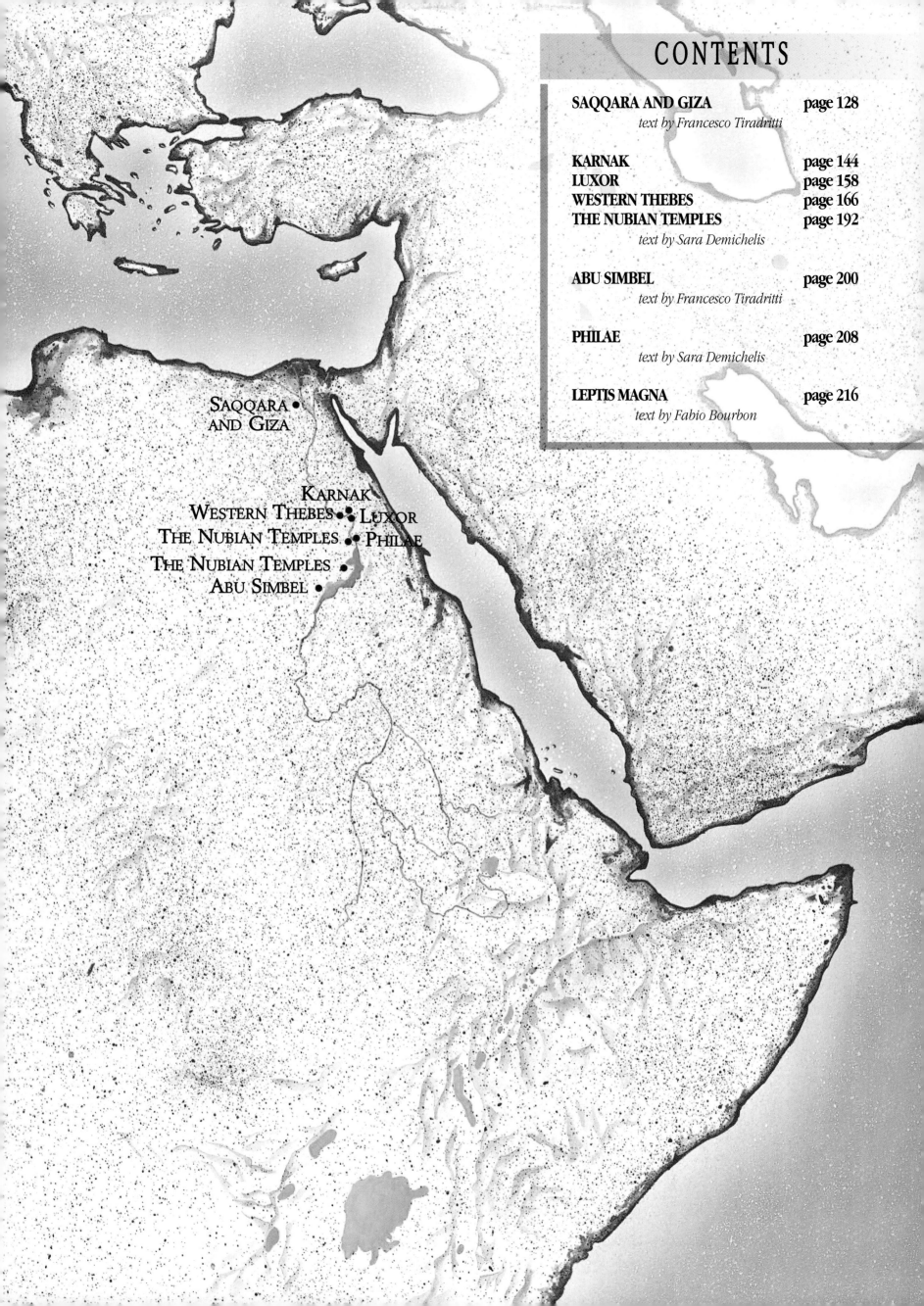

CONTENTS

SAQQARA AND GIZA page 128
text by Francesco Tiradritti

KARNAK page 144
LUXOR page 158
WESTERN THEBES page 166
THE NUBIAN TEMPLES page 192
text by Sara Demichelis

ABU SIMBEL page 200
text by Francesco Tiradritti

PHILAE page 208
text by Sara Demichelis

LEPTIS MAGNA page 216
text by Fabio Bourbon

SAQQARA •
AND GIZA

KARNAK
WESTERN THEBES •• LUXOR
THE NUBIAN TEMPLES •• PHILAE
THE NUBIAN TEMPLES •
ABU SIMBEL •

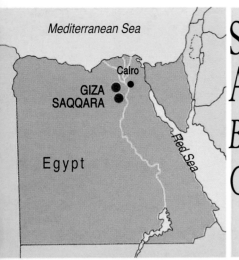

SAQQARA AND GIZA, BURIAL GROUNDS OF MEMPHIS

128 top The pyramid of Djoser, in Saqqara, almost 190 feet high, is the result of five successive additions to an initial mastaba built over a burial trench 93 feet deep.

128-129 The stepped pyramid, here seen from the northwest, dominates the archaeological site of Saqqara and is incorporated in a monumental group of buildings that form the so-called "complex of Djoser", which extends over an area of 38 acres.

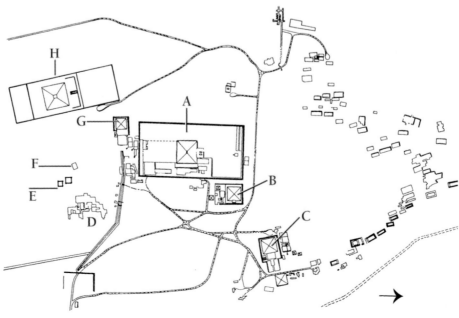

A Burial complex
   of Djoser
B Pyramid of Userkaf
C Pyramid of Teti
D Monastery of St. Jeremiah
E Tomb of Horemheb
F Tomb of Maya
G Pyramid of Unas
H Burial complex of
   Horus Sekhemkhet

The founding of Memphis, the most ancient capital of the land of the pharaohs, is attributed to Menes, mythical sovereign believed by the Egyptians to have united the country into one kingdom. Even though the role of political and administrative center later passed on to other cities, Memphis kept its pre-eminence and authority long afterward.

The Nubian ruler Pye (750-712 BC) for instance, after sailing all the way up the Nile to the north of the fourth cataract, only considered his journey over when he entered the temple of Ptah, patron of Memphis. With this, Pye believed he had conquered all of Egypt as he had reached its deepest heart, where the royal leadership of the Pharaohs had lasted for millennia. It didn't matter to the Nubian king that descendants of Menes continued to rule to the north, for the true essence of Egypt was in Memphis. Today, little remains of the past glory of Memphis. Among the palm groves of Mit Rahina, 20 miles south of Cairo, an extensive heap of rubble covers the remains of a huge temple complex, very difficult to recognize as the temples have been repeatedly ransacked over the course of the centuries. Many of the stones, used in building the sanctuaries for the Egyptian gods, are now found in the buildings of Islamic Cairo. And yet, Memphis must have been very beautiful, if we are to believe the many descriptions of the Ramses papyri dating from the 14th and 13th centuries BC, saying such things as "Nothing can be compared to Memphis. . . Its granaries are bursting with grain and barley, its lakes are covered in flowers and lotus blossoms, the oil is sweet and fat abounds. . ." The most important testimony to the greatness of the Pharaohs' Memphis are its tombs, stretching out over a strip of desert more than 24 miles long, to the west of the Nile, from Abu Roash, just north of Giza, to Dahshur, about 10 miles south of Saqqara. The rulers of the II dynasty were the first to exploit the desert sands to the west of Saqqara as a site of royal burial. Only a few

traces remain of their tombs, spacious enclosures with a tomb in the center, now barely visible beneath the desert sands. Before these tombs, the area had been used as a cemetery by functionaries who lived during the I-dynasty, while the government of the pharaohs was still in formation and whose bureaucratic headquarters had been set up in Memphis. The tombs of these functionaries could compete with and even exceed in size those of their rulers, who were buried in Abydos in Upper Egypt, the area from which the ruling house originally came. The III-dynasty ruler Djoser (2630-2611 BC) may have decided to have his tomb built upon the infrastructure of a previous royal burial place. The entire funerary complex, designed by the architect Imhotep, was revolutionary for its time. The fulcrum of the structure was the Stepped Pyramid, around which a complex of buildings developed which were used as a backdrop for the jubilee festivals of the sovereign. One of the innovations was the building material used by Imhotep. The funerary complex of Djoser must be the first building of importance constructed entirely in stone. The abandonment of reeds, wood and Nile lime was sudden and the formal language of the structures develop from the oldest buildings in these materials. The stone architecture reveals the reference models from which its inspiration is taken. For example, the columns are reproductions of bundles of reeds which are not completely detached from the walls to the rear, and the top parts of the outer walls show decorative designs inspired by the mud-coated reed palisades. The initial plan was altered on various occasions. The stepped pyramid takes its origins from a tomb which was similar to the one of previous dynasties. This was raised five times, by superimposing five other tombs of decreasing size to reach a total height of almost 200 feet. To the south of the sovereign's tomb a spacious courtyard opens up. This is where the most important of the

ruler's jubilee celebrations took place. Djoser's funerary monument set up a process of transformation in the conception of the royal tomb in Egypt. Within the space of a few generations this led to the pyramid form which is now so familiar to us. An important stage in this development took place during the reign of Snefru (2575-2250 BC), when three pyramids were built. The first of these was erected well to the south of Memphis, in the Meidum area, while the other two, known as the "double sloping pyramid" and the "red pyramid" were located in Dahshur, about 10 miles from the capital. The last of these, despite its excessive slope, was used as a prototype for the Great Pyramid of Cheops, the son and successor of Snefru, in Giza. With Cheops (2550-2528 BC), the royal cemetery moved north, to Giza and Abu Roash. It was the rulers of the V-dynasty who once again selected Saqqara as the burial ground. To them, we owe above all the continuation of the Egyptian religion of deifying the sun,

which had already emerged during the reign of Chefren. The interests of Userkaf (2465-2458 BC) and his successors were mainly in the construction of temples dedicated to the sun. Ruins of these temples can still be admired today at Abu Ghorab, between Giza and Saqqara. The return to Saqqara as the site of the last resting place shows the evident desire of these rulers to move away from tradition. The remains of the pyramid of Userkaf are not far from the funerary complex of Djoser and show a willingness to create an ideal connection with the famous III-dynasty sovereign. The design of the pyramid reached its final form under Userkaf. From a costly structure built entirely in limestone it moved toward a funerary chamber covered with a mound mainly of rubble with an external covering of limestone slabs. The monumental appearance of the royal tomb is in this way

guaranteed with a reduced expenditure of energy. The successors of Userkaf chose to be buried north of Saqqara in Abu Sir. Here, among the remains of the bare brick buildings annexed to the funerary temples, numerous papyrus documents were found showing useful light on the administration of this remote age. Unas, the last ruler of the V-dynasty, chose Saqqara once again as his burial place. His pyramid is now only rubble, but the walls of his funerary apartments contain the inscriptions of the Texts of the Pyramids for the first time. This is a collection of texts that would have been of use to the dead king when he arrived in the next world. A great variety of subjects are covered, from the hymns to the gods to incantations against snakes and other magical texts still not understood by us. In Saqqara, as well as the pyramids of the VI-dynasty rulers, are the tombs of the functionaries who lived between this dynasty and the previous one. These are divided into a number of rooms, just like the houses they had lived in when they were alive. The walls are decorated with painted reliefs showing scenes from everyday life. These are works of very high artistic quality and provide us with a very precise picture of ordinary life, with all its customs and unpredictable events, both serious and amusing. The tomb of Ty is especially notable in this sense, while the tombs of Mereruka and Kagemni are considered less original and vivid although, in a sense, richer.

The necropolis of Saqqara was used continuously during the periods when Memphis no longer dominated all Egypt. Many tombs of functionaries linked with Akhenaton and Tutankhamon date to the New Kingdom. Among these, splendid decorations in the Amarnian style can be found in the tomb of General Horemheb (1319-1307 BC) who was soon to take power and become Pharaoh. During the reign of Ramses II (1290-1224 BC) the total repositioning of the Apis bulls, a few miles north of the Djoser funerary complex, took place on the order of Prince Khaemuaset.

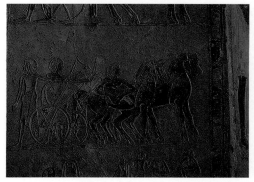

The cult of the bull had been practiced since remote antiquity and it was mentioned in the burial treasure of Hemaka, the functionary who lived under the ruler Den in the I-dynasty. In this period, the bull was considered a personification of the generating force of nature. As time passed, it came to be seen as the earth manifestation of the protector god of Memphis, Ptah. The cult was seen as offering salvation and this led to its wide-spread popularity in Egypt in the late period. When the bull died, it received honors identical to those given the ruler. It was subjected to the complex ceremony of mummification and buried with a rich treasure in a large stone sarcophagus with long, deep galleries. During the Greco-Roman Period, the place was known as Serapeus and was mentioned in the accounts of many travelers who visited the Nile Valley at this time. Among these was Strabo, whose description influenced the Frenchman Auguste Mariette (1821-1881) to carry out a number of excavations in an attempt to bring the entrance to Serapeus to the light. After considerable effort, he succeeded in 1851. With this discovery, the systematic, scientific exploration of the tombs of Memphis, the most ancient capital of the Egypt of the Pharaohs, began.

132 top left The western wall of the tomb of Irukaptah, in the Saqqara site, is adorned with eight large multicolored statues of relatives of the dead.

132 bottom left In the mastaba of Mereruka, in Saqqara, in a deep niche of the six-columned hall, we see the life-size statue of the deceased in front of an offering table. Alongside the niche are two other images of Mereruka.

132 top right Inside the mastaba of Ptah-Hotep, in Saqqara, are sumptuous multicolored bas-reliefs. In the foreground on the right, Ptah-Hotep is shown seated and wearing the skin of a feline as he sniffs perfume from a stone container.

132 bottom right This splendid battle chariot is shown in a multicolored bas-relief in the necropolis of Saqqara.

133 In the pyramid built by Unas, last king of the V-dynasty, the walls of the inner chambers are covered with hieroglyphics in the first known example of them. These contain invocations and magical formulas, the Texts of the Pyramids.

134-135 Ptah-Hotep was immortalized in this low relief as he receives offerings from processions of bearers.

A Downstream Temple
B Temple of the Sphinx
C Sphinx
D Eastern Cemetery
E Satellite pyramids
F Ditch of the solar boats
G Pyramid of Cheops
H Western Cemetery
I Second solar boat
   (still to be unearthed)
J Funerary Temple
K Pyramid of Chefren
L Funerary Temple
M Pyramid of Mycerene
N Satellite pyramids
O Procession ramps
P Museum of the
   solar boat

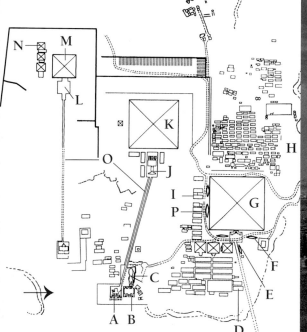

The construction of the Pyramid of Cheops marked the transfer of the royal tombs to the north of Memphis, on the plateau of Giza. The funerary monument of the successor to Snefru was included among the seven wonders of the ancient world and, with its height of nearly 500 feet, is undoubtedly one of the most fascinating monuments in the history of the world. Often wrongly believed to be the highest architectural achievement of Egyptian culture, this is merely one more stage in the development of the Egyptian funerary monument. The rulers continued to be buried in pyramids but with smaller dimensions and less expensive building methods up to the Middle kingdom and beyond. Nevertheless, the Great Pyramid has always thrilled the imagination and all kinds of legends have been built around it, from those reported by Herodotus to some of the absurd tales that continue to arouse the interest of the news media today. All this is because, separated as it is from the culture that produced it, this enormous mound of stone, concealing the mummy of the ruler, loses its real meaning and leads us to make up theories developed without taking into account the great distances in both time and space between our way of

136 top left This ivory statue, found at Abydos and now in the Cairo Museum, is the only image we have of Cheops, the pharaoh who had the largest of all the Egyptian pyramids built and who ruled from 2550 to 2528 BC.

136 top right The Sphinx, 190 feet long, was sculpted at the time of Chefren by modeling a limestone rock that was in front of the eastern side of the pharaoh's pyramid. A male figure and a symbol of the sun god, it also was the image of the deified king.

136-137 About 50 miles from the center of Cairo, at the edge of a high desert plain, the three pyramids of Cheops, Chefren and Mycerene are aligned from northeast to southwest in size order.

thinking and that of the Egyptians of almost 5,000 years ago.

The pyramid, like many other symbols of Egyptian culture, is open to many interpretations. It is a sign in the desert, a marker of the body of the deceased ruler. Its ordered geometric perfection is an impressive contrast to the disorder that surrounds it. Even after his death, the sovereign continued through the pyramid to play the role as a defender of order (cosmos) against the invasion of disorder (chaos). This dogma, which is basic to understanding the royal nature of the pharaoh and extends to all of Egyptian civilization from its beginnings to the end, can be used as a key to interpretation and help us understand why the pyramid shape itself was chosen to mark the burial site of the ruler. The pyramid is also reminiscent of a mountain, the first hill of earth that emerged from the primordial seas and from which the entire process of creation originated. The pyramid can also be compared to a materialization of the sun's rays, come down to bathe the earth with their light. Finally, the pyramid can be seen as all this and more. And it owes its success among the Egyptians, so keen to detect signs that could conceal more than one meaning, to this ability to give rise to a whole series of readings. In the final analysis, the pyramid is exactly this, a sign. Around the pyramid of Cheops the functionaries who had served under him also had their tombs built. In an age when eternity was the exclusive prerogative of the sovereign, being close to him in the Afterlife was the only hope for a life after death.

137 top The sacred face of the Sphinx is more than 13 feet wide and still keeps traces of color.

137 center This picture gives some idea of the long galleries that are inside the pyramid of Cheops.

137 bottom In a trench near the pyramid of Cheops, an intact ship was found in 1954.

138-139 The Sphinx, in the foreground, appears between the pyramids of Chephren (left) and Cheops (right).

Giza

Giza

141 top right This aerial photograph gives an excellent view of the summit of the pyramid of Chefre, which was once topped by a pramidion.

141 bottom right In this view of the archaeological site of Giza, the shadow of the pyramid of Chefre stretches to the pyramid of Cheops behind.

Cheops also wanted the body of his mother, Hetepheres, wife of Snefru, originally buried in the sands of Dahshur, beside him. Her tomb was discovered along the eastern side of the Great Pyramid and although the body of the queen was never found it was possible to recover part of her burial treasure. The furniture is covered in gold leaf, and the vases used for her toilet were also in gold while two of her bracelets were silver. All these objects, together with an alabaster sarcophagus, are now in the Egyptian Museum in Cairo. Along the southern side of the pyramid of Cheops, a sailing vessel made from Lebanese cedar was recently found. This had been taken apart and placed with care at the bottom of a trench covered in slabs of limestone. It shows signs of wear and must have been placed close to the pyramid for the possible use of the ruler on voyages after his death.

140 and 141 left This imposing diorite statue of Chefren (2520-2494 BC) was found in 1860 by the French archaeologist Auguste Mariette in the temple downstream from the pyramid of Chefren, in Giza.

141 center This famous group of statues, discovered in the temple downstream from the pyramid of Mycerene in Giza, shows the pharaoh flanked by two gods. On the left is the goddess Hathor, who is linked to abundance and fertility, and to the right is the tutelary divinity of the 17th administrative district of Upper Egypt. Upper Egypt is identified by the symbol on the head of the god.

Restored and perfectly reconstructed, it is now exhibited in a special museum at the foot of the pyramid, above the ditch in which it was found. Research on the site has proven the existence of another trench, containing the pieces of a second vessel, but it was decided not to open this trench. The pyramid of Chefren (2520-2494 BC) is smaller than that of his father Cheops, but as it is built on a slight rise it looks slightly higher. Its summit still shows part of the white limestone covering that was systematically removed from the base and from the other pyramids for use in some of the buildings of Cairo during the Arab period. The burial complex of Chefren is in better condition than that of Cheops. On the eastern side of the pyramid we can still see the remains of the temple where the rites for the deceased ruler were held. From here, across a downward-sloping covered ramp, it was possible to reach what is called the "downstream temple", where the body of the ruler was mummified and purified. This structure consists of granite

141

blocks weighing several tons, whose red color contrasts with the white of the alabaster floors.

The emptiness of the halls is balanced by the heaviness of the walls, pillars and architrave, and is a clear example of IV-dynasty work. Inside this temple a beautiful diorite statue of Chefren was found. The ruler is seated on a throne and a falcon, a symbol of the god Horus, is behind him. The wings of the falcon embrace the head of the king in the usual gesture of protection and have a variety of geometric designs illustrating trends in abstract art during this period of Egyptian history.

Alongside the downstream temple was a mound of limestone, all that remained of a place where the building stone for the pyramid of Cheops was obtained. The shapeless mass of rock was worked and transformed by the craftsmen of Chefren into a fantastic animal, with the body of a lion and a human head, the personification of the power of the sovereign. Later, the colossal statue was deified and identified with the god Ra-Harakhti, the morning sun. During the XVIII-dynasty (1550-1295 BC), a temple was dedicated to it, and Thutmose IV (1401-1391 BC) had it freed from the sand after being told in a dream to do so. The first Greek travelers identified the huge sculpture with a being from their own fantastic mythology as the Sphinx. The Islamic people called it Abu el-Hol, meaning "Father of Fear", and it is still known by this name today.

The pyramid of Mycerene, although smaller than that of his immediate predecessors, had its base covered in slabs of syenite, the special quality of granite found at Aswan. The summit was covered on the outside with limestone slabs.

In later periods, especially during the reign of the Ramses rulers, the granite was reused as sculpture material. The burial complex of Mycerene was richly decorated with statues of the ruler, many of which were found during excavations.

The so-called "Triad of Mycerene" where the king is shown between the goddess Hathor and the personification of an Egyptian region is especially famous.

142 top and 143 bottom The mastaba of the functionary Merynepher Qar, in the necropolis of Giza, is outstanding for the series of statues of the deceased and his family. These are sculpted in haute-relief on the southern wall of the first room where there are also a number of fine bas-reliefs.

142 bottom In the mastaba of Idu, also in the cemetery of Giza, are numerous haute-relief statues of the deceased.
The false pillar at the center of the eastern wall of the great hall is also decorated with the image of Idu, shown with his hands open and pointed upward to receive offerngs.

The greatest masterpiece of the art of this period is a sculpture that shows Mycerene and his wife. She has her arm around her royal spouse in a gesture of affection, rare in the works of art of this period.

With the end of the Ancient Kingdom and the beginning of a period of a divided Egypt, Memphis lost the primary role it had held from the very start of Egyptian history. From that point on, the plateau of Giza was almost completely abandoned as a burial site. It came to be used once again during the 1st millennium and during the same period the pyramid of a wife of Cheops was identified as the burial site of Isis, to which goddess a temple was built and dedicated along the eastern side.

KARNAK,
THE KINGDOM OF AMON

Karnak is the great temple complex which developed around the sanctuary dedicated to the god Amon of Thebes, situated to the north of the modern city of Luxor. The complex also includes the temple of Montu to the north and the temple of Mut to the south. A ceremonial street links Karnak with the temple of Luxor, about two miles further south, and with a pier on the Nile, from which processions started out for the royal temples on the opposite bank. During the New Kingdom (1552-1069 BC), the temple of Karnak became the most important religious center of ancient Egypt. Retracing the history of the temple means going back through a great deal of Egyptian history, as nearly all the rulers of the age were involved in both the architectural and decorative work that made the temple, first built on a base from the Middle Kingdom of 1991-1785 BC, a combination of different styles illustrating Egyptian art through the

144 left The first pylon of the temple was built at the time of the pharaoh Nectanebo I (378-361 BC) and left unfinished. The enormous structure has a 370 foot front and is 144 feet high. On the façade eight large channels can be seen into which huge pennants on standards were placed.

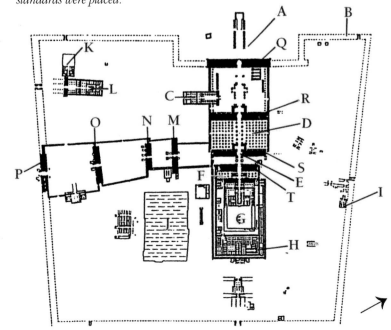

A Access road with serpent-headed sphinxes
B Walls of Amon
C Temple of Ramses III
D Great colonnaded hall
E Obelisks
F Uagit (small colonnaded room)
G Courtyard of the Middle Kingdom
H Akhmenu
I Temple of Ptah
J Sacred Lake
K Temple of Opet
L Temple of Khonsu
M Seventh pylon
N Eighth pylon
O Ninth pylon
P Tenth pylon
Q First pylon (of Nectanebo I)
R Second pylon
S Third pylon
T Fourth pylon

centuries. The temple was important not only religiously but also economically in direct proportion to the prestige it enjoyed. Each time an Egyptian temple was built it was given possessions and income to guarantee the support of the priests and ceremonies. Continuous donations and tributes from the rulers made Karnak the most important economic center in the country, a state within a state.

The oldest building, of which only traces remain, dates to the period of Sesostris I (XII-dynasty, 1962-1928 BC), who had a limestone temple built inside a wall facing southwest. The front section contained a sacred garden surrounded by colonnaded rooms while the sanctuary itself consisted of three rooms in a line. This nucleus was virtually unchanged until the start of the XVIII-dynasty. Throughout the New Kingdom and into later periods up to the times of Ptolemy the original part

144 right In the first courtyard of the temple is an enormous statue of Ramses II, 45 feet high. The image of the queen consort is sculpted at the feet of the pharaoh.

144-145 and 146-147 The temple of Amon-Ra, seen here in two spectacular aerial views, covers an area of 360,000 square yards. The complex of Karnak, called Ipet-isut by the ancient Egyptians, was built in stages over a period of 1,600 years, from the time of Sesostris I (XII-dynasty) to the reign of Nectanebo I (XXX-dynasty). The temple is built on two axes running from east to west and north to south which are believed to stand for the sky and earth and divine and royal power. The sacred lake,

begun under Thutmose II and completed on the order of Taharqa (690-664 BC) was supplied from underground springs. This lake supplied water for the purification rites and was a place where the sacred birds of the temple could swim.

145 bottom The famous Valley of the Sphinxes leads to the first pylon, where the main entrance to the temple opens up.

148-149 The aerial photograph shows the First Pylon and courtyard in the temple.

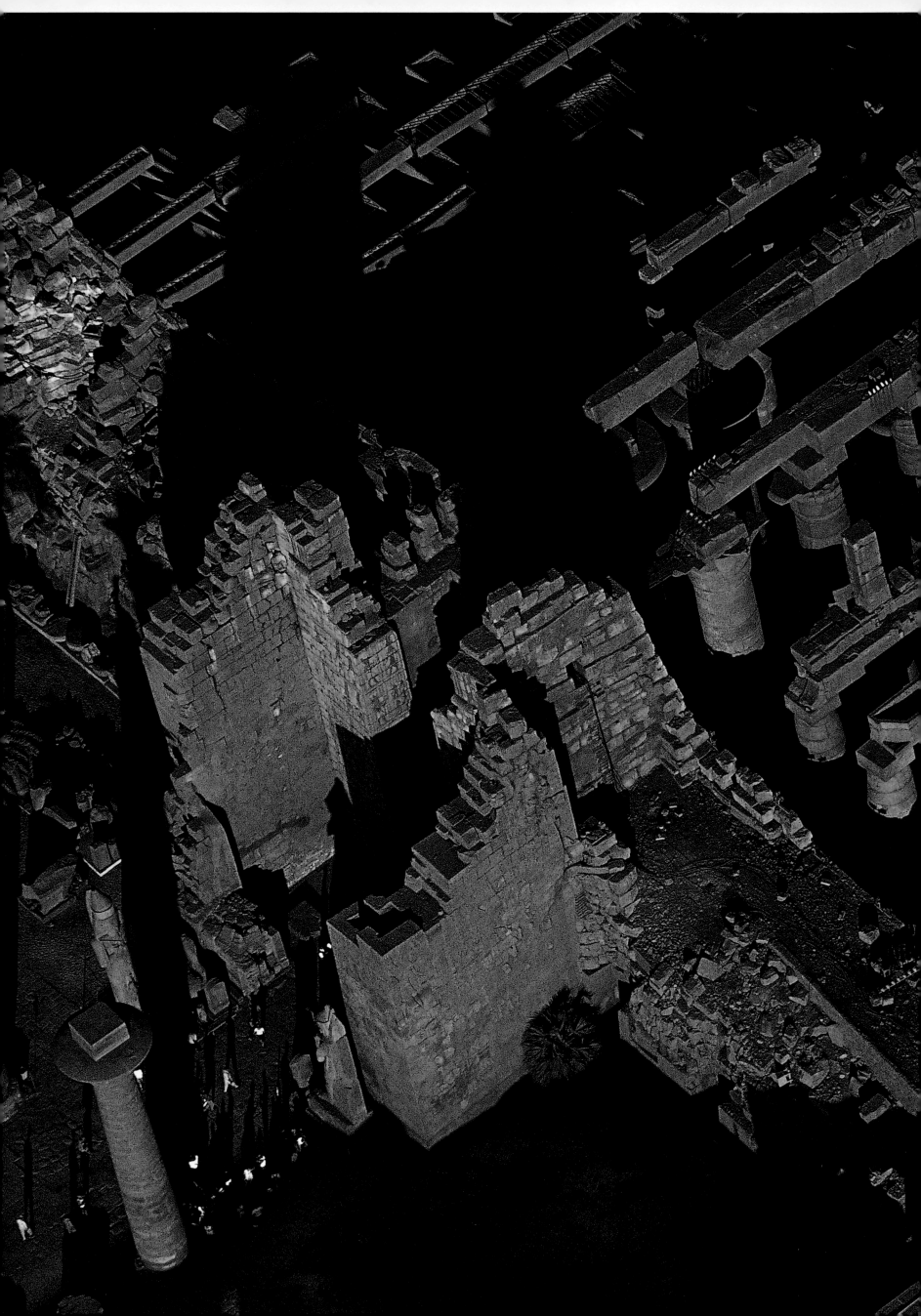

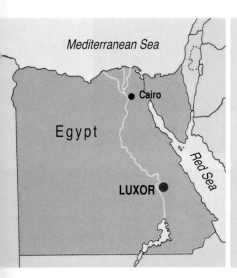

Mediterranean Sea

Cairo

Egypt

Red Sea

LUXOR

LUXOR,
ETERNAL BEAUTY

A Sphinx-lined road
  of Nectanebos I
B Shrine of Serapi
C Obelisk
D Pylon of Ramses II
E Shrine of
  Hatshepsut
F Mosque
G Courtyard
  of Ramses II
H Great
  colonnade
I Courtyard of
  Amenophi III
J Position
  of the hide
K Other colonnade
L Room of birth
M Shrine of the
  sacred vessel
  of Alexander
N Sanctuary
  of Amenophi II

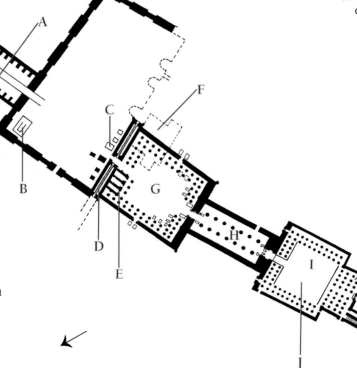

Ancient Thebes, now Luxor, is situated in Upper Egypt, about 300 miles to the south of Cairo. This ancient city was built on the eastern bank of the Nile, with the tombs and important temple complexes on the western side. During the Ancient Kingdom (c. 3150-2200 BC) Thebes played a secondary political role and only became a provincial capital at the end of the VI-dynasty (c. 2460-2200 BC). During the First Intermediate Period (c. 2460-2200 BC) it was the nerve center of the expansion policy that led the Theban princes to reunite the entire country under Mentuhotep II as a result of which it became the capital. In the Middle Kingdom that followed (1990-1785 BC) the capital was transferred to the north, but Thebes continued to be the administrative center of Upper Egypt and the rulers continued to

158 top The photograph shows a detail of one of the enormous seated statues of Ramses II in front of the pylon of the temple.

158 bottom left This sacred head of Ramses II was part of the other four colossal statues that stood in front of the temple.

158 bottom right The surviving pink granite obelisk before the pylon of the temple has a long commemorative head of Ramses II on the four sides which stretches over three columns. The two scrolls at the bottom bear the name of the great ruler who was so important in extending the empire.

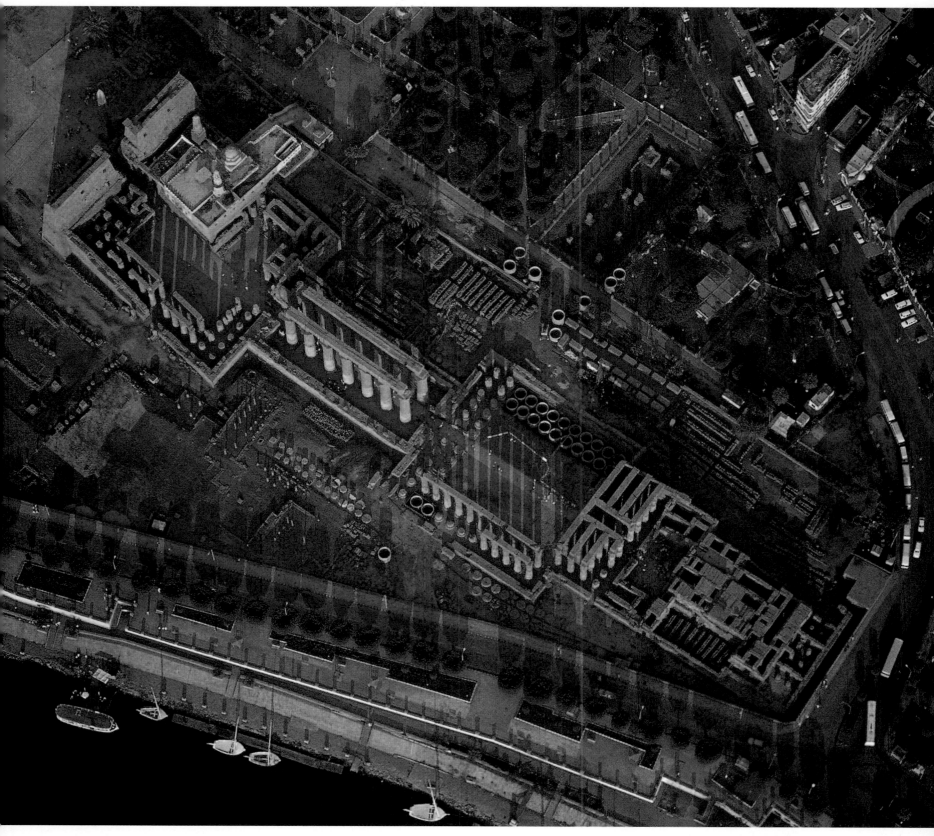

view it as of being of major importance as can be seen from various architectural projects. The Second Intermediate Period (c. 1785-1550 BC) brought about a new split in Egypt, with the southern part remaining under the control of Thebes which eventually was once again the starting point for the movement which led to the reunification of the country. It was, however, during the XVIII-dynasty (1552-1295 BC) that the city enjoyed its greatest prosperity, as the grandiose complexes testify. This was also the period when the Valley of the Kings was created on the western bank of the Nile behind the rocky amphitheater of Deir el-Bahari as a burial ground for sovereigns. The Amarnian religious reform promoted by the pharaoh Ikhnaton led to the transfer of both the

capital and royal tombs to the city of Amarna briefly. However, the period of restoration that followed not only led to the return of Thebes to the role of religious capital of the country but it is also likely that the administrative center was transferred to the north, first to Memphis and then to Pi-Ramses. In spite of its distance from political power, Thebes retained its importance in the religious life of Egypt and this is where kings were crowned, receiving divine legitimacy in the temples, and this is where they were buried.

During the third Intermediate Period (1069-332 BC), a genuine theocracy developed around the great temple of Amon in Karnak. This went on to further extend its control over the southern part of

158-159 and 160-161 The temple structure is clearly visible from these aerial views which show the pylon and courtyard built by Ramses II, the colonnade dating from the end of the XVIII-dynasty, the courtyard of Amenhotep III, the court and the sanctuary itself.

159 bottom The great courtyard built on the orders of Ramses II was bounded by 74 papyrus-shaped columns, arranged in a double row. Sixteen statues of the pharaoh are still standing in the spaces between the columns.

159

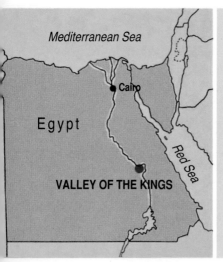

WESTERN THEBES, THE PHARAOHS' LAST HOME

A	Karnak	H	Colossi of Memnon
B	Luxor	I	Temple of Thutmose IV
C	Malqatta	J	Ramesseum
D	Site of the palace of Amenophes III	K	Temple of Thutmose III
E	Temple of Ramses III	L	Temple of Ramses IV
F	Medinet Habu	M	Temple of Sethi I
G	Temple of Merneptah		

N	Temple of Mentuhotep
O	Temple of Hatshepsut
P	Valley of the Kings
Q	Valley of the Queens
R	Deir El-Medina

On the west bank of the Nile at Thebes, where the cultivated zone meets the desert, were a number of temples dedicated to the cult of Amon and the dead kings. The oldest of these temples is that of Mentuhotep (XI-dynasty, 2100-1955 BC) built at the foot of the rocky amphitheater of Deir el-Bahari. This consisted of an access ramp leading to a courtyard enclosed by walls on three sides, which in turn led to a terrace. At the center of the terrace there was probably a colonnade with a mastaba in the center. The temple also included an inner part dug from the rock with a long corridor leading to the king's tomb. The temples to the rear, all dating from the New Kingdom, have no royal burial chambers. The separation of the place of funeral worship and the burial site in the Valley of the Kings is one of the changes made during this period, and seems to be

the result of the transformation in the Egyptian view of death. At Deir el-Bahari, beside the temple of Mentuhotep II from which it takes its inspiration, is the temple of Queen Hatshepsut. This includes three terraces resting against the mountain, connected with each other by an access ramp. The last terrace was occupied by various chapels dedicated to the most important gods worshipped in the temple. The scenes on the walls tell the story of the divine birth of the queen and the great deeds of her reign, such as the expedition to the county of Punt and the transport of two great obelisks for the temple Karnak. The temples at the rear are all similar in structure to buildings of the same period that were dedicated to divine worship. All that remains of the temple of Amenophes III are two colossal statues, the famous Colossi of Memnon, which flanked the entrance.

166 top left The colossi of Memnon adorned the first pylon of the memorial temple of Amenhotep III, which has been entirely destroyed.

166 center left Several very famous bas-reliefs showing the expedition to the land of Punt can be found in the southwestern corner of the first portico in the temple of Hatshepsut.

166 bottom left The intermediate portico in the temple of Hatshepsut, also known as the "portico of Punt", is held up by a row of square pillars and decorated on the north with scenes showing the divine birth of the queen. On the south, it is decorated with images of the famous expedition to Punt.

166 right This splendid painted limestone head shows Hatshepsut with the false beard that was one of the symbols of royalty. It belongs to one of the colossal statues of Osiris in the upper portico of Deir el-Bahari. There are only a few statues in which the queen appears in women's clothing.

166-167 The spectacular temple of Queen Hatshepsut rises from the base of a valley sacred to the goddess Hathor. The building, a succession of three terraces with deep porticoes resting on the rock wall, is the work of the famous architect Senenmut.

167 top On the supporting wall of the first terrace of the temple of Hatshepsut, in Deir el-Bahari, the effigy of the god Horus appears several times in the form of a falcon. Behind, we can see some of the surviving Osiristyle statues of the queen.

Western Thebes
Western Thebes

The funerary temple of Ramses II, known as the Ramesseum, is surrounded on three sides by an imposing complex of bare brick warehouses.

The temple itself has two courtyards and a large colonnaded hall which leads through three antechambers to a sanctuary dedicated to the cult of Amon. The complex of rooms to the south was used for the cult of the ruler.

To the south of the Ramesseum is the most imposing architectural complex of the western bank, which is known as Medinet Habu.

Inside the surrounding walls are temples, warehouses, houses and tombs, all made of bare brick, a genuine town which was inhabited up to the 9th century AD.

The oldest of the temples is the one dedicated to Amon, built by Hatshepsut and Thutmose III, and altered from that point all the way through to the Ptolemic period.

Behind this is the huge funerary temple of Ramses III, a larger version of the Ramseon. Against the southern side of the first courtyard is a palace that was used by the king during the religious celebrations that took place in the temple at certain times during the year.

168 top left In this aerial view can be seen the second courtyard and the colonnaded hall of the Ramesseum, the memorial temple built on the orders of Ramses II.

168 center left In the first court of the Ramesseum was the colossal monolithic statue of the pharaoh, 66 feet high. Today it is only fragments.

168 bottom left The memorial temple of Ramses III, in Medinet Habu, is the best preserved in Western Thebes.

168 top Splendid bas-reliefs adorn what remains of the great colonnaded hall of the Ramesseum (left). The poor condition of the temple is the result of the fact that in ancient times it was simply used as a source of building materials. This superb black granite head of Ramses II (right) was one of the statues of the pharaoh as Osiris which rested on the pillars of the second courtyard in the Ramesseum. The temple was known for its imposing form.

168-169 and 170-171 The first pylon of the temple of Medinet Habu, over 200 feet long, is decorated with bas-reliefs commemorating the victories of Ramses III. The ruler is shown sacrificing his enemies before the gods Amon-Ra (left) and Amon-Ra-Harakhti (right). Inside the right-hand structure of the pylon is a staircase that leads to the terrace above the great portal. The channels on the façade were used to hold flagpoles from which the divine insignia flew.

168 bottom left The pillars of the second courtyard in the temple of Medinet Habu are decorated with scenes of the pharaoh making ritual offerings before various gods.

169 bottom right The stems of the columns in the second courtyard of the temple of Medinet Habu are covered with bas-reliefs and hieroglyphics. Clear traces of bright coloring remain which give us today an idea of the vibrant colors of Egyptian temples.

Western Thebes

Western Thebes

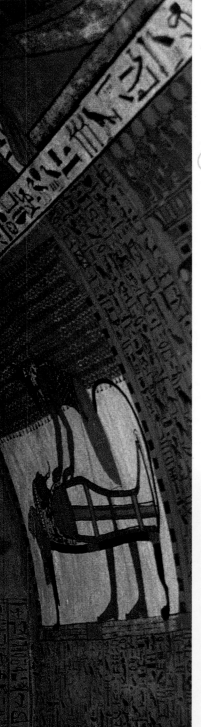

Near the Valley of the Queens was the village of Deir el-Medina, where the building workers and decorators of the royal tombs lived. Both the residential part and the necropolis of the village remain. We should also mention the burial grounds for the court functionaries and nobles, who were buried near the tombs of the pharaohs they had served. However, the occupation of the entire area as a cemetery continued up to a much later date, with the grandiose tombs of the functionaries of the XXV- and XXVI-dynasties (712-525 BC), built by Asasif in front of Deir el-Bahari. Eventually, even the great funerary temples were invaded by later burials which took place in a totally different religious context, although the rites were still considered sacred.

186-187 The famous paintings that decorate the burial chamber of the tomb of Sennegem are in perfect condition and can be considered the finest in the Necropolis of the Artificers. On the western wall, seen here, Sennegem and his wife Inypherti worship the gods of the afterlife. In the gable is a double image of Anubis crouching on a shrine.

186 bottom left Heliopolis's cat kills the serpent Apopis under the sacred ished tree. This impressive picture is part of the decorations on the walls of Inherkhau's tomb in the Necropolis of the Artificer.

186 bottom right In this detail, the god Anubis prepares the mummy of Sennegem, respected functionary of the Theban necropolis.

187 top left The tomb of Sennefer, a senior functionary at the time of Amenhotep II, is one of the richest in the Necropolis of the Nobles. In this detail, the deceased is shown with his wife.

187 top right This detail of the vaulted ceiling in the tomb of Pashedu in the Necropolis of the Artificers shows the gods Ra-Harakhti (left) and Hathor (right).

187 bottom left The narrow passage that leads to the burial chamber in the tomb of Pashedu is decorated with two identical images of Anubis, portrayed as a jackal.

187 bottom right The wife of Pashedu, Negemtebehdet, is portrayed in the fresh, lively style typical of the Ramses period. She wears her hair in small curls.

188-189 The tomb of Pashedu – a stonecutter who lived during the reign of Ramses II – is famous for its splendid paintings.

190-191 Sennegem is often shown on the vault of his tomb; he was a worker during the reigns of Sethi I and Ramses II.

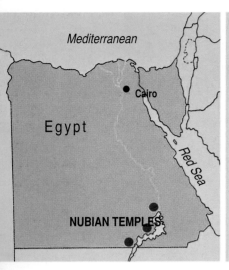

Mediterranean

Cairo

Egypt

Red Sea

NUBIAN TEMPLES

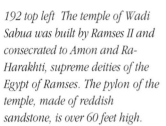

A
C
D
B
F
E
G

THE NUBIAN TEMPLES, SAVED FROM THE WATERS

The region that spreads out to the south of the first cataract of the Nile was under Egyptian control from the time of the Ancient Kingdom (c. 2670-2150 BC). Originally, the Egyptians limited their activities to military and trading expeditions in the area, but from the Middle Kingdom onward (2100-1750 BC) they set up direct military control as far as the second cataract, building strong fortresses. During the New Kingdom (1500-1076 BC) the Egyptian empire extended its boundaries beyond the fourth cataract. The Egyptian presence in Nubia was marked by the building of temples as a natural result of the cultural processes which followed the conquest of the region. The temples were dedicated not only to the gods in the Egyptian pantheon, including deified pharaohs, but also to the Nubian gods. This influence on the region diminished at the end of the Ramses period. At the start of the first millennium the entire region was independent of Egyptian control, to the extent that in the 8th century BC it was the Nubians who conquered Egypt and founded the XXV-dynasty. The clash with the Assyrians marked the end of this dynasty, which returned to the area of its origins, in Napata, near the fourth cataract. In the centuries that followed a local kingdom developed that combined certain indigenous elements of African origin with others from Egyptian and Greco-Roman traditions, from the Ptolemaic period on. The reign of Meroes took this kingdom to its highest levels along with the Greek domination of Egypt, causing trouble for the

A Aswan Dam
B High dam
C Phyllo
D Kalabsha
E Sebua
F Hamada
G Abu Simbel

192-193 and 194-195 A long avenue flanked by a row of sphinxes and preceded by two colossal statues of the pharaoh led to the temple of Wadi Sebua. This building, like most of the other Nubian monuments, was only saved from the waters of the artificial Lake Nasser by being dismantled into numbered blocks and later reassembled about forty miles from its original site. The new location is called New Sebua.

193 top and 196-197 The temple of Dakke, compact but with excellent dimensions, was built at the end of the 3rd century BC on the orders of the Ethiopian king Arqamon and Ptolemy IV Philopator, the Macedonian pharaoh who reigned at the same time. Later, Ptolemy VIII Evergetes II (146-117 BC) added the portico, but the Romans gave it its final appearance. The sanctuary, dedicated to the god Thoth, was rebuilt near New Sebua.

Roman Empire. In Lower Nubia, the region between the first and second cataract, the valley of the Nile was very narrow, forcing the Egyptian architects to build temples wholly or partially dug from rock. With the intended building of Lake Nasser in the 1960s all these sanctuaries were threatened with destruction. UNESCO developed a major plan which involved technicians and archaeologists from all over the world. It was found possible to dismantle most of the temples in the area, including Abu Simbel, Amada and Kalabsha, and rebuild them on higher ground. Some of the temples were then donated by the Egyptian government to the countries that had taken part in these operations, which explains why the Ellesiya, a shrine dug from the rock by Thutmose III and dedicated to various gods, including the pharaoh Sesostres I is now in the Egyptian Museum in Turin, Italy. The most active Pharaoh in the area was Ramses II, who was responsible for building not only the famous temple Abu Simbel but also Beit el-Wali, Gerf Hussein, Uadi es-Sebua and Derr. The temple of Sebua, partially dug out of the rock, was built on the western bank of the Nile, near an older building by Amenophes III. The temple consists of two pylon entrances leading to courtyards, the

second of which gave access to the part of the temple cut from the rock, including the colonnaded hall, an antechamber which had four shrines off to the sides and the sanctuary. The building was dedicated to Amon and the deified Ramses II.

Derr was the only temple of Ramses II to be built on the eastern bank of the Nile, and was dedicated to the cult of Ra-Harakhti. Completely dug from the rock, this had very much the same structure as Abu Simbel but without the colossal statues that decorated its façade.

Temples of the traditional kind were built in Upper Nubia. At Soleb, to the south of the third cataract, is the great temple of Amenophi III, dedicated to Amon and the deified king. The temple, which is in an east-west position, had two porticoed courtyards, a colonnaded hall with 20 foot high columns shaped to look like palms, and a sanctuary of several rooms.

The building, which is today in ruins, still has part of the decorations and the reliefs which show stages in the jubilee celebrations of the king are of particular interest. The jubilee was a very old tradition, first celebrated when a ruler had been on the throne for thirty years and then repeated more frequently.

In the course of the ceremony, a complex system of rites was celebrated to reconfirm the royal power. At a point slightly further north, in Sedeinga, the king built another temple, dedicated to his wife Teie. Both these sites were explored in the 1960s by archaeological expeditions led by the Italian M. Schiff Giorgini and many of the finds are now at the University of Pisa.

Further south is the grandiose temple of Amon at Jebel Barkal, perhaps begun under Thutmose III, although most of it was built under Ramses II. Built against the mountain which was probably the seat of a primitive cult, the temple was an active cultural center around which other temples were built and a flourishing city emerged, home of the kings of the XXV-dynasty and capital in the following period of Meroes.

198 top The small temple Wadi Kardassy, to the left in the photograph, is a small square building of 26 feet to a side, begun in the late Ptolemaic period and completed under Roman rule. This building was dismantled to save it from Lake Nasser and rebuilt near the temple of Kalabsha (far right in the photographs) 24 miles from the original site.

198 bottom Before being moved to New Sebua in 1964 the rock temple of el-Derr was the only sacred Theban building on the right bank of the Nile. Built under Ramses II, it was dedicated to the god Ra-Herkhti and was known as the "House of Ramses in the Dominion of Ra". The pylon and courtyard have been lost. The four pillars of the rear row of the portico on which the Osiric statues of the pharaoh rest have been partly saved.

198-199 Considered the second greatest Nubian monument (after Simbel), the temple of Kalabsha was built in the Ptolemaic period and dedicated to the local god Mandulis, associated with Isis and Osiris. Rebuilt during the Augustan empire, it remained almost entirely undecorated. Between 1961 and 1963 the temple was dismantled and rebuilt 24 miles south in New Kalabasha, at the western end of the Great Dam.

199 top Begun by Thutmose III (1468-1436 BC) and continued by Amenhotep II (1436-1412 BC), the temple of Amada is not large but has elegant proportions and is covered with lovely reliefs. During the salvage operations of the Nubian monuments the small sanctuary was completely closed in a steel and concrete frame weighing 900 tons and moved to its new site, nearly two miles away and over 250 feet higher up, by a specially built three-track cog railway. Originally, the portal of this temple was enclosed by two brick towers, now lost.

199 bottom left Only the colonnaded hall, supported by 16 columns, remains of the temple of Wadi Maharraka. The building, from the time of the Romans, was rebuilt on the New Sabua site.

199 bottom right The so-called Hall of the Festivals in the temple of el-Derr is a huge colonnaded room supported by six pillars whose bas-reliefs show Ramses II before a number of gods.

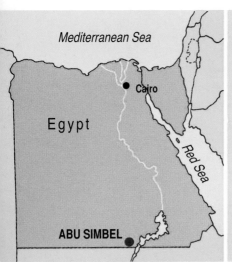

ABU SIMBEL,
HONORING RAMSES II

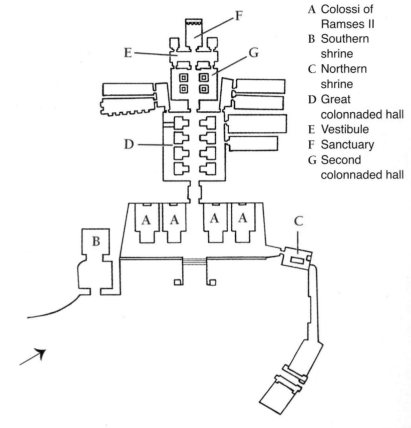

A Colossi of
  Ramses II
B Southern
  shrine
C Northern
  shrine
D Great
  colonnaded hall
E Vestibule
F Sanctuary
G Second
  colonnaded hall

*200 top This aerial view shows
the new position of the temples of
Abu Simbel with respect to the
waters of the artificial lake built
in the 1960s and honoring the
Egyptian president, Gamal Abdal
Nasser.*

*200 center left The portico of the
great temple of Ramses II,
completely dug from the rock, is
60 feet long and decorated with
eight Osiric pillars, about 30 feet
high, showing Ramses II in the
form of Osiris.*

The discovery of the two temples of Abu
Simbel was made by the Swiss traveler
Johann Ludwig Burkhardt (1784-1817).
While he was staying on Malta in 1809,
where he had gone to improve his
knowledge of Arabic, Burkhardt was
converted to Islam, and took the name
Ibrahim ibn Abdullah.

He became a Muslim in every sense and
traveled throughout Egypt and the Near
East, reaching places where no other
westerner had been. In 1813 he set out to
explore the region south of Qasr Ibrim, in
Nubia. On the way back he decided to
stop in the village he wrote of in his notes
as Ebsambal (this was what Abu Simbel
sounded like to him) as the local
inhabitants had told him there was an
extraordinarily beautiful temple in the

area, not far from the Nile. It was thus that
Burkhardt found himself face to face with
the splendid rock sanctuary dedicated to
Queen Nephertari, decorated with six
colossal statues.

Before leaving the area, he decided to
explore it further. He headed toward the
desert where he discovered a second
temple, dedicated to Ramses II, almost
entirely buried in the sand. Only the upper
part of the southern colossus was visible,
and Burkhardt made an ecstatic
description of this wonder in his notes.
When he returned to Cairo, Burkhardt told
what he had seen to Giovanni Battista
Belzoni (1778-1823) who visited Abu
Simbel the next time he visited Nubia.
There, after a great deal of work, he was
able to free the entrance to the Greater

200 center right This famous bas-relief showing Ramses II in his war chariot during the battle of Qadesh is on one of the walls of the portico. The bow and the arms of the pharaoh, shown as he fires at his Hittite enemies, appear to be doubled, as if the artist had second thoughts and covered his first version with a layer of plaster, now lost.

200 bottom The most secret and holy part of the great temple is 214 feet from the entrance door. In this small room, 13 feet wide and just over 23 feet deep are the seated statues of Amon-Ra, Harmakhis, Ptah and Ramses II.

200-201 The façade of the great temple of Abu Simbel, decorated with four immense statues of Ramses II, is of gigantic proportions. It is 125 feet wide and almost 110 feet high, the equivalent of a nine-story building. The second colossus from the left collapsed in the thirty-fourth year of the ruler's reign, possibly because of an earthquake. The third was restored by Sethi II (1214-1208 BC).

201 bottom From this photograph we can appreciate the dimensions of the two artificial hills that house the reconstructed temples of Abu Simbel. The entire complex was dismantled and reassembled between 1964 and 1972 to save it from the waters of the artificial Lake Nasser.

Temple from the sand and penetrate its interior. From that moment on the rock sanctuaries of Abu Simbel became an essential stopping place for every traveler to Egypt.

The local inhabitants were hired to remove the sand that blocked the entrance to the Great Temple. When the tourists and explorers left, the locals returned and covered over the entrance with sand again, so they could be hired by the next group that came to see the sight! Toward the end of the 19th century the Antiquities Service in Egypt decided to put an official end to the this practice and the façade of the Greater Temple was entirely uncovered.

At the start of the 20th century the construction of a dam on the Nile at Aswan made the river waters rise, and it became necessary to protect the site of Abu Simbel from flooding. The situation became even more perilous toward the end of the 1950s, when the decision was taken to build the Great Dam. On March 8, 1960, UNESCO asked for international cooperation to safeguard the rock sanctuaries of Abu Simbel. Among the projects presented, the one chosen was to dismantle the temples block by block and reconstruct them on higher ground.

The difficult, huge-scale operation took many years.

The two sanctuaries were first carefully shored up and covered in sand to protect them from damage and then sectioned off into hundreds of blocks. Finally they were rebuilt 500 feet from their original site about 200 feet higher up. The two hills the temples had been dug from were replaced by reinforced concrete domes covered in sand.

During the rebuilding operations every effort possible was made to keep the setting, position and distances between the two monuments as they had been originally.

On September 22, 1968, the official opening ceremony marked the conclusion of this dramatic salvage operation.

The two rock sanctuaries built on behalf of Ramses II (1290-1224 BC) must have been originally located near an Egyptian colonial settlement, of which no trace remains. This would have had the dual function of controlling the southern borders and handling trade with the

Nubian peoples.

The Greater Temple is preceded by a terrace in front of which there is a broad, level area. There are four colossal statues on the façade, arranged in pairs on either side of the main entrance, showing a seated figure of Ramses II.

The upper part of the southern statue closer to the interior is no longer upright, the result of an earthquake which occurred only a few years after the building of the temple. Other damage was caused by this event, so some part of the façade and a number of internal structures were restored.

The enormous statues, nearly 60 feet high, were sculpted out of the rock in the hill behind, and are seated heavily on their thrones. Their majesty is emphasized by

the crown worn by the figures which combines the crowns of Upper and Lower Egypt. Their imposing form contrasts with the mild, calm expressions on the faces, expressions which seem to symbolize the image of a just, generous ruler, prepared to listen to the needs of his subjects.

At the feet of these great statues are various members of the king's family. There are statues of princes, princesses and queens filling all the surrounding space, creating a rich, varied, and almost confusing composition typical of the artistic tastes of the Ramses period.

There are various inscriptions on the surrounding rock, including one that tells the story of the marriage of Ramses II with a Hittite princess.

Above the main entrance to the temple is an

image of Ra-Harakhti, sculpted in strong high-relief. The god is shown walking, from the front, with his arms by his sides. His right hand is resting on a scepter-user, his left on an image of Maat, the goddess of justice.

The presence of these two elements leads to a secondary interpretation of the entire composition that, interpreted as a rebus, makes its meaning to be "Powerful in justice is Ra". The fact that the sculpture can be interpreted as an effigy of Ra or as the name of Ramses II is extremely significant, and forms part of the attempt at self-glorification which is a constant feature of this ruler's reign, and finds its most complete manifestation here at Abu

203 bottom right The colossal statues of Ramses II wear the double crown of Upper and Lower Egypt and the urea, a regal symbol.

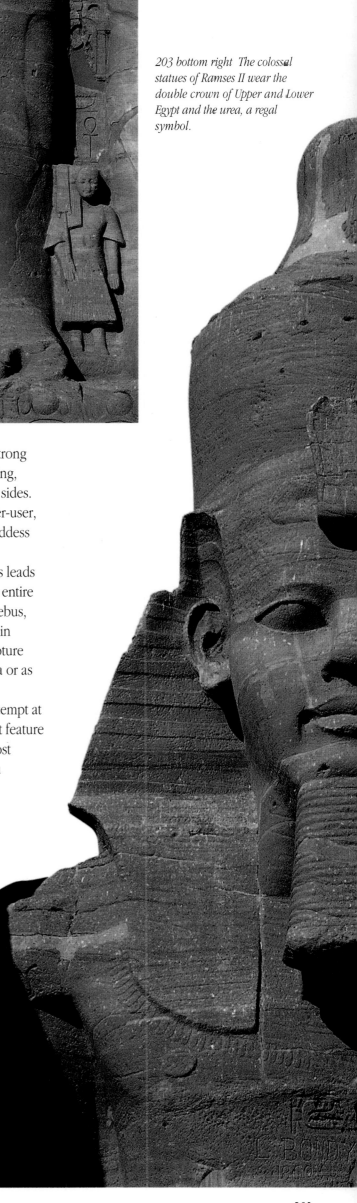

202-203 The statues of Ramses II which are on the façade of the great temple, well over 60 feet high, are believed to faithfully reproduce the face of the sovereign.

203 left A group of sandstone falcons, symbol of the god Horus, adorn the balustrade in front of the great temple.

203 top right Between the legs of each colossus are other similar statues of members of the royal family.

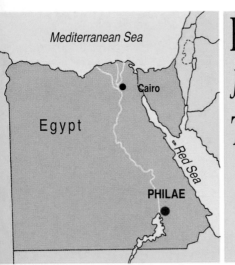

PHILAE, JEWEL OF THE NILE

208 *The Kiosk was built on the island of Philae by the Roman emperor Trajan in 105 AD as the site for the sacred vessel of Isis, in which the statue of the goddess was carried during the procession to the southern Nubian temples. The structure is in the form of a four-sided pavilion made up of 14 columns with floral capitals. They are joined at the bottom with inter-columnar walls mainly without decoration.*

The temple complex of Philae is a special one, different from the true Nubian temples. It is situated on an island of the first cataract, which had always been a point of contact between Egypt and Nubia, as it was the most important center of worship dedicated to the goddess Isis. Designed and built almost completely during the period when Greece dominated Egypt, the temple complex of the island became a place of worship venerated not only by the

the time of Justinian in 535 AD that the temple was finally closed and four churches were built on the site in the years that followed.

The first evidence of the cult of Isis on the island of Philae dates back to the era of Psammeticus II (XXVI-dynasty, 6th century BC). The king probably stayed on Philae during his Nubian campaign, and there he built a small building honoring the goddess who was worshipped in his home town of

208-209 *This splendid aerial view shows the whole island of Philae including the temple dedicated to the goddess Isis, the colonnade in front of the first pylon, the Kiosk of Trajan and other minor structures. Most of the buildings are from the Ptolemaic-Roman period.*

Egyptians and inhabitants of Nubia but also by the cosmopolitan citizens of the capital, Alexandria. The special position of Philae made it particularly important for the southern part of the area and it was a favorite place of worship for the Nubian people, who continued practicing their religion here even after the arrival of the Christianity. In fact, the temple of Philae was the only one throughout the entire Roman Empire that remained open following the edict of Theodosius in 378 AD prohibiting "pagan" practices. It wasn't until

Sais. Later, Amasis (XXVI-dynasty, 6th century BC) built a small temple which was then extended by Nectanebos (XXX-dynasty, 4th century BC). The same king also built a monumental portal which was later incorporated into the first pylon of the temple of Isis and a smaller building that remained unfinished on the southern side of the island. But the great temple to which the island owes its fame was designed by Ptolemy of Philadelphia (3rd century BC). This king and his successors built an original complex in which the elements of

A Vestibule of Nectanebos I
B Temple of Arsenuphi
C Western colonnade
D First pillar
E Mammisi
F Second pillar
G Temple of Herendote
H Gate of Diocletian
I Temple of Augustus
J Coptic church
K Temple of Isis
L Cloister of Trajan

209 top In front of the first pylon are two long colonnades, running almost parallel.

209 bottom At the southern end of the island is the Kiosk of Nectanebus, consecrated to the goddess Hathor.

210-211 This general view shows the island of Philae dominated by the First Pylon of the temple of Isis.

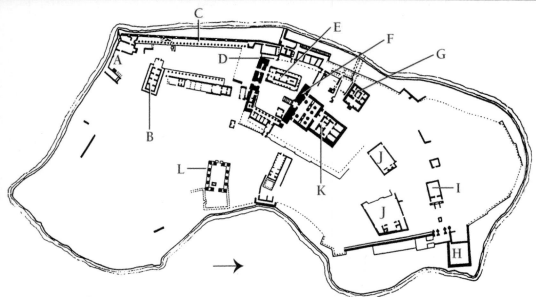

Mediterranean Sea

Tripoli ●
LEPTIS MAGNA

Libya

LEPTIS MAGNA, *THE ROME OF AFRICA*

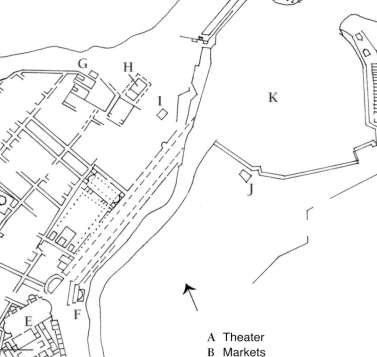

A Theater
B Markets
C Arch of Septimus Severus
D Baths of Hadrian
E Gymnasium

F Nympheon
G Temple of Rome and Augustus
H Forum
I Curia
J Temple of Dolychene Jupiter
K Harbor of Severus
L Lighthouse
M Amphitheatre
N Circus

216 bottom left The intense building activity ordered by Septimus Severus, born in the city, transformed Leptis Magna into a metropolis with a luxurious appearance. The picture shows one of the mermaids in the medallions that are part of the decoration of the Severian Forum.

216 bottom right Scrolls of acanthus decorated the pillars that frame the apse of the Severian basilica.

216-217 The great basilica of the Severian Forum reflects the new aesthetic styles that came into the Roman world at the end of the 2nd century AD. The columns are of red granite with white marble capitals and a number of niches give a sense of movement to the massive walls.

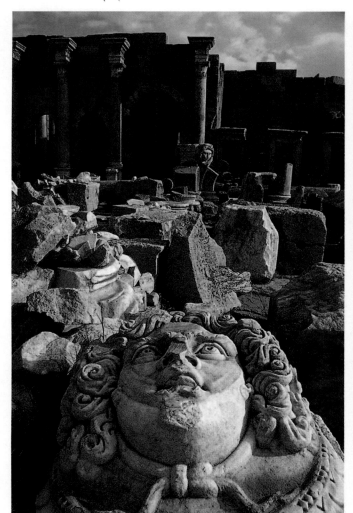

Archaeology is often seen as a heroic and even dangerous field. This is partly the fault of Hollywood, which has created epic characters prepared to stop at nothing to save their extraordinary discoveries from the villains. Many people seem to see archaeologists as Indiana Jones personalities, half scientists and half adventurers, while the archaeological sites are considered to be found only in remote areas, difficult to reach, buried in tropical forests or burning deserts and perhaps under the control of treacherous warriors and hostile tribes. Certainly, there are such places as Piedras Negras and Angkor, which are located in difficult or even dangerous areas, and the history of archaeology lists the names of such people as Hiram Bingham, John Lloyd Stephens

and Frederick Catherwood who were extraordinary people deserving of being called explorers. In most cases, however, archaeology is less romantic than this picture. Today, it is mostly a question of careful study, rigorous methods and long periods of research in the field using advanced technology. While it is true that in the early days of archaeology both research and excavation could turn into real adventure, today technological progress and modern communications have brought us to a point where there are no really inaccessible places left. Even excavations in the tropical rain forests take place in relative comfort with the help of logistical support services that would once have been unimaginable. The use of motor vehicles, helicopters, satellite

communications, echo soundings, self-inflating tents, thermal clothing, portable water purifiers, long-life foods and many other innovations have change the course of archaeology over just a few decades. But this does not mean that it has lost anything of its fascination. It is still a fascinating, intriguing science but it is important to view it realistically from today's point of view. Even Heinrich Schliemann, often mentioned as the great amateur archaeologist, prepared carefully for his expeditions. Actually, it's important to remember that even in the past the great archaeological discoveries were rarely made as a result of stunning human heroic actions. To take one example, the excavations that brought to light one of the most important Roman cities on the African

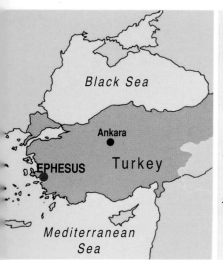

EPHESUS, PHILOSOPHERS, MERCHANTS, AND EMPERORS

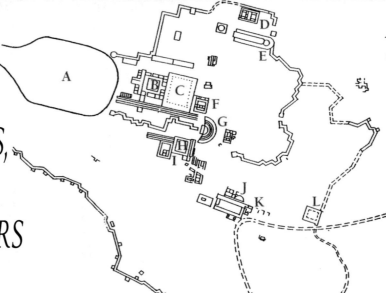

A Harbor
B Harbor bath-house
C Square of Verulanus
D Gymnasium of Vedio
E Stadium
F Gymnasium of the Theater
G Theater
H Square
I Library of Celsus
J Odeon
K Baths
L Eastern Gymnasium

"Men do not understand this eternal Word, either before they hear it or after they have heard it once. Although everything is based on this Word, they are as unskilled men, even though they are skilled in words and works such as those I display, distinguishing everything according to its nature and showing what it is. Men, however, are unaware of what they do when awake, and have no memory of what they do when asleep."

With these words, Heraclitus of Ephesus, in what is today Turkey, who was called "the obscure" but was actually considered one of the greatest of pre-Socratic philosophers (6th-5th centuries BC) urged his fellow citizens of Ephesus, one of the finest and richest Greek cities in Asia Minor, to look

beyond appearance and to recognize the fundamentals of being, to find the logos, the Word, the Reason for all things.

Centuries later, Paul of Tarsus attempted a similar thing in letters to the Christian community of Ephesus and similar urgings that mankind look to the logos, the word, is found in other places in the Christian Bible. Ephesus was an extremely important city in both periods. Today, it is a popular place for tourists to visit with its superb extensive ruins only a few miles from the Aegean Sea. These ruins can still reveal to us the wealth and luxury, the intense trading and other business, the brilliant cultural life of this ancient Ionian city which flourished from the 6th century BC onward under various governments and political influences, including oligarchies, tyrannies, Persian satraps, democratic colleges, Hellenic dynasties and Roman governors.

It is impossible to mention briefly all the fantastic and amazing monuments that can be found in Ephesus not to mention the many other treasures to be found in the ultramodern museum in the nearby town of Selçuk.

At the gates of Selçuk, far from the ancient center as was the usual Greek practice, was the sanctuary of Artemis Ephesia, goddess of fertility, with numerous breasts on her bare torso. This colossal temple, measuring 500 feet by 150 feet was built around the middle of the 6th century BC and was considered one of the Seven Wonders of the ancient world. Herodotus, the Greek historian, said it was built as a gift by

246 top left This dancing flower girl is one of the surviving reliefs of the classic monument of Caius Memmius in Ephesus.

246 bottom left A great colonnaded avenue on the edge of the marketplace leads to the graceful small square overlooked by the famous library of Celsus.

246 top right The classic statue of Aretes, personification of Virtue according to the Greeks, is modestly dressed in a niche in the Library of Celsus.

246 bottom right The remains of the nymph's shrine and fountain of Trajan are a fine example of the elegant decorations and service structures of the town. They date back to the start of the 2nd century AD.

247 Admirers come from all over the world to see the sumptuous, dynamic front of the Library of Celsus, perhaps the most famous ancient monument in Ephesus.

248-249 The imposing theater dominates the ruins of the colonnade in Verulanus Square.

Croesus King of Lydia, a man of enormous wealth. The grandiose monumental nature of the structure and the decorative exuberance of the architects Kersiphrones and Metagenes of Knossos assisted by Theodorus of Samos has been reconstructed only in drawings. Very little remains of the ancient Artemision and its reconstructed version from two centuries later, about 350 BC. The two differently columned plan (21 by 8 columns in one section with a triple row of columns while another section was nine-columned) gave the impression almost of a stone forest similar to that found in the densely columned halls of Egyptian sanctuaries. The temple, built entirely in pale blue marble, is one of the earliest examples of how the use of marble transforms the traditional clay of earlier times. The columns, above all, were overwhelming, measuring 60 feet high, grooved and usually covered up to nine feet from the base with bas-reliefs showing processions of women or warriors. The remains of some of these bases and some other finds are in the British Museum. Only one column survives on site from the reconstructions that took place during the 4th century BC. This rises almost intact from the extension of the foundation and is half-hidden among the wild vegetation.

Ephesus

Ephesus

Ephesus

250 top The grandiose water supply system of Ephesus was set up by order of Caius Sestilius Polliones in the Augustan period. It involved the building of reservoirs, nymphs' shrines and fountains, such as the one shown in the photograph with its splendid Ionian front.

250 center Many statues honoring people and events were among the works of art from Roman times decorating the public areas of Ephesus.

250 bottom left Here, we can still see the remains of the temple of Domitian (end of the 1st century AD), the eight-columned outer colonnade and three-columned inner sanctuary. Here were applied the most advanced principles of Roman engineering.

250 bottom right This view of the ruins of the acropolis of Ephesus shows a cylindrical monument with decorations in the high Imperial style.

250-251 Resting against the hill as is Greek tradition, the theater of Ephesus was built in the 3rd century BC but was extended and modified in the 1st century AD for staging Roman games, including gladiatorial combats and hunts. It held 24,000 spectators. Partially restored, it faces the old harbor, now buried. This view did not exist when the stage rose in front of the semi-circular auditorium.

Another exciting building is the beautiful theater, which acted as a spectacular arrival point for those who reached the city from the port of Ephesus along the Arcadian Way. It was built in the 3rd century BC and extended on various occasions during the Roman period. The huge terraced area is on the lower slopes of the ancient Mount Pion (also known as Panacir Dag) and opens up a view toward the sea, although it was apparently originally screened from this by a high building, part of which remains. This theater could hold at least 24,000 spectators. In the city center the road network is scenic and sumptuous, with intersections of colonnaded streets, magnificent fountains and temples in Hellenistic style, typical of the influence of Greece and Rome on architecture, and lined with the homes of the wealthier classes, with mosaics and marble carvings designed to augment the luxury of the paintings and household basics. The most elegant monument in Ephesus, the splendid Library of Celsus, belongs to the Trajan era and was dedicated by Julius Aquila to the memory of his father Julius Celsus Polemeanus, senator under Trajan. It was built in a small square at the edge of the agora in 115 AD. This combined the functions of both a public cultural service and a tomb and sanctuary honoring the deceased, raising him almost to divine rank. The sarcophagus of Celsus was placed in a burial chamber beneath the floor of the single, grandiose, apsed, quadrangular hall. This was enclosed by a double wall with the air space between acting as a way of protecting the precious volumes from damp. The purchase of these volumes was at least partially financed by the heirs of Celsus. The hall contained access stairs to the underground funeral chamber and the two upper balconies, supported by a double, airy peristasis.

The façade introduces a new artistic feature. This was designed as an elaborate theatrical backdrop, with its double arrangement of composite columns placed on staggered levels so that the upper ones protrude less than the lower. In addition, the highly decorated entablatures and the color effects with their dramatic use of light and shade according to the relation of the colonnades to the door and window openings make this façade something very special. Deep gables, alternately curved and triangular, enhance the effect.

Ephesus

Ephesus

While every element belongs to the classical architectural base, the imaginative plastic movement of the entire façade, which stresses the aesthetic over the structural, makes it stand out.

The glorification of the culture and generous action of those who had the building constructed is clear from the texts of the epigraphs and the allegorical statues of the Virtues. Despite these noble ambitions, it was found necessary to place on the wall a warning to those who visited the shadows offered by the library not to leave ill-smelling mementos behind!

A miniature jewel of the site of Ephesus is the temple of Hadrian (127 AD) which was built in Hellenistic-Roman style with a Corinthian two-columned front between pure Corinthian pillars and an entablature of mixed lines. The horizontal lines of the architrave are broken by a highly decorated Syrian-style arch. A single inner section, which can be reached through a wide rectangular gate with a relief showing a Siren coming out of an acanthus chalice, apparently had a barrel-vaulted ceiling, marble decorations on the walls, and a cult statue, now lost.

In front of the temple, however, we can still see the four bases of the statues of the tetrarchs: Diocletian, Maximianus, Galerius and Constantius Chlorus (the second of these was later replaced by the statue of Theodosius I).

252 top The figures on this bas-relief which decorates the space over the entrance door to the Temple of Hadrian in Ephesus are almost baroque in their styling. This is typical. Note the siren emerging from entwined acanthus branches.

252 bottom The style of this mythological frieze in four slabs is definitely late-Ancient. It was inserted in the restorations of the Temple of Hadrian at the end of the 4th century AD.

252-253 This fine overall view of the Temple of Hadrian stresses the harmony and elegance of its proportions and decoration.

253 right Another view of the acropolis of Ephesus shows the Gate of Hercules, marked by two massive pillars decorated with haute-relief figures of the god dating to the 4th century AD.

254-255 This detail shows the trabeation of Hadrian's temple with the typical curved element known as the 'Syrian arch' that was used throughout mid-imperial architecture.

HERODION, STRONGHOLD OF KING HEROD

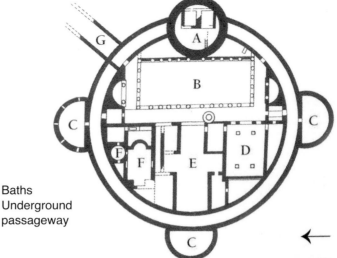

A Main tower
B Colonnaded courtyard
C Semi-circular towers
D Synagogue
E Cross-shaped hall
F Baths
G Underground passageway

256-257 and 258-259 This aerial view gives us a clear idea of the strict symmetry of the various parts of the building. The tunnel that gave access to the fortified palace emerged near the sumptuous inner garden. Josephus Flavius said that the access staircase had 200 marble steps.

257 left Herod had the palace built as a refuge, but he also intended it to be his mausoleum. However, no trace of a royal tomb has been found in the ruins. Archaeologists discovered the remains of a synagogue and a mikveh, the ritual Jewish bath, as well as some small ovens used by the Jewish rebels.

257 right The unusual conical shape of the fortress built for Herod dominates the high plains of Judea. The Herodion, considered one of the most extraordinary monuments in the western world, was built on the summit of a semi-artificial hill, with the second residential complex, possibly for guests, built at the foot.

With the emergence of the Hasmoneon state in 142 BC, the Jews began to expand their territory, and during the reign of John Hirkan they took control of a wide part of the Negev region. Later they conquered what later became Transjordan, the land that stretched as far as Banias and the coastal plain south of Ashkelon. Between 67 and 63 BC, however, a bloody civil war raged caused by a conflict over the succession to the throne. At this time the Roman general Pompey, who had recently created the nearby province of Syria, attacked and destroyed the Harmoneon empire with his armies and went on to occupy much of the territory. Only Judea was granted the right to remain an autonomous Jewish state, governed by the Hasmoneon Hirkan II, who had been proclaimed leader of the people and high priest. The Romans, however, also reinforced their presence by appointing Antipatros regent, his son Phasael as governor of Jerusalem and his other son, Herod, tetrarch of Gelilee. These were the most influential members of an Idumenean family that had been converted to Judaism, although they showed more loyalty to Rome than to their own people. In 40 BC the Parthians, a people of Persian stock, invaded Judea and deposed Hirkan. Nevertheless, the new conquerors left the control of the region in the hands of the

Hasmoneons and Matthatias Antigonus was crowned. However, this state of affairs only lasted three years. During the Parthian invasion Antipatros's son, Herod, fled to Rome, where he was proclaimed King of Judea. With the help of Roman troops, he returned home in 37 BC to put the invaders to flight and take control of Idumea, Samaria and Galilee. He then marched on Jerusalem, which fell into his hands after a

five month siege. The Hasmoneon dynasty came to an end with the execution of Matthatias Antigonus. Although Herod was a Jew and may even have adhered to the customs and laws of the religion he was never accepted by the Jewish majority in Judea, who considered him a slave to Rome. Ambitious, a lover of luxury and anxious to please Rome, Herod became famous for the splendid architectural works that sprang up during his reign. He was responsible for the construction of the fortress of Masada, on the Dead Sea, a

luxurious winter palace, in Jericho, a modern harbor and a new barracks for troops loyal to him in Sebastes, near the ancient capital Samaria, and the model city of Caesarea, built in honor of his protector and patron, Caesar Augustus. Jerusalem itself was transformed. Here, Herod built a palace for his own use, with three huge monumental towers, and then in 19 BC he started work on an immense, spectacular temple for the Jews. However, his most outstanding and original creation was the grandiose palace he had built to the south of Jerusalem and named Herodion. Seen from the distance in the arid landscape of the heights to the south of Jerusalem, it looks like a strangely regular conical, flat-topped hill, with the ruins of a great palace, an immense swimming pool, warehouses and bathhouses at the foot.

This superb building was a fortified palace and was designed to become the mausoleum of its founder. However, despite the description of the king's funeral procession by the historian Joseph Flavius, Herod's tomb has never been discovered. The building is at the top of a semi-artificial hill about 200 feet high and is enclosed inside two concentric circular walls with a

diameter of just over 200 feet. The walls were dominated by a circular tower which must have been about 50 feet high, and three smaller towers that protruded from the outer wall. The hill took on its unusual shape from the rubble dug up to lay the foundations and left over from the construction of the palace, tossed onto the slopes, along with other excess material, to make the incline steeper. Access was possible only by way of a vaulted underground passage that opened from the base of the hill. The interior of the circular

palace was divided into two sections. One had a garden, surrounded by columns, a true oasis in the desert, and the other consisted of luxurious apartments with refined baths on the ground floor. The floors were covered in mosaics with geometric motifs, and the walls were coated in stucco with multicolored reliefs. The lowest part of the Herodion was dominated by a huge pool in the center. This was used as an artificial lake and was big enough not only to swim in but also to sail small boats. An ornamental garden with several buildings and a large bath complex surrounded the pool. Inside the semi-artificial hill was discovered an intricate network of secret passages, partly making use of Herod's underwater supply system. The passages were dug out by the followers of Simeon Bar Kokhba during the Second Jewish Revolt, which erupted all over Palestine in 132 AD. Among the finds are many tools and weapons as well as coins minted during the uprising. Later, in the Byzantine period, a monastery was founded on the ruins of the palace. Now, the isolated position of the area makes the structure seem even more unusual, a memorial to Herod's architectural imagination.

MASADA, THE CHALLENGER OF ROME

260-261 The fortress of Masada stands on an isolated rock overlooking the western shore of the Dead Sea. The main buildings and the fortifications of the level area, almost 1,000 feet long and 400 to 800 feet wide, were built by King Herod in 37 AD. A large area of the plain was cultivated, using the water in the large underground tanks for irrigation.

260 top The grandiose northern palace of Masada was built as the personal residence of King Herod. The apsed hall of the highest level and the circular room beneath were used for important receptions. The lowest level, built around an inner courtyard, was the private quarters of the king and contained a small bath complex.

261 top In a building near the western palace this large space was used as a mikveh, the ritual Jewish bath.

261 bottom The long, narrow rooms of the northern complex were used as an arsenal and warehouses for foodstuffs necessary for the considerable garrison of the king.

Masada, the fortress in the Judean desert built by Herod the Great, is still today one of the greatest living symbols for the Jewish people. On this site, in 73 AD, 960 men, women and children committed suicide rather than surrender to the Tenth Roman Legion. This was the last episode in a rebellion that had reached its height three years earlier with the destruction of Jerusalem by the armies of Titus.

In the Hasmoneon period this rocky site, situated in an ideal position near the Dead Sea, with steep escarpments and a huge flat area at the top, was transformed into a military stronghold. In 40 BC it took on a special significance for Herod who had to ensure the safety of his family during his flight from the forces of Antigonus, the Parthian pretender to the throne, during his journey to seek military aid from Rome. His friends and family, along with 800 men charged with protecting them, were

suffering from extreme thirst and only saved by a timely downpour that filled empty water tanks. Later, when he was able to take back his kingdom with the help of the Roman army, Herod transformed Masada into a palace-fortress complex to defend himself from both the threat of a Jewish rebellion and the queen of Egypt, Cleopatra. The entire perimeter of the citadel was surrounded by a turreted defensive wall fortified at strategic points with huge tanks, dug from the bare rock, designed to supply the troops with water. But the most imposing structure at the site is the splendid royal palace at the most northerly point of the complex.

This shows quite advanced architectural concepts and admirable distribution of the rooms. The upper floor consisted of a huge rectangular hall which opened up onto an apse bounded by a Corinthian colonnade, and giving a magnificent viewpoint over the Dead Sea. A covered stairway connected this wing of the palace with the intermediate section, which was formed by a structure with a rounded floor plan, surrounded by columns and topped by a bell-shaped roof.

The lower level was roughly square in plan with an inner courtyard at the center surrounded by a portico supported by pillars with Corinthian half-columns. Alongside was a small but luxurious bath complex. The inner walls and the columns of the palace were covered in lively multicolored stucco, mainly imitating precious marble decoration, some of which can still be seen today. The floors were covered in black and white mosaics with geometric patterns. The large, four-roomed bath complex on the upper floor is

particularly interesting as it is among the best preserved of the sites in Israel dating from Roman times.

The dressing room was decorated with stucco and black and white tiles covered the floor. We can also recognize the lukewarm room and the cool room, with its large seated bath. In the warm room, we can still see the hypocauston, or floor held up by small pillars beneath which the hot air from the boiler circulated. Near the bathhouse was a large complex of rooms used to store food and wine and as a safe deposit area for weapons and valuables. This sector of the fortress, including the palace itself, the bath complex and the warehouses, was separated from the rest of the citadel by a wall and gate.

This luxurious complex was clearly used for banquets and as a showpiece for the wealth and power of Herod, but at the same time it was designed to offer a last line of defense

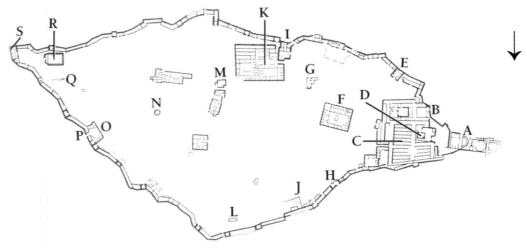

A Northern Palace	F Large Building of uncertain use	J Residences of the Zealots	O *Mikveh*
B Gate of the Water	G Byzantine Church	K Western Palace	P Southern Gate
C Warehouses	H Gate of the Serpent's Path	L Open water tank	Q Covered tank
D Baths	I Western Gate	M *Mikveh*	R Great Pool
E Synagogue		N Dovecote	S Southern Bastion

against invaders who succeeded in scaling the walls.

The western palace, on the other hand, had to be more functional. Because of this need for functionality, it consisted of the royal apartments, guest quarters, service rooms, workshops and warehouses, as well as rooms with certain administrative functions including state receptions. Here, too, the floors were covered in mosaics and it is known that some parts of the building were several floors high. Nearby are three other, smaller buildings, one of which contained a mikveh, the Jewish ritual bath.

The most serious problem for Masada, a complex where it might be necessary to accommodate as many as a thousand people at once, was the supply and storage of water. Not only was the fortress in the desert, with only occasional, seasonal rainfall, but it was also on a high plateau at the top of a mountain surrounded by steep escarpments.

For this reason, a drainage system was installed that took the rainwater from the dams of the surrounding valleys to a complex of twelve tanks at the base of the fortress.

These tanks had an enormous capacity and from them water could be taken by men or on mules along a difficult path to the tanks inside the fortress. Despite the fact that Masada was virtually inaccessible, in a remote position surrounded by high, steep walls, it was also fortified with thick walls that enclosed all the buildings on the plateau, with the exception of the northern palace.

The defensive perimeter consisted of an outer and an inner wall, with the space between the two occupied by rooms for various purposes.

The walls of Masada are 5,000 feet long, with 70 turrets, 30 towers, and four gates. When the Zealots conquered the fortress during the six-year-long Jewish uprising against the Romans, they made a number of changes to Herod's complex. To house a large number of families, all the rooms between the two walls were transformed for domestic use and many halls in the palace were subdivided to create extra rooms. The Zealots also built two mikvehs,

Mediterranean Sea

Amman

Egypt

PETRA

Jordan

Saudi Arabia

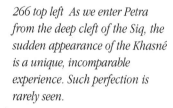

PETRA, THE ROSE RED CITY

266 top left As we enter Petra from the deep cleft of the Siq, the sudden appearance of the Khasné is a unique, incomparable experience. Such perfection is rarely seen.

266 bottom left The interior of the Khasné consists of a great cubic hall, whose sides measure almost 40 feet. Three smaller rooms open onto this room through enormous doorways.

The ruins of Petra in Jordan are one of the most fascinating monuments of the ancient world. The combination of the exceptional quality of the architectural work of the city, the extraordinary location of it, lying as it does among steep hills and narrow spaces between rocks, add to the rose color of the rock itself to make this one of the most extraordinary sights in the world. Petra is situated in southern Jordan and is mentioned in the Bible occasionally as Sela which is the Hebrew for rock. The Arabs called it Wadi Musa, which means the Valley of Moses. The name given to the city by its original inhabitants is unknown. Petra, of course, is simply the Greek word for rock.

Although it is known that the site was inhabited during the Iron Age its major importance is linked to the Nabatean occupation, during the second half of the 4th century BC.

The Nabateans were originally nomads from the Arabian peninsula who later became settled and, eventually, grew to become a solid monarchy which grew rich through trading. Their stronghold was on one of the rocky spurs of the area and in 312 BC they were able to resist the attempt at conquest by Antigon I, thus confirming their independence and establishing the foundations for a period of tremendous splendor.

266 top right The Nabatean carvers reached amazing heights in molding the bare rock into a wide range of shapes. These subtle plant motifs are part of the complex decorative designs found here.

266 bottom right After crossing the threshold of the Khasné, the visitor enters into the cool vestibule, a room 46 feet long and almost 18 deep, which leads to the great hall and two smaller rooms opening out on the short sides.

267 The Khasné, a superb funerary temple probably built by King Aretas IV between 85 and 84 BC, is extremely well preserved.

A Florentine
  Tomb
B Corinthian
  Tomb
C Tomb
  of the Urn
D Roman triumphal
  Arch
E Temple
F Theatre
G Kashné
H El-Deir
I Wall remains

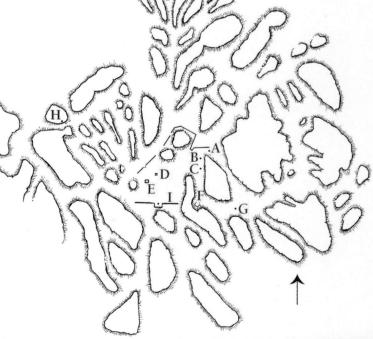

268 top left The pinnacles that give their name to the Tomb of the Obelisks were a typical Nabatean grave marking.

268 top right The Tomb of the Lions owes its name to the sculpted figures at the side of the door.

268 bottom The Tomb of the Urn, believed to date to 70 AD, is one of the most elaborate structures in Petra. The finishing is of a high quality and the façade is set back from the natural face of the mountain.

The Roman occupation and creation of the province of Arabia under Trajan in 106 AD slowed the development of the city but did not stop it. It was only when other major centers for trading, notably Gerasa and Palmyra became increasingly important and the capital was moved to Basra in the 3rd century AD that Petra lost its importance. For several centuries after that it continued important as a Bishopric and under the reorganization of the empire by Diocletian it became capital of the province of Palestina Taertia. With the Arab conquest of the region it fell into decay, although it was briefly fortified and defended by the Crusaders. After the 13th century it was finally abandoned and forgotten in the West until 1812 when it was rediscovered by Johann Ludwig Burkhardt, a Swiss explorer and authority on the East.

Petra developed as a hill town at a central point of three steep valleys, gradually becoming the place where nearby tribes gathered for meeting and defense. It was named as the capital of the area for safety reasons. Since it was concealed among the mountains with only a few, easily guarded, entry points, it was an ideal place for both refuge and the regrouping of forces. Its links with the Red Sea made it possible to establish trading with Arabia and Mesopotamia while the route across the Negev to Gaza gave not only access to the Mediterranean but also to Syrian ports.

It is because of this continuing connection with the major trading routes and the ever-increasing prosperity of Petra that there was such a strong Greek influence, especially evident in the monuments dug by the Nabatean rulers in the rock walls during the 1st century AD. At the moment of Petra's greatest importance it would have had between thirty and forty thousand inhabitants, most of them involved with trade.

He was unable to thoroughly study the ruins, however, as the local Bedouin tribes stopped him. Twenty-seven years later, David Roberts, a Scot artist, was one of the first Westerners to obtain permission to camp in Petra and to study its buildings. He was one of the first, also, to produce an exhaustive graphic documentation of the site.

A highly gifted man, he was considered one of the best artists of his day and an excellent landscape painter, skills which he used when he made several journeys

Petra

through Europe and followed them by going to Egypt in 1838. Early in the following year he visited the Sinai Peninsula, Palestine, Jerusalem and the coasts of Lebanon and Baalbek. Lithographs made from his drawings of this journey were published in London between 1842 and 1849 and are still valuable. In addition to drawing what he saw, Roberts also wrote down his impressions and practical information about his travels in a diary, describing what seems like an almost incredible adventure

268-269 The Palace Tomb (center) and the Corinthian Tomb (right) are important examples of the construction skills of the Nabateans.

269 bottom The Theater, dating to the 1st century AD, could hold over 6,000 spectators.

270-271 The skimming light picks out the unusual facade of the Tomb of the Obelisks.

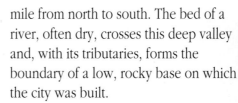
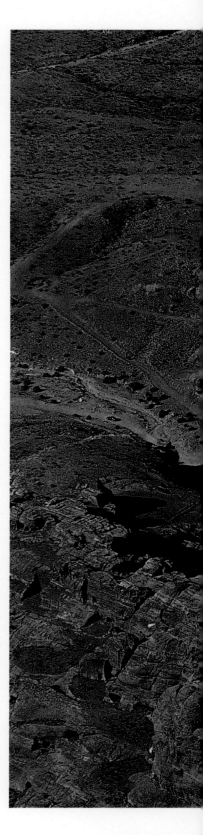

272 top The first rock tombs of Petra, mainly dating to the 2nd century BC, usually have high fronts crowned with stepped battlements which show Egyptian and Assyrian influences.

272 bottom A splendid example of its genre, The Tomb of Silk is also known as the Rainbow Tomb because of the many shades of fine sandstone in the façade.

to today's tourist.

Roberts reached Petra on March 6, 1839, and through the influence of his local guides and, of course, the payment of a considerable bribe he was allowed to remain for five days in what was then the territory of a fairly war-like Arab tribe. What he saw was breath-taking. Petra is built on a site which is in the shape of an amphitheater enclosed by rocks measuring about a mile from east to west and half a mile from north to south. The bed of a river, often dry, crosses this deep valley and, with its tributaries, forms the boundary of a low, rocky base on which the city was built.

Although the river is often dry it occasionally floods and some of the city has been washed away by these floods. The rock walls that surround the valley, in some places as much as nine hundred feet high, were used by the Nabateans as both tombs and houses. They have been compared to enormous theatrical backdrops of great beauty. On the summits of the peaks which surround this area were several places of worship and small fortresses overlooking the access routes to the city.

What is now the bed of the Wadi Musa was the main street of Petra. It was fully paved and began at the site of a bathing pool which was part of a temple. Further on, there were three market places on terraces. The stalls of the markets were along the sides and there were also such buildings as a large Corinthian temple, bathhouses, the Roman arch and a gymnasium of several floors. The rock wall opposite the theater shows a number of magnificently carved structures. The theater itself is amazing as it seated over six thousand people and was carved completely from the rock.

Rogers was thrilled, and wrote "I continue to be amazed and overwhelmed by this extraordinary city. . . Every ledge, and even the summits of the mountains, were inhabited. The valley is scattered with temples, public buildings, triumphal arches and bridges. The architectural style is different from any other I have seen, and in many places we can see a curious combination of the Egyptian, Roman and Greek styles. The stream still flows through the city.

"Lush shrubs and wild flowers abound. Each cleft in the rocks in full of these and the air is perfumed with their delicious fragrance." As soon as his camp was set up, Roberts decided to visit the Khasné, the most famous monument in Petra.

272-273 *This spectacular aerial view of the Road of Façades shows how the rock tombs flank the main street on terraces at various levels, with great effect. They were originally linked to each other with stairs.*

273 top *An inscription states that the Tomb of Aneishu belonged to a minister of Queen Shuquailat II, who lived in the 1st century AD. Extremely dignified, this tomb contains exquisite Nabatean architectural features, such as these two typical capitals.*

To understand the tremendous impact this monument has on the visitor we have to remember that the only easy entry into the city is from the east, through the narrow bed of the stream which is here bound by a narrow path between two rock walls which at some points are only nine feet or so apart. The passage, which is called the Siq, is about five miles long. In ancient times the water in this stream flowed through two channels dug from the bare rock and then into the town's aqueduct. This gorge itself is permanently shadowed and the rock shows evidence of having been shaped over the centuries by wind and running water. The water in the stream increases rapidly during summer thunderstorms. In some places the path opens up to show spots where caravans might have stopped. Halfway through the

274 top On the inside, these rock tombs are usually large bare rooms, furnished only with niches which held the bodies. Spacious and clean, many of these chambers were lived in by Bedouin peoples in the past.

274-275 The Tomb of the Roman Soldier is given its name because of the bas-reliefs showing Roman legionaries which decorate the niches on the front. It is believed it was prepared for the body of a high ranking individual.

path the Siq suddenly changes direction and the KhasnJ appears, a funeral temple cut from the rock that is unlike any other monument in the world. The dramatic contrast between the gloom of the Siq and the delicate pink façade of the monument is one of the highlights of Petra. The façade itself is symmetrical in form and the proportions are magnificent.

Roberts, thrilled by the sight, wrote ". . . I don't know whether I was most surprised by the appearance of this building or by its extraordinary position. It rises intact from an immense niche in the rock, and the pale color of the rock together with the perfect conservation of the tiniest details give the impression that the work has only recently been completed." The façade, about forty-five yards high and twenty-five yards wide, is divided into two floors.

The lower floor has a gabled portico with six Corinthian columns thirty-six feet high. Between the two pairs of outer columns there are two very large groups of horses in high-relief which over the years have become extremely worn. The frieze on the portico shows a series of griffins facing each other while the gable, which had an eagle with outspread wings at its center, is finished with a scroll. In the corners of the architrave are two lions. The second floor is divided into three sections. At the center, there is a tholos which looks like a miniature rounded temple. It is typical of the local architecture and has a cone shaped roof with an urn on top.

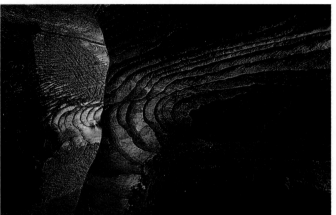

275 top and center The builders of the rock structures of Petra often achieved extraordinarily beautiful results, skillfully incorporating the natural veining of the sandstone to achieve special colorful effects.

275 bottom Near the Tomb of Aneishu are many structures in the rock wall that date to the oldest period in the building of Petra. They all have a very simple, smooth façade topped by a stepped battlement. A door, framed by half-columns, is sometimes inserted in this.

For years there has been controversy among scholars about the real purpose served by the buildings lined up along the valley. From detailed excavations and careful studies it now seems as if many of them were residences, often with a large hall with columns and niches on the sides and a raised area in the center which perhaps served for dining. Some of these houses are decorated with vine-leaf frescoes and floral patterns.

The building styles throughout Petra differ considerably from each other, each indicating a different historical period and cultural influence.

The earliest rock monuments of the Nabatean city had a smooth, very simple façade with only one or two rows of

This has given the building its Arabic name, which means "treasure." The Bedouins believed that immense riches were hidden inside this and they fired at it with their rifles, trying to break it up to reach these treasures. The tholos is flanked by two half-gables, each supported by four columns. Within the niches are reliefs of female figures, also very eroded. Finally, four gigantic eagles balance the ends.

The inside of the building consists of a

large entrance hall which leads by eight steps to the central hall. This, a huge cube of thirty-six feet on each side has small niches on each of three sides. The arrangement of the inner rooms and the lack of an altar as well as the fact that this monument is placed where it is in the narrow trench, which would not have encouraged religious rites, have led recent scholars to believe that the Khasné was a monumental tomb rather than a temple as had been once believed.

battlements, a door at the base with perhaps half columns. This type of tomb, whose earliest examples can be dated to the 3rd century BC, was a typical adaptation by the Nabateans of styles used throughout nearby Syria at that time. During the following two centuries more complex models developed, starting with those which showed a strong Greek influence in the use of the frieze, the architrave and the protruding columns. Meanwhile, a special type of capital,

276 This building, called el Deir which means "the Convent", is considered the most impressive monument in Petra. It stands in a n isolated position at the top of a spur of rock at a distance from the center of the rose red city. The face of the temple, deeply set into the rocky mass in order to create a spacious level area in front, is of unusual size. It is almost 162 feet wide and 129 feet high.

known as the Nabatean, had been developed and purely ornamental structural elements were increasing in use. The extremely provincial nature of the local art, developed in a desert region that was far distant from the Mediterranean basin did, however, mean that certain local and in a way obsolete elements in decoration remained, such as rosettes and heraldic animals facing each other. In the second half of the 1st century AD a new type of façade appeared and developed further over the following decades. The basic architectural style was accompanied now by a decorative grandeur that was influenced by Roman developments. The rock façades reached colossal dimensions, with rows of columns overlapping so that they imitated temples and theatrical curtains. The so-called Tomb of the Palace

rough path that soon turned into a steep upward path which rose over one thousand feet before finally arriving at what is probably one of the least visited of all the monuments in the Nabatean city, although it is one of the most imposing and interesting.

This monument is completely dug out of the bare rock. The façade of the temple is one hundred fifty feet wide and one hundred twenty feet high. The decoration is similar to the Khasné but less elaborate.

On the lower floor, which is bounded by pillars, there are eight half-columns framing two niches formed by arches on the sides and a gabled door in the center. The entrance leads into a large, square room, in the bottom wall of which was the altar which is now almost completely

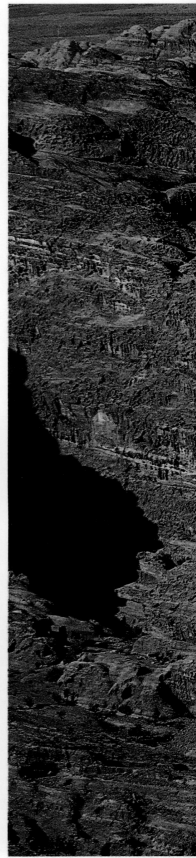

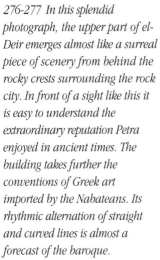

276-277 In this splendid photograph, the upper part of el-Deir emerges almost like a surreal piece of scenery from behind the rocky crests surrounding the rock city. In front of a sight like this it is easy to understand the extraordinary reputation Petra enjoyed in ancient times. The building takes further the conventions of Greek art imported by the Nabateans. Its rhythmic alternation of straight and curved lines is almost a forecast of the baroque.

and the adjacent Corinthian Tomb, similar to the Khasné but with a lower intermediate level between the gable and the tholos, belong to this period of great flourishing.

The remarkable building known as el-deir, Arabic for The Convent, belongs to the Graeco-Roman period. In a sense, it is so rich in its way that it could almost be called baroque. Roberts came to this on the morning of March 8, accompanied by a small group of armed men.

He stepped into a deep gorge along a

destroyed. In the upper level, the façade contains a central tholos and a split gable, as well as two pillars at the corners, while a Doric frieze runs across the entire front. Roberts was thrilled by the view from that balcony of rock, looking down over the valley of El Ghor. "From here," he wrote, "the view is marvelous, the gaze extends over the valley, to Mount Hor which, one tradition says, is crowned at its peak by the tomb of Aaron, and the entire mountain gorge, which weaves in and out amidst dizzying rocky peaks.

The ancient city, in all its extension, stretches out along the valley."
In spite of all this enthusiasm Roberts's stay in Petra had its unfortunate side although the annoyances were certainly minor. Some dishes were stolen and, on the fifth day, the plunderers carried off a number of rifles and cartridges along with other goods.
Given that, there was nothing to do but to leave as the local tribes were considered and, indeed were, quite dangerous.

277 bottom The tholos, of the Convent, almost 30 feet high, emerges from the bare rock in a way that seems to announce the triumph of human genius over the raw materials of nature. With the possible except of Abu Simbel, there are few monuments in the world comparable to el-Deir. The temple, dating to the 1st century AD and originally dedicated to the deified King Obodas I, got its name in Byzantine times when it became a place for Christian worship.

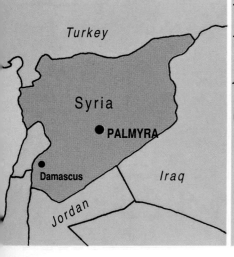

PALMYRA, PRIDE OF QUEEN ZENOBIA

A Field of Diocletian
B Great Colonnade
C Agorà
D Tetrapylon
E Sanctuary of Ba'alshamin
F Theatre
G Monumental Arch
H Temple of Bel
I Monumental Tombs

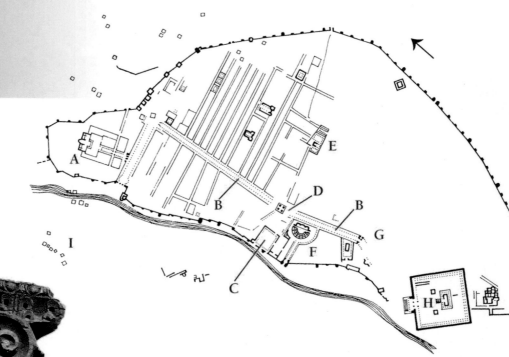

278 top and bottom The art of Palmyra is a distinctive combination of the figurative world imported from the Greco-Roman west and local style. Here, in the compound capital from one of the columns of the main road and the refined funerary relief, dating from the final years of the 2nd century, we can see this combination clearly.

History has tended to favor men over women, and great women are relatively rare in chronicles, but this does not mean that there have been no outstanding women down through the centuries. For example, Queen Hatshepsut not only ruled Egypt with all the rights and privileges of pharaohs, but extended the sanctuary of Karnak, ordered the construction of the funerary temple of Deir el-Bahari and organized major trading expeditions to distant lands which greatly expanded the geographical knowledge of her time. Less well known, perhaps, but not less important was Zenobia, whose history is bound with the city over which she reigned and which she took to the dizziest heights of splendor. Palmyra, now in Syria, is one of the most famous archaeological sites in the Middle East with its spectacular and well-preserved monuments. The ancient city, built on a desert oasis halfway between the Mediterranean and the Euphrates, is far from any other source of fresh water. It was inhabited from Neolithic times, as was proven by a series of careful excavations in 1996 during which a village five thousand years old was found. The area was strategically important because of the abundant supply of water. In Babylonian, it was known as Tadmuru and as the Old Testament refers to the foundation of a city called Tadmor or Thadamora by Solomon it was believed for some time that there was a connection between the two. However, the biblical mention almost certainly refers to a site in Judea known as Tamar. This is one of the many examples which can be found in archaeology in which the study of written sources proves less meaningful than may at first be believed.

The oldest certain historic mention of this settlement is to be found on an Assyrian tablet written in cuneiform characters, dating to the early 2nd millennium BC. Equally certain is the mention of Tadmuru in the annals of Tiglatpileser I, an Assyrian

278-279 The main axis of the town center in Palmyra was the famous colonnaded road, which ran from the northwest to the southeast and was built primarily during the 2nd century AD. This long road consists of three straight sectors with an unusual triangular arch with three openings at the junctions (left) and a tetrapylon, which can be seen in the center of the photograph. This was a square monument with two points of passage along the medians, usually placed at the crossing of two roads. They originally were built in the great eastern caravan towns during the Hellenic period, but later became very common throughout the Roman Empire.

279 bottom The layout of Palmyra underwent intense restructuring from the first Imperial period onward, and reached its current appearance in the Severian period and under Zenobia, when the second stretch of the Great Colonnade, seen here from the west, was built. Along this road were the sanctuary of Nabu, the great theater and the palace of Zenobia which recent excavations have found beneath the later Dicoletian bath complex. Large shelves can be seen on the columns which probably held statues of the city dignitaries, a typical feature of the local architecture.

monarch who ruled in the 11th century BC. Unfortunately, if we want to know more we have to wait for the appearance of the classical sources written a thousand years later in Greek or Latin, in which the city finally appears with the name Palmyra, "The Place of Palms". A great deal of time passed, therefore, with no written documents produced, so that the only indications we have on the development of the city are from the archaeological findings. However, we do know that from the 11th century BC onward Palmyra was an important Assyrian caravan center whose wealth grew constantly as a result of its crucial position between the Mediterranean basin and the fertile Euphrates valley along the Silk Route. The city came under Greek influence because of the expansionist policies of

Alexander the Great, but was able to keep a degree of independence and continued to flourish. In short, Palmyra's excellent geographical position made it an ideal halfway house between east and west, but also placed it in the role of a buffer state between the Persian empire and the growing imperialism of Rome. Relations between Palmyra and Rome were always rather uncertain.

In 41 BC, during the civil wars, Anthony allowed the sacking of the wealthy city, although the inhabitants were able to flee to the other side of the Euphrates with some of their riches. Augustus, on the other hand, granted Palmyra autonomy from the province of Syria, which guaranteed its neutrality with regard to the Parthians. Thanks to the taxes which the city levied on

the caravans that transported precious goods from the Arabian peninsula and even further afield to the markets of the Mediterranean, the city returned to a position of great prosperity. But there was a further change in diplomatic relations with Rome around 114 AD, when Trajan occupied Palmyra with his armies to use it as a strategic base during his successful campaign against the Parthian empire. His successor, the refined, learned Hadrian, restored the city's privileges once more. Following his visit in 129, the city gained fiscal autonomy and the name Hadriana. Caravan traffic crossing Syria reached enormous heights due to the constant Roman demand for luxury goods from the east. The so-called "Tariff of Palmyra", a bilingual stelae in Greek and the Palmyran

Palmyra

language dating to 137 and now in the Hermitage Museum in St. Petersburg, gives us an idea of the quantities of goods that were normally carried by the constant caravan traffic. From Arabia came incense and myrrh, from India aromatic essences, dyes, gems, cotton and other fabrics, from China came silk and precious hides. Going in the opposite direction, Asia Minor exported colored wool, silver and gold, and purple dyes, while colored glass and wine arrived from Phoenicia. There is nothing surprising about all this movement. The Romans, highly skilled merchants and great travelers, went as far as Zanzibar and Samarkand, did business in Begram, in Afghanistan, and along the Ganges, reached the banks of the Huang-Ho in China and the southern tip of India. Together with spices

280-281 The archaeological site of Palmyra is the largest and most spectacular group of ruins in present-day Syria. Its glorious monuments reflect the prosperity that the center enjoyed from the 1st to 3rd centuries AD due to the fact that it was an almost obligatory stopping point on the caravan route between the Euphrates basin and the Mediterranean.

The great colonnaded road, common to all the great cities during the Imperial age, is a typical expression of the artistic influence of Greece and Rome. Here, however, the style is somewhat unusual. Monotony is avoided with great care and arches break up the succession of columns that mark the junctions with the roads that cross the main road.

A distinctive triangular arch (shown here are a few of the most interesting details) marks the change of direction of the route. When we view these monumental remains it is easy to imagine the superb appearance of this city in the desert, its broad streets, its many important monuments with their splendid marble, the forests of columns and the shining roofs of gilded bronze.

P a l m y r a

282 top *The architecture of Palmyra manages to combine western building methods with a feeling of independence. Here, for example, in the great sanctuary of Bel, whose layout is quite different from classical ones, the columns of the portico marking the perimeter of the huge inner courtyard are nevertheless topped by Corinthian capitals.*

and the finest fabrics, precious metals and works of art, they also brought back an enormous variety of ideas and notions to Rome and the other cities of the empire, in turn influencing distant people and cultures. A statuette of Lakshmi, the Hindu goddess of fertility, was found in Pompeii, for example, while archaeological expeditions in China, India and southern Arabia have unearthed glass and bronze objects and coins showing the faces of Roman emperors.

Palmyra reached the height of its economic power and monumental glory during the

282 center This view of the inner sanctuary of the temple of Bel emphasizes some of its outstanding differences from other buildings, such as the presence of windows (behind the second column from the left) and the Syrian type battlement which surmounted the cornice.

282 bottom The great agora, which was originally surrounded on four sides by a colonnaded portico in typically Roman-Eastern style, dates to the second half of the 2nd century AD. The agora was the meeting and marketplace of the residents of Palmyra.

282-283 In this aerial view of the sanctuary of Bel, we can clearly see a concept extensively used in eastern religious art. Notice the positioning of the temple at the center of a spacious courtyard closed along its entire perimeter by a colonnade.

rule of Septimus Severus (193-211) partly because this Roman emperor, who was born in Leptis Magna, had considerable personal interest in Syria. Julia Domna, his wife, was the daughter of the high priest of Emesa, in fact. In 217, under Caracalla, the city was made a colony of the empire but was still able to continue its trading activities which had made it one of the wealthiest cities of its time. A highly sophisticated irrigation system was installed, enabling large expanses of land around the city to be cultivated. Meanwhile, the social organization, which was originally based on tribal systems, had been transformed into a model similar to that of the Greek colonies, with Palmyra becoming a kind of aristocratic republic in which the members of the most important families along with the representatives of the merchant corporations holding the power. In the 3rd century, the new rulers of Persia, the Sassanides, began to pose more and more of a threat, and the increase in hostilities with the Romans caused severe repercussions on the city's economy, while at the same time reinforcing its political and military prestige, its military reputation in particular benefiting from the amazing skill of its archers mounted on dromedary camels. It was for this reason that when the Sassanide sovereign Shahpur I inflicted a terrible defeat on the emperor Valerian in 259, in the battle of Edessa, the army of Palmyra under Prince Odenatus was able to stabilize the situation. As a token of gratitude, the emperor Gallienus granted Palmyra its independence in 261. The city's influence soon extended to Syria, Palestine, Mesopotamia and part of Armenia, while Odenatus acted like an eastern king and at the same time proclaimed his support for

the Romans. On his death in 267 following a palace uprising, his widow Zenobia showed strong hostility to Rome. She became regent in the name of her young son Vaballatus and embarked on a strong policy of expansion. Thanks to the daring courage of General Zabda, she gained possession of Egypt, Anatolia and other neighboring territories, and the imprint of her strong independent character shows in the conquests. She also gave her son the title Imperator Caesar Augustus, thereby placing him in direct opposition to Aurelian, the Roman emperor, who obviously could not tolerate such arrogance. Heavily defeated in

the battle of Emesa, Zenobia's armies had to abandon all their claims and beat a hasty retreat. Victory on the battlefield was not enough for Aurelian, however, and he took further revenge. In 272 Palmyra was put to the fire and sword and the proud queen was taken prisoner. Taken to Rome as a symbol of the emperor's triumph, Zenobia was held prisoner in a villa near the Eternal City where she died. Palmyra fell into a rapid decline as the continuous hostilities had severely reduced the trading traffic. There was a brief period of recovery during the principalities of Diocletian and Justinian, who had the walls rebuilt in 528. But these

were the last sparks of a greatness that had vanished. Conquered by the Arabs in either 634 or 638, Palmyra was finally burnt to the ground by the last Omayyad Caliph halfway through the 8th century during a period of civil unrest. As a result of its privileged position between east and west, and the extremely varied origins of its population, Palmyra in its centuries of maximum splendor had created a number of quite unique artistic and cultural forms, combining Aramaic, Semitic, Greek and, finally, Roman influences. The architecture reflects this mixture, especially in the imposing sanctuary dedicated to Bel and in

285 The temple of Bel, consecrated in 32 BC but finalized in the shape it took on in the 2nd and 3rd centuries AD, stands at the center of a square of 660 feet per side. As can be seen in the photograph, the entrance was placed on one of the building's long sides rather than the more usual short side. Another peculiar feature is that the capitals of the surrounding colonnade, probably Corinthian although there is no trace remaining to indicate this, were each made up of two halves of gilded bronze applied to the columns with metal fasteners.

the temple of Ba'alshamin, both of which had inner sanctuaries lit by windows, which is most unusual in a Roman-influenced setting. Palmyra also had a great colonnade avenue, the main street which cut the town in half with various other roads leading off at right angles. The temple of Bel, a supreme deity of Babylonian origin with similarities to Jupiter, was built in the 2nd century AD on a traditional Syrian plan, at the center of a huge porticoed courtyard reached from Corinthian-style colonnaded antechambers. It was clearly influenced by Greco-Roman styles. The temple was very elegant in its decoration and in its structural

284 One of the biggest and best preserved monuments of Palmyra, the temple of Ba'alshamin, was built in 132 AD under Hadrian, to complete an older monumental complex. The sanctuary is formed by a series of courtyards, at the center of which is the temple itself, shown in the photograph. The building has four Corinthian columns in the façade, with no podium. Here, too, the columns at the front have shelves, which may have held statues of gods.

286-287 *The great theater in the middle section of the Great Colonnade is typically Roman. This splendid building, of which part of the front can still be seen, dates to the first half of the 2nd century AD.*

287 top *This grandiose Corinthian six-columned temple stands in what is called the Field of Diocletian. It was dedicated to the goddess Allat and built at the end of the 3rd century AD to house the local garrison.*

287 bottom *The current appearance of the tetrapylon (four-columned) front in Palmyra is the result of careful analysis of the columns themselves. This type of monument, elsewhere crowned with four openings in the form of a square-fronted arch, is typical of the Syrian region.*

solutions of non-classical origin. These include having the entrance on one of the long sides, giving the cornice triangular patterns and having the roof be formed by a terrace with a turret at each of its four corners. The Temple of Ba'alshamin, built in 132 during the time of Hadrian, consisted of a Corinthian style four-colonnaded building at the center of a complex system of courtyards. Again a wide range of cultural influences can be seen. Although the building is decorated with Ionian and Corinthian capitals, the temple overall seems closer to eastern models. The same is true of the sanctuary of Nabu, another local god, built between the 1st and 2nd centuries. The most spectacular monumental features of Palmyra, however, are the two great colonnaded avenues. The first of these, known as the Transverse Portico, running from northeast to southwest, dates back to the first imperial period, while the Great Colonnade, running northwest to southeast, dates mainly to the 2nd century AD. Just about a mile long, this street consists of two parallel rows of Corinthian columns with entablatures. About halfway along, this is broken by a huge pylon of obviously Greek influence with, at the eastern end, a Roman style arch of triumph with an unusual triangular plan. The most interesting detail of these two colonnaded avenues is the presence of ledges halfway up the columns which were probably used as bases for the statues of local dignitaries, another typically local element adapted from the models of classical art. Typically Roman, on the other hand, are the theater, still in relatively good

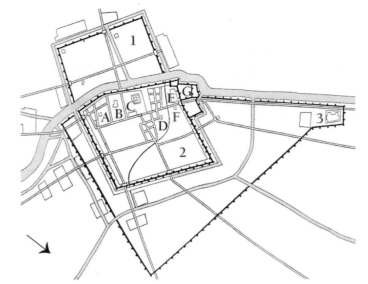

1 Western City
2 Eastern City
3 Northern Citadel

A Temple of Ishara
B Hexagila - Temple of Marduk
C Etemenanki - Ziggurat of Marduk
D Temple of Ishtar Agade
E Southern Palace
F Temple of Ninmah
G Northern Palace

289 center This terra-cotta relief, today in the Louvre in Paris, dates to the beginning of 2000 BC and shows an elegant and natural portrait of a woman weaving.

three centuries earlier. The completeness and breadth of the code make it the main source for the reconstruction of Babylonian society.

No statue from the Babylon of Hammurabi has ever been found on the site of the city. The only known ones are those taken to Susa by the Elamites after they defeated the dynasty of the Kassites, whose kings had absorbed Babylonian culture. It is just as difficult to assess the achievements of the first Babylonian dynasty in the field of town planning and architecture, as the Babylon of this period is inaccessible, buried beneath later reconstructions of the city. At the end of the 12th century, the Babylonians, led by Nebuchadnezzar, put the Elamites to flight

Babylon, a name which means "The Gate of God", was the center of the cult of the god Marduk. An administrative capital of some importance when Ur dominated the whole of central and southern Mesopotamia (2112-2004 BC), in the 18th century Babylon became the spiritual and temporal capital of southern Mesopotamia under the Amorite king Hammurabi (1792-1750 BC). Hammurabi, fifth king of the first Babylonian dynasty, was without doubt its most prestigious ruler. He built up an important empire which included the south of Mesopotamia and coincided with the territory which had been under the sovereignty of Ur in the past. A diorite stone slab discovered in Susa at the start of the twentieth century, on which a code was inscribed, was to reveal the genius of this unifying action. A bas-relief shows King Hammurabi receiving the texts of the law from the god Shamash, patron of justice. The slab, which must have been erected in the temple dedicated to Shamash in Sippar or in Babylon itself, was transported to Susa as booty by the king of Elam, Shutruknakhunte, around 1200 BC. The code issued by Hammurabi was not the oldest as the Sumerians had created another

289 bottom The inner walls of Babylon had eight entrance gates, the most famous of which is the Gate of Ishtar. The brick walls of the gate are decorated with reliefs of dragons, symbol of the god Marduk, and bulls, the symbol of the storm god Adad.

290 top This picture shows a detail of the kudurru stone of King Melishihu with the ruler shown presenting his daughter to a god. This type of stone, sculpted with symbols of deities, was used in Babylon, especially during the Kassite period, to mark land boundaries.

290-291 The gate of Ishtar, dedicated to the goddess of war, was reconstructed in the Pergamon Museum in Berlin using enameled bricks found on the site. An inscription tells of the works carried out by King Nebuchadnezzar II, an enthusiastic builder. On the gate of Ishtar is inscribed "... I dug the base of this gate, strengthened the foundations from the river with tar and enameled bricks in the color blue, on which wild bulls and dragons were shown... I placed intrepid bulls and furious dragons at the entrance".

and destroyed their capital, Susa, and recovered the statues of the kings of Babylon that had been taken away.

In the first millennium, the city fell to the Assyrians, but the rebellions continued and the city was destroyed twice by the Assyrians during the 7th century BC. In 625, the governor Nabopolassar declared the independence of the city and himself king, then formed an alliance with Meda to defeat Assyria and destroy its capital, Nineveh, in 612 BC. Nebuchadnezzar II, his son, overcame the last outposts of the Assyrian resistance and dedicated his reign (604-562) to intense building operations. The remains of the city, still visible today, belong to this period of reconstruction. The exploration of Babylon took place only at the end of the 19th century (1899) by German archaeologists, led by the architect Robert Koldewey who, for eighteen consecutive years until 1917, systematically brought to light the monuments from the eastern part of the city, significantly increasing our knowledge of the architecture and town planning techniques. The city stretched along both banks of the Euphrates, but the most important buildings were on the eastern bank. An outer wall roughly 10 miles long enclosed an almost uninhabited territory that could be used as a shelter for the peasants in time of war.

This outer line of defense was reinforced to the north by a fortress, still over 70 feet high today, which protected the king's palace. A double, four-sided wall five miles long, flanked by a canal which was used as a moat, defended the city itself.

The inner wall had eight gates, each protected by its own god, the most famous of which is the one dedicated to Ishtar, the god of war.

This was a double gate, crossing two walls, flanked by two forward towers and doors that opened inward on the walls themselves, used as guard posts.

The main gate was decorated with the figures of dragons, the emblem of the god Marduk, in smoothed brick, and bulls, associated with the Adad, the god of storms, on enameled bricks. The gate, of which only the foundations were found, was rebuilt to a height of 48 feet, a figure

and capitals topped by palms. The famous hanging gardens described by Diodorus Siculus as one of the seven wonders of the world but not found in any Babylonian text may have been in the northwestern corner of the royal palace with vault-covered parallel corridors. From the palace, the avenue continued to the great temple of Marduk, the most important god in the Babylonian religion. The temple was a fortress with a square floor plan and central tower containing the statue of the god, which was carried during the processions. At the side of the temple, but isolated by a wall, was the famous ziggurat or Tower of Babel. This was an almost 300 foot high square tower, built in bare brick covered in baked

brickwork. This was repeatedly robbed for its materials over the centuries, and all that remains of it today is its enormous square base. At one time, however, it loomed over the city with its seven stories, crowned by a temple where, according to a passage in Herodotus, the holy marriage of the god and goddess took place, imitated by the king and the high priestess as part of the new year celebrations.

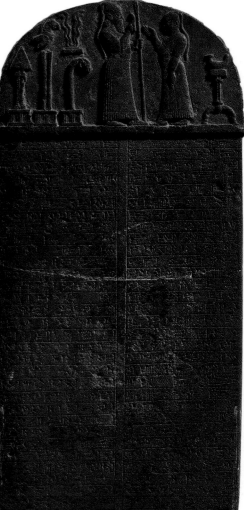

derived from the base of the enameled bricks found on the site.

An avenue used for processions, with enameled bricks and figures of lions, emblems of the god Ishtar, passed beneath the gate of Ishtar, followed the double wall that protected the palace and led into the heart of the city, where it connected the Heragila, a word meaning "the high-roofed temple" or temple of Marduk to the new year temple outside the city walls where celebrations marking the beginning of the year and lasting 12 days took place each spring.

The royal palace of Nebuchadnezzar was defended by the River Euphrates and a massive fortification on one side, and was protected by high walls on the others. It had five courtyards which opened onto state rooms on the southern side. The main courtyard opened onto a large throne room with its walls covered in blue and yellow enameled bricks showing scrolled columns

291 top left The walls of the processional avenue that passed through the gate of Ishtar were decorated with enameled bricks showing lions, the emblem of Ishtar, goddess of war.

291 bottom left The Code of Hammurabi, now in the Louvre, shows the king receiving the laws from the god of justice Shamash.

291 right This kudurru stone, made from limestone, belonged to King Marduk Zakir Shumi.

carried out a number of surveys in the area and, as a result of several inscriptions discovered there, the site was identified as the Ur of the Chaldeans, the land of Abraham. In 1922, a joint expedition was organized by the British Museum and the University of Pennsylvania, led by L. Woolley, who was assisted on the site for 12 years by other internationally known archaeologists and epigraphists including M.E.I. Mallowan, C.J. Gadd and L. Legrain. The most sensational discovery was undoubtedly the royal tombs (3rd millennium BC) in 1927, which were excavated from then through 1931. The burial zone, next to the sacred area, contained the tombs of common people in rectangular trenches, over 2000, and 17 graves of high ranking figures, which consist of burial chambers in stone and brick. Many of these tombs were opened and robbed in ancient times but nevertheless what remained was extraordinary.

The best known are those of Arbaji and Queen Puabi, which was named the "Great Trench of Death" as it contained the remains of at least 74 people, and the tomb

of King Meskalamdug. The splendid funeral treasures found include gold vessels, jewelry, hundreds of objects made from lapis lazuli, harps decorated with bulls' heads, golden arms including the helmet of Meskalamdug worked in relief and his dagger with a golden blade and lapis lazuli handle, and even a panel made in shells and red limestone set in a background of lapis lazuli embedded in bitumen. This panel shows a war scene on one side and a banquet on the other. The banquet may be part of the victory celebration. Animals and men bearing offerings are also part of this panel.

The funeral ceremony for these proto-dynastic kings was reconstructed by Woolley on the basis of the findings and the many human and animal sacrificial victims found in the tombs. The dead ruler was accompanied to the hereafter by a large escort of dignitaries and warriors, who were drugged and killed together with the animals that hauled the carriages, a comparable practice to those in Egypt during the same period. To the north of the city, a sacred enclosure contained the ziggurat, or temple tower, and the temple

294-295 and 295 bottom The "Standard of Ur", an oblong wooden chest which may have been the sound box of a musical instrument, shows the main activities of the king and his court on the decorations on the sides, with shells and limestone inlaid on a background of lapis lazuli, attached to the wood with tar.

The panels should be read from the bottom to the top. The upper panel shows scenes of war with the victorious king (above, the large figure) passing through the ranks of his enemies. The other panel, known as the panel of peace, shows the spoils of war and scenes of the victory banquet.

of the moon god Nanna. The buildings, erected by the kings of the 3rd dynasty, were restored by later governors. The ziggurat built by King Ur-Nammu and completed by his son Shulgi on the site of an older temple consisted of three floors and the sacristy of the god, which crowned the building. The bottom floor, over 60 feet high, was entered from three broad staircases which met at the top. To reach the main temple built at the foot of the ziggurat the goddess had to first come down from the heavens to arrive at the temple at the top of the tower dedicated to her. In this way, the ziggurat stressed the connection between the earth and the sky, man and his god. The great courtyard of Nanna, in which offerings for the deity and the clergy were collected, occupied the remaining northeastern part of the sacred area. In the corner formed by the courtyard and the sacred enclosure is the building that was probably the residence of the divine couple Nanna-Ningal. At the opposite side of this enclosure there was a large square building which may have been the royal palace of Ur. Alongside this was a residential quarter, suddenly abandoned

when King Samsu-Iluna of Babylon destroyed Ur in 1729 BC. The houses were generally of two floors, built with walls which, as there was no stone, had baked brick bases and bare brick, hardened by the sun, on the upper part. These houses had a central courtyard onto which the rooms opened. Typically, a chamber for the burial of the dead was located beneath the ground level, and here various offerings were consecrated in a kind of chapel at one end of the courtyard.

294 bottom The lion-headed eagle Anzu, with lapis lazuli wings and a gold head and tail, is part of the treasure of Ur, discovered at Mari and dating to 2600-2400 BC. This mythological animal is the incarnation of the warrior-god Ningirsu.

295 top This gold and lapis lazuli bull's head is the ornament on a harp that belonged to Princess Shub-Ad, found in the royal tombs of Ur. The instrument, which dates to 2800-2700 BC, is an indication of the Sumerians's great love of music.

PERSEPOLIS, CAPITAL OF THE ACHEMENIDIAN KINGS

Persepolis was the ceremonial capital of the Achemenidian Persians, founded by Darius I around 500 BC and later destroyed by Alexander the Great. Its imposing remains are 30 miles from Shiraz in the province of Fars, and over 300 miles from Susa, the administrative capital. Plutarch, the Greek writer, confirms that this fabulous residential complex must have been truly splendid and luxurious. He tells us that Alexander had to organize a caravan of 10,000 mules and 5,000 camels to take the riches he found in Persepolis to Ekbatana. European travelers were attracted to the site from medieval times onward. The first detailed description was by the Roman Pietro della Valle, who brought inscriptions from Persepolis that he had copied back from a journey of 12 years to Mesopotamia from 1614 to 1626. In the 17th century, new documents were added to the older ones, and inscriptions from Persepolis were copied and distributed by the Danish mathematician Carsten Niebuhr. In 1887, the governor of Fars, Mu'tammad al-Daula, conducted some surveys in the Hall of a Hundred Columns which was built by Xerxes I.

In 1931, at the request of the Iranian government, the German archaeologist Ernst Herzfeld carried out the first of four cycles of excavation on behalf of the Oriental Institute of Chicago. It is to him that we owe the discovery of the porticoes of Xerxes I, the great stairway to the east leading to apadana, and other discoveries. From 1935 to 1939 the excavation continued under the direction of Erich Schmidt then, from 1939 on, the Iranian Archaeological Service continued the work, first with the help of the French expert on Iran, A. Godard, then with the assistance of M.T. Mustafawi. Recently, excavations have slowed as a result of political changes within the country and war in the area itself. The monumental site of Persepolis shows the signs of a complex architecture linked with the history of the Persian empire. The formation of this empire was the work of Cyrus II. The Persians had replaced the Elamites in the region of Anshan (ancient Parthia, now known as Fars), and a family belonging to the Achemenides had been reigning there for several generations, with the title of King of Anshan (Theispes, head of this tribe, ruled around 670 BC), related and subordinate to the royal house of Medea. After proclaiming himself king of the Medes and Persians, Cyrus II took control of Lydia, the

296 left Persepolis was the capital of the Achemenidean empire from the 6th century until 330 BC, when Alexander the Great burnt it down. The royal palaces, the only buildings remaining in the city, had great stone portals with columns and frames. The walls were made of brick which is much more perishable than stone and they have been almost entirely lost.

296 bottom This superb golden rhyton, now in the archaeological museum in Teheran, shows the high degree of refinement achieved by Achemenidean art. The winged lion was one of the heraldic animals of the reigning Persian dynasty.

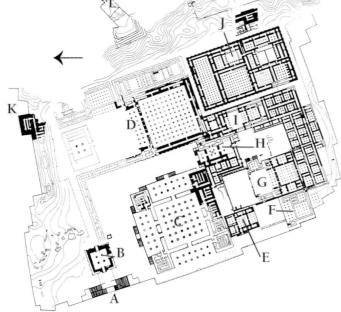

296-297 *The building of Persepolis was based on a strict plan designed by Darius, who arranged for every single part of the construction. His successors, Xerxes and Arthaxerxes I, followed his plans. All the buildings on the great raised terrace, seen here from above, were built and decorated in accordance with their role in the important new year ceremonies.*

297 bottom *Griffins are fantastic creatures that appear frequently in Persepolis. The royal architects made capitals with decorative heads of these animals for the great palaces.*

A Access stairway
B Gate of Xerxes
C Apadana
D Hall of the Hundred Columns
E Palace of Darius
F Palace of Arthaxerxes IIII
G Residential palace of Xerxes
H Tripylon
I Harem
J Treasury
K Part of the fortified walls
L Tomb of Arthaxerxes II

298 top It is usual to consider Persepolis as the main artistic center of the pre-Islamic Near East. However, this belief is largely due to our modern idea of beauty. The ornamental features that decorated the various monumental structures of the royal palaces were primarily designed to make an impact on the onlooker and create a sense of the grandiose, with artistic importance only secondary. Official Archemenidean art shows no trace of the typical Greek or Roman theories of good taste.

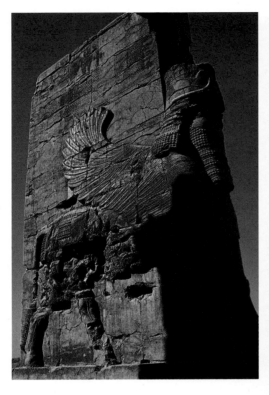

298 center This photograph shows one of the enormous bulls on either side of the Door of the Nations. These enormous statues were designed to defend the palace from the forces of evil. It is interesting to note the way in which Achemenidean art moves away from its usual formal and rigid base to a more realistic view when producing animal figures.

298 bottom and 298-299 Access to the terrace of the royal palaces was from the Gate of Nations, an imposing structure built by Xerxes and consisting of a huge square hall, whose ceiling was held up by four columns with elaborate animal-headed capitals. The three great entrances opening to the west, east and south, were decorated by enormous figures of bulls, some human-headed, taken from traditional Assyrian imagery. The "throat" that crowned the crossbeams of each portal were typical Egyptian. This mix indicates the way in which Persian architecture combined a large number of different influences.

kingdom of Croesus, in 546 BC, and then conquered the Greek cities of Asia Minor. Finally, in 539, he also defeated Babylon, thus taking over all the territories not only of Mesopotamia but also of Syria and Palestine. The conquests of Cyrus were then extended by his successors. In 525, his son Cambises annexed Egypt and Cyprus. After the power struggle that followed his death, Darius I (521-485 BC), who belonged to another branch of the Achemenides, continued and completed the expansion of the empire but devoted his efforts above all

to its structural reinforcement. The Persian empire also continued to make use of the ancient imperial notion of the inward movement of resources and the outward flow of ethical and political services. The palaces of the Achemenides and those of Persepolis are the clearest examples. They are built using materials from every part of the known world and are the work of craftsmen from all the provinces of the empire. Every group contributed its best to the construction of the capital which was seen as the nucleus of the world. In the

opposite direction, safety, respect for the law, agreement with the divine world and civilization moved outward into the world from this central point. Darius I chose Susa, the ancient Elamite metropolis, as the administrative capital of the empire, as it not only possessed consolidated administrative structures but was also located where the highlands of Iran, Armenia and Anatolia and the lowlands of Syria and Mesopotamia met between the Iranian and Semitic worlds. These worlds had always been opposed to each other and now found themselves within

301 top The two monumental staircases that led to the apadana were decorated with bas-reliefs showing delegations from the 25 nations subject to the Persian crown, all offerings gifts to the sovereign. From Susa came weapons and lions, the Armenians were bearing metal vases and horses, the Lydians precious metals and horses, and so on. Each delegation is separated from the others by cypress trees, the Persian "tree of life". All the reliefs were originally multicolored.

301 bottom All the reliefs of Persepolis are designed to exalt the greatness of the empire through a repetition of people and objects. They show foreign delegations, servants, heroes, guards and officers as seen here.

300 top and bottom Gottfried von Herder wrote in 1780 about the long rows of reliefs that cover the staircases of the Apadana that the processions showing bearers of gifts were a "kind of statistical map of the lands that formed part of the Persian empire, a living representation of its provinces and the peoples that lived in them." Furthermore, these images are also of tremendous documentary value as they show in incredible detail the clothing, hairstyles, personal ornaments and weapons, means of transport and everyday objects in common use in the empire.

300-301 The apadana was used for audiences that the "king of kings" granted to the Persian and Medean lords. The enormous hall was reached by two monumental staircases decorated with bas-reliefs showing combat between lions and bulls and, above, a procession of people bearing tributes, some of which we can see here.

a single political entity. On the other hand, as the site for the new capital which would reflect imperial splendor, Darius I chose the fine plain of Marv Dasht, in Anshan, dominated by a rocky spur of Mount Kuh-I Rahmat, but he did not live to see the completion of the work he had started. His son Xerxes continued the work of his father, followed by his grandson Arthaxerxes. Nevertheless, the complex of Persepolis was never finished. In 330 BC a violent fire caused, accidentally or through arson, by the army of Alexander the Great, destroyed the city once and for all. The Persian empire was then made up of 20 provinces or satraps, whose representatives came to Persepolis for the new year which, in the calendar of Mazda, the religion of Ahura Mazda and the Prophet Zarathustra, corresponds to the spring equinox. They all brought tributes and offerings to the king at this time. Delegations from the vassal states, like travelers in the 19th century, reached Persepolis on horseback, as described by Jeanne Dieulafoy in *La Perse, la Chaldée, la Susiane*, Paris, 1884.

"The steps are so slightly inclined that it is easy to go up and down them on horseback, and they are so broad that ten men can walk along them side by side." The horsemen stopped at the foot of an immense terrace upon which monumental buildings stood. This huge platform measuring 500 yards by 330 yards was built of carefully squared limestone blocks. Its height above the plain varied from 20 to 9 yards. An enormous staircase made of two diverging ramps parallel to the supporting wall led to the upper level, directly in front

of the Gate of Nations, built by Xerxes I and guarded to the east and west by two winged genie, with the bodies of a bull, bearded human heads and the crowns of the king, showing a strong Assyrian influence. Over each of these is a cuneiform inscription in which Xerxes says, "Ahura Mazda is a great god. He created the earth, the heavens and man. To man he gave happiness. He made Xerxes the only king over thousands of men. . .this portico. . .from which all nations can be seen, I built, like many other monuments, as built

by my father, and this magnificent work and all these splendid buildings we have erected for the grace of Ahura Mazda. . . May Adhura Mazda protect them!" The Persian and Medean nobles who reached this monumental entrance then turned south, before the apadana, the hall set aside for official audiences with the king. The palace was begun by Darius and completed by Xerxes. It had a central hall with a square plan of over 80 yards, and 36 columns, only three of which are still standing. These are almost 70 feet high and are arranged in six rows to support the ceiling.

From the columns that are left we can see that each was surmounted by a capital in the form of two bull's, lion's or griffin's heads (the griffin was the traditional symbol of balance for the Babylonians and the Elamites). On these columns a structure made of Lebanese cedar rested, brought to Fars from that far distant part of the empire. Three sides of the hall opened onto porticoes made up of rows of six columns. The fourth side opened onto adjoining rooms and a staircase that led to the upper terrace. Access was gained to the apadana from two huge staircases on the east and west sides, both covered entirely in bas-reliefs showing a long row of Persian, Medean and Susean dignitaries, accompanied by infantry, cavalry and archers marching toward a procession of tribute-bearers coming from all parts of the empire to pay homage to the king on the occasion of the new year. Every ethnic group in the procession is preceded by a Medean or Persian dignitary. The ethnic features and the costumes of the various people are so exactly depicted that we can identify the origins of most of the groups. Separated from each other by cypresses, the tree of life, we see Ethiopians, Egyptians, Babylonians, Indians, Libyans, and so on. At the center of the staircase is an image of Ahura Mazda in the form of a winged god above the solar disk, while at the ends of the ramps are motifs of a lion attacking a bull. The bas-reliefs show how Persepolis was entirely dedicated to the power of the Achemenidean king and to the celebration of the new year, under whom these events took place, protected by the god Ahura Mazda. Behind the apadana to the north is the palace begun by Darius and completed by his son Xerxes. We reach the terrace on which it is built by two staircases decorated with scenes showing the guards of the king. These guards were known as the "immortals" because each time one died he was immediately replaced by another. Also shown on these staircases are scenes of vassals bringing offerings. The palace consists of a central colonnaded hall behind a 16 column portico which is flanked by smaller room. The slabs of gray porphyry that covered the walls were so highly polished that the rooms was called "The Hall of Mirrors". The reliefs on the six doors of this hall show the king in a variety of situations. He is seen marching, escorted by servants, or fighting a lion or a mythical animal as a symbol of the king's power over the spirit of evil. Leaving through what is known as the Tripylon, or Triple Gate, we finally reach the immense Hall of the Hundred Columns which covers the entire northeastern part of the terrace. The building was begun by Xerxes I and completed by Arthaxerxes I.

It consisted of a central hall with an over 80 foot square plan which contains a forest of a hundred column in rows of ten. The hall is preceded by a vestibule with two rows of eight columns and was completely destroyed by the fire caused by Alexander's army. Inside, only the bases of the columns remain, while the door frames are for the most part conserved and the bas-reliefs, which repeat the themes seen in the palace of Darius, are still clearly visible. Diodorus Siculus, a contemporary of Augustus, says that a drunken Alexander, instigated by

Thaida, an Athenian courtesan, decided to burn down the palaces of Persepolis as if he was performing a ritual, with a riotous musical cortège parading from one room to the next. In this way, the profanation of Xerxes when he burnt down the Acropolis in Athens was revenged. The nearby civilizations of Mesopotamia, Uratu, Egypt and Greece had a significant influence on the stone and bare brick architecture and the sculpture of Persepolis. The Achemenidean empire took the inspiration for many of its forms, including animals

302 bottom Persepolis was, apparently, divided into two distinct areas for functional purposes. To the north is the ceremonial part while to the south are the private residences in which the nobles lived. The two sectors were joined by a monumental hall, the Tripylon, which could be considered a hinge between the apadana and a small palace situated to the south. The reliefs on the eastern door show Darius on the throne, supported by the subject nations.

302-303 and 303 top The staircase that leads to the palace of Darius, in the southern section of the great terrace, has a relief showing servants bringing food to the royal table. Several scholars believe that this sequence indicates this was the route taken by participants in the new year festival when they left the apadana to go to the banquet offered by the sovereign in his private residence.

303 bottom The haute-reliefs that decorate the sides of the two doors of the Tripylon, to the north and south, show the "king of kings" followed by a parasol bearer and a fan bearer. Studying these pictures, in which solemn gestures are repeated over and over, we can understand commentators who have said that Achemenidean art was virtually without evolution. It never developed the concept of three dimensions, or moved away from the rigid limits of profile portrayals. However, it is important to remember that court art is always based on the archaic and has a severity considered necessary for representations intended to be passed down to posterity.

facing each other, guardian bulls, military parades, stylized cypresses and so on from the art of Sumeria, Assyria and Babylon. The monumental complex on the terrace had to represent the center of the empire, the symbol of the power of the king as mediator and interpreter of the god Ahura Mazda, supreme divinity, who incarnated the principle of good in his fight with other, opposing gods which represented evil. The symbolic and magical nature of the reliefs and motifs shown throughout this complex emphasize the importance of religion. The rosette decorations, the stepped battlements symbolizing the sacred mountain, source of fertility, the columns representing sacred palms and those of the Hall of the Hundred Columns, representing a sacred wood, the struggles between the lion and the bull, believed to have a zodiacal meaning linked to the changing seasons, show the continuing importance of ancient, naturalistic, polytheistic traditions based on adoration of the mountain, the bull and fertility amid a consolidated state religion.

305 top right This head in lapis lazuli paste, found in Persopolis and probably produced there, can be considered a symbol of the ideal of youthful beauty in the Achemenidean court.

305 center right Basically, Achemenidean art is designed as a means of ornamentation. It therefore repeats objects over and over without concerning itself with the risk of monotony.

305 bottom right Although Achemenidean art has been accused of copying the styles of the people they conquered or other nations such as Egypt, Babylon and Greece, therefore making it an art with no roots or evolution, it can surprise. Remarkable plastic solutions, lightness of anatomical details.

306-307 This low relief shows several offerings' bearers belonging to the delegations of states subjected by the Persians.

304 The portraits in Persepolis show few traces of realism. The figures, whether servants or royal guards as shown here, have the same globular eyes, the same long thin eyebrows, the same curls of hair and beards, the same solemn expressions. They all are part of the desire to make art serve power, even at the cost of making it pompous.

305 left As in this relief showing a royal guard, the many works of art in the sumptuous decorations of Persepolis were designed and executed exclusively to glorify the "king of kings".

Not far from Persepolis, in Naqsh-I-Rustam, are the spectacular royal cemeteries of the Achemenides. The four rock tombs have cross-shaped façades and belong to Darius I and probably three of his successors, Xerxes, Arthaxerxes I and Darius II.
The façade shows the images of the kings in adoration of the fire of Ahura Mazda. The thrones of the kings are held up by representatives of the nations that were subject to the empire.

The Sassanide rulers decided to emphasize their link with the ancient empire by carving some of the most famous reliefs of the time beneath the tombs of the Achemenidean kings. These include the investiture of Ardeshir (224-240 AD), a battle fought by Bahram IV (388-399 AD), or perhaps by Hormuzd II (302-309 AD), and the famous scene of the submission of the Romans, in which two figures, probably the emperor Valerian and Philip of Arabia bow humbly

before the horses of Shahpur I (240-272). Below the tombs and the Sassanide reliefs below is a tower popularly called Kaaba-I Zardust, or the Cube of Arathustra, perhaps an Achemenidean funerary temple dedicated to the royal cult.
Other royal tombs dug from the rock appear near the terrace of Persepolis to the east, and have been attributed to Arthaxerxes II and Arthaxerxes III (405-361 and 361-338 BC).

308-309 Beneath the Achemenidean tombs, the rulers of the Sassanide dynasty, founded by Ardashir I in 224 AD, had huge bas-reliefs sculpted to bear witness to their deeds. The selection of the site was highly symbolic, as it emphasized the continuity of Persian Imperial power.

309 top At Naqsh-i-Rustam are the tombs of Darius, Xerxes, Arthaxerxes I and Darius II, but the last three Achemenidean rulers preferred to be buried near the terrace of Persepolis.

309 bottom Beneath the tomb of Xerxes, a Sassanide relief shows Hurmuzd II defeating an enemy.

308 About six miles from Persepolis is the rock of Naqsh-i-Rustam, the site chosen by four Achemenidean rulers for their inaccessible rock tombs. Each of these was modeled on the tomb of Darius I and has a cross-shaped façade showing a stylized palace, surmounted by an enormous bas-relief throne, held up, as always, by the representatives of the nations forming the Persian empire. Above, we see the king (detail above) before Ahura Mazda, the great god of the Persians. At the center of the colonnade is the entrance to the burial chamber, which is dug out of the rock.

310-311 The best known Sassanide relief in Naqsh-i-Rustam, sculpted near the tomb of Darius I, shows the triumph of King Shapur I over the Roman emperors Philip the Arab in 244 and Valerian, defeated in the battle of Edessa in 260. A long inscription on the right celebrates the king's victories.

310 bottom This relief shows the investiture of Ardashir I, founder of the Sassanide dynasty. The king, to the left, receives the royal crown from the god Ahura Mazda, on horseback. These symbols appeared throughout the 3rd century and were often used by successors to the king on the rock walls of Naqsh-i-Rustam.

311 left The Achemenidean rock tombs of Naqsh-i-Rustam have identical cross-shaped façades just over 72 feet high. The door is framed by columns with ram-headed decorations. Inside, each tomb contains a number of chambers cut out of the rock designed to hold the royal sarcophagus and the burial treasure, stolen many years ago. In the tomb of Darius I the rooms have sloping roofs.

311 right Sassanide sculpture was still of high quality under Bahram II (276-293) when the range of subjects covered was enlarged to include more than investitures and military victories. There is, for instance, a monumental bas-relief showing the king from the front with his head in profile and his hands on the hilt of a sword while he receives homage from the court. The same ruler is shown in another relief beneath the tomb of Darius I, portraying two duels on horseback.

SANCHI, CENTER OF THE WORLD

312 left The voluptuous figure of a shalabhanjika, a tree nymph also known as yakshi, juts out dramatically from the side and the eastern portal of the main stupa. This dryad symbolizes the fertility of the earth and the vital sap of the trees as well as the Indian ideal of female beauty while suggesting in esoteric and subtle ways the sweep of consciousness that leads to enlightenment. This motif is also repeated in reduced dimensions as the element between the beams.

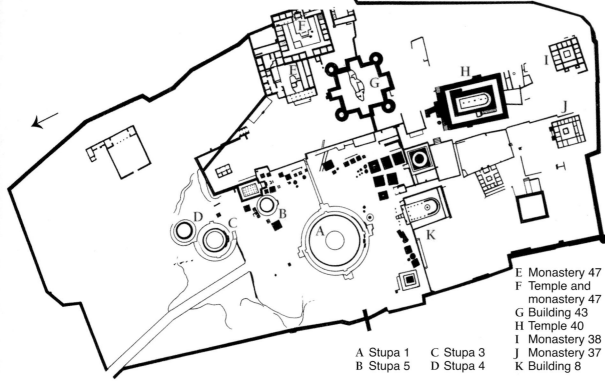

A Stupa 1   C Stupa 3
B Stupa 5   D Stupa 4

E Monastery 47
F Temple and monastery 47
G Building 43
H Temple 40
I Monastery 38
J Monastery 37
K Building 8

The most significant feature of Buddhist architecture is the *stupa*, a reliquary or place to hold sacred remains, derived from the ancient burial mound. After the cremation of Buddha, his remains were divided up among the most important warrior tribes that had taken part in the funeral rites and, it is said, that the first ten stupas were built over these sacred remains. In the state of Madhya Pradesh, about 28 miles from the capital Bhopal, is the best conserved stupa complex in all India, Sanchi. Sanchi is at the junction of two rivers, in an idyllic spot perfectly suited to the monastic life, and near the prosperous trading town of Vidisha on a caravan route. Founded during the reign of Ashoka, a great Buddhist emperor of the 3rd century BC, the site remained important up to the 13th century, when the

general decline of Buddhism in favor of Hinduism caused it to fall into decay.

The site on the hill was almost forgotten, only to be discovered by mere chance by a General Taylor in 1818. The buildings were still intact, but the area would soon be devastated by amateur archaeologists and treasure hunters. In 1881, Major Cole began proper restoration work which was continued by John Marshall, head of the Department of Archaeology from 1912 to 1919. Over 50 monuments in Sanchi were numbered by Marshall which can be divided into two groups, those at the summit of the hill and those lower down, on the western slope. The main stupa, which currently has a diameter of 122 feet and a height of 56 feet plus an additional 56 feet if we include the series of parasols, incorporates a smaller building in baked brick and mortar, attributed to Ashoka. In the 2nd century BC the building was reconstructed and enlarged with a surrounding wall of blocks in the local sandstone, covered with a thick coating of plaster and given an addition in the form of the terrace at the base with its double access staircase, the balustrades, the corridor and the *harmika* in the form of a reliquary.

313 bottom right The toranas, the splendid portals of Sanchi, are two tiled pillars into which the triple architrave is set. These are supported by elephants in the northern and eastern toranas and by yakshas, pot-bellied good luck genies, in the west and lions in the south, as shown here. The inscription states that they were crafted by ivory carvers of Vidisha as a celebration of the Shakya, the warrior tribe of the Buddha.

312-313 Of the four entrances to the main stupa in Sanchi, the best preserved is the northern one. The first architrave shows a scene from the Jatakas, the collections of the earlier lives of the Buddha, and the Enlightened One appears there in the form of the generous Prince Vessantara. In the second architrave is the temptation of Mara, god of love and death, who clashed with the Buddha, shown symbolically on the left in the form of the tree of enlightenment. In the final architrave there is another episode from the Jakatas, with the Buddha appearing as a six-tusked elephant.

313 top right The architraves of the toranas are separated by four cubic blocks and a double row of riders on horses and elephants, interspersed with small columns with floral symbols. Sanchi stood near the ancient Vidisha, a prosperous caravan town, and it is therefore probable that the rider motif is a celebration of the mercantile world.

313 center right Sanchi is not l inked with episodes from the life of the Buddha, but is connected with Mahendra, an historic figure who spread the message of the Enlightened One to Sri Lanka. He was apparently the son of the great emperor Ashoka, patron of Buddhism, and Queen Devi, born into a family of rich Vidisha merchants.

At the base of the structure is a precise set of cosmic symbols. These include the high circular base or *medhi*, representing the earth, with the cupola body or *anda* above it representing the heavens. The square platform with balustrade, or harmika, that tops the structure represents the mythical cosmic mountain at the center of the universe, while the world beyond, hidden, the domain of the ultimate truth, is symbolized by the central pillar, or *chattravali*, the pivot around which the stupa rotates, compacting itself like a three-dimensional spiral. This element is formed by three parasols and celebrates the three jewels or aspects of Buddhism which are Buddha the Enlightened One, the Sangha or the Community, and the Dharma, or the Doctrine. The cosmic mountain, the axis of the universe, the world's umbilicus, stands in the form of the stupa for the totality of Being and, therefore, the Buddha himself.

Around the stupa is a stone enclosure or *vedika*, which marks off space set aside for holy processions, known as the *pradakshina* and a central rite in Buddhism. The processions take place with the object of worship always on the right of the walkers. The vedika extends to the four points of the globe, with projecting bodies ending in splendid portals, the *toranas*, topped by a triple architrave and built in the 1st century AD. The heart of the stupa is the reliquary, which may or may not be housed in a special chamber at the center of the anda, while the toranas are arranged on the arms of a cross that extends outward from the center, emphasizing the concept of cosmic and, above all, doctrinal rays, in the sense that the Buddha's message, since his stone body is the stupa itself, extends out to every corner of the universe. There are no images of Siddhartha, the historic Buddha, on the portals of Sanchi.

Sanchi *Sanchi*

314 *The pillars of the* toranas *show the main events in the life of the Buddha and the stories of his previous lives. A panel on the left shows a scene from a hunt, the favourite pastime of nobles during that period. In the top right we see the Buddha's conversion of three hermits, the Kashyapa brothers, followed by their disciples. In the bottom right, a prince, recognised by his parasol (a symbol of royalty), has garlands of flowers placed by his handmaidens on the* bodhi *tree, or* ficus religiosa, *under which Siddhartha Gautama achieved enlightenment.*

315 *After his enlightenment, Buddha was not sure whether or not to preach the doctrine that had led him to supreme knowledge. He realized it was difficult to communicate such an intangible experience to others. It was the gods themselves who asked him to teach humanity the way to salvation and they persuaded him to do so. The second panel in the southern pillar of the western torana is a reminder of this event, known as adhyeshana. The Buddha is never shown in human form in Sanchi, but always by symbols. Here he is symbolized by the tree of enlightenment.*

316-317 *This is the first architrave of the north portal in Stupa 1.*

318 top right Stupa number 2 stands on an artificial terrace over 1,000 feet below the summit of the hill and its older parts can probably be dated to the 2nd century BC. Although there is no torana, the balustrade is beautifully decorated with splendid floral and animal groups. The chamber where the reliquaries were placed, in the west rather than in the more usual central position, contained a sandstone reliquary with the remains of at least three generations of Buddhist teachers, confirming the theory that the stupa had been used as a burial tabernacle.

318 top left The architectural complex of Sanchi contained various other buildings as well as the stupas, such as temples and monasteries. In this photograph, we see part of temple 45 with its monastery annex, dated to the 7th-8th centuries AD but rebuilt in the 9th-10th.

318 bottom right Stupa number 3, built in the 2nd century BC and therefore contemporary with the greater one, has a single portal which was probably built by the corporations of carvers, ivory workers and jewelers in the 1st century AD, like the toranas of the great stupa. Although the work may be less elegant, this stupa is of great importance as this was where the remains of two Buddhist saints were found, Shariputra and Mangdalyayana, contained in two sarcophaguses in the chamber of the reliquaries. All around are the remains of other stupas of various sizes, built as votive offerings by the pilgrims.

The followers of Hinayana, the oldest form of Buddhism, looked upon him as the supreme enlightened master, and within the bas-reliefs he is seen only through symbols, each connected in some way with specific events in his existence. The creative skill of the artists did find great inspiration in the *Jatakas*, the literary collections of the prior lives of the Buddha, in which he often appeared in the form of an animal. The structure of the toranas consists of two pillars surmounted by four lions, elephants and *yakshas*, plump tree genies which hold up three curved architraves ending in spirals and separated from each other by square blocks and rows of riders on elephants and horses. Jutting outward from the jamb toward the spiral of the first architrave are delightful figures of the yakshis enriching the entire effect. The final architrave is topped by the remains of the wheel of law flanked by two fan-bearers and two *triatnas*, the triple jewel motif of Buddhism. Smaller and simpler, the nearby stupa number 3, built at the same time as the great one, is preceded by a single portal, while stupa number 2, built on an artificial terrace below the top of the hill, has no torana although its balustrade is decorated with splendid medallions.

318 bottom left Temple number 17 is a typical example of the Gupta architecture of the 5th century AD. It is in hall form, with a portico in front supported by four pillars and a flat roof. It is one of the oldest temple prototypes.

319 *The stone balustrade of stupa number 2 is enriched by these outstanding medallions. In this picture Gajalakshmi, a special version of Lakshmi, goddess of fertility and beauty and wife of Vishnu, god of the conservation of life, is bathed by two elephants symbolizing the earth being freshened by the rain.*

MAMALLIPURAM
AND THE MINIATURE TEMPLES

320 top In this detail we see the god Shiva, who made the River Ganges, the mythical goddess Ganga, come down to Earth.

320-321 Beside the rock of the Descent to the Ganges is the Mandapa of the Five Pandavas, the mythical brothers from the great epic poem the Mahabharata. The manapa, or pavilion or place of worship, is preceded by columns of lions, symbol of the Pallava kings.

The site of Mamallipuram also known as Mahabalipuram, in what is now India was known to the Ancient Greeks and visited by the Romans. Between the 7th and 8th centuries AD this became the main port of the Pallava dynasty. The name of Mamallipuram means City of Malla, a name which refers to one of the titles of Narasimhavarman I, one of the most important Pallava sovereigns who reigned from 630 to 670 AD. The closest town is Madras, capital of the state of Tamil Nadu, about 20 miles away.

321 top and 322-323 Within the mystical geography of India where stones, trees, caves and mountains all stand for the divine, the River Ganges holds the key role. The main artery of the sub-continent, Ganga Ma, or Mother Ganges, the goddess who came down from heavy to bless the Earth, is celebrated in a grandiose bas-relief carved from the rock at Mamallipuram.

321 center The myth says that 60,000 young sons of King Sagara were killed and cursed by an enemy. Their salvation was accomplished by a descendent, Bhagiratha, who persuaded Ganga to come down to Earth and purify their remains.

321 bottom At the right to the Descent to the Granges is this realistic group of three granite monkeys. The male is removing fleas from the female who is feeding the baby.

The archaeological complexes are divided into three groups. These are the monumental reliefs of the *Descent of the Ganges*, with a series of pictures sculptured in an enormous spur of diorite, the complex of the five *rathas*, about 500 yards further south, and the so-called "Temple of the Bank."

Facing eastward, the 90 by 25 foot *Descent of the Ganges* panel has been dated to the middle of the 7th century AD and contains a powerful stone fresco believed by many experts to tell of the mythical descent of the Ganges to the earth, although other scholars believe it shows the penitence of Arjuna, one of the five heroes of the great epic poem *Mahabharata*, in order to obtain invincible weapons from the god Shiva. Nevertheless, the theory that the bas-relief is a celebration of India's holiest river is probably the most commonly believed one. The rock is, in fact, split at the center and a tank which was originally at the top of the spur made it possible for a stream of water

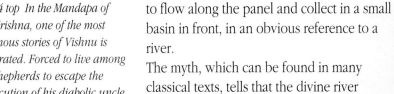

to flow along the panel and collect in a small basin in front, in an obvious reference to a river.

The myth, which can be found in many classical texts, tells that the divine river Ganges was only persuaded to descend to earth by the strict penitence of the holy man Bhagiratha who wanted to remove a curse from his ancestors.

Crowded with figures, the Descent of the Ganges shows scenes of idyllic life in the woods with hunters, hermits, local inhabitants and wild animals in various poses. The scene is dominated by the court of the gods with the beautiful nymphs, the magic spirits of the air, the half-animal celestial musicians, and many other mythical figures watching. Baghirata is shown in the yoga position representing the tree, on one leg with his arms raised upward. In the split along which the water flowed are the sinuous *nagas* with their spouses, the *naginas*, part human and part serpent and connected with water, fertility and knowledge. Beside them, a girl is drying her long hair by twisting it gracefully in a movement still seen among Indian women. The wild animals are illustrated with a vivid freshness. A young elephant holds its mother's tail with its trunk, and an antelope crouching on the ground scratches its nose with its leg.

Among the many monuments scattered around the *Descent of the Ganges* are rocky sanctuaries dug out into caves or beneath overhanging rocks which house splendid reliefs. Balconies and columns are often held up by lions, the symbol of the warlike Pallava dynasty. Among the most important is the *Grotto of the Five Pallavas*, *The Mandapa of Varaha*, which contains an image of the god Vishnu as a varaha, the boar that freed the goddess Earth from the muddy ocean bed, *The Mandapa of Krishna*, another image of Vishnu, *The Mandapa of Mahishasuramardini* dedicated to Durga as the killer of the buffalo-demon Mahisha, and *The Grotto of the Tigers*, with animal heads carved from the rock.

To the south is the famous group of five monolithic temples in the form of wooden ceremonial carriages of a design which is still used today to carry the images of the gods when they are moved from the temples.

Mamallipuram

Sculpted around the middle of the 7th century from the diorite blocks emerging from the beach, it has been suggested that these temples may be test pieces for a local school of architecture or votive offerings. They are completely unique in the history of Indian art and not completely finished. They have been given the names of the heroes of the *Mahabharata*, the great epic poem that describes the positive forces of the gods against the demons, all incarnated on the earth.

Draupadi is the wife of all five Pandavas, the champions of good, and gives her name to the smallest of the temples, which was probably dedicated to the goddess Durga.

324 bottom center This view shows the main panel of the Mandapa of Krishnu, in which the god raises the mountain Govardhana and uses it as a shelter to protect the local shepherds from the flood released by the god Indra.

324 bottom In this scene of the Mandapa of Mahishasuramardini, Vishnu is shown asleep on the serpent Ananta at the moment between the end of one universe and the birth of another. The Indian vision of time is cyclical and worlds originate and dissolve continuously.

324-325 In the Hindu world there is one Divine Being projected into an infinity of forms that perform specific functions. At the summit of this pantheon is the Trimurti, the Triple Image of Brahma, who begins the universe, Vishnu who preserves it, and Shiva who dissolves it. In the Mandapa of Varaha, Vishnu is shown in one of these persona as a wild boar. In this form the god saved the Earth when it was held prisoner by the Ocean and restored it to man.

325 bottom The Mandapa of Mahishasuramardini is dedicated to the goddess Durga, warlike wife of the god Shiva, celebrated in this case as "She who kills the demon Mahisha" who took the form of a buffalo. The many arms symbolize her great strength.

326-327 *The five rathas grouped in the southern part of Mamallipuram, although not completely finished, were given the names of heroes of the Mahabharata, the great Hindu epic poem, said to be of Indo-European origins, which depicts the conflict between gods and demons. In the photograph, from left to right, are the Dharmaraja dedicated to Yudhisthira, the Bhima, the Arjuna and the ratha of Draupadi, the common wife of the five brothers, with the bull Nandin, the mount of Shiva.*

This temple is a stone reproduction of the hut of an ascetic, taking the form of a simple square room with a straw roof and wooden decorations at the edges. An access stairway leads to the entrance, flanked by two guardians and topped by an architrave with motifs showing mythical sea creatures which are also shown above the niches containing statues of the goddess on the other three walls. The bull Nandi, the mount of the god Shiva, consort of Durga, and the lion carriage of the goddess are sculpted alongside.

The next temple is named after Arjuna, the great horseman, and is probably dedicated to the ancient god Indra, who is shown on his elephant on a base supported by lions and elephants. It has an entrance portico and two lion columns. The other three walls are divided into five panels with various

statues, including pairs of lovers. On a ledge decorated with small horseshoe-shaped arches containing laughing faces an upper section, pyramid shaped, is in two levels, bordered by miniature pavilions ending in an octagonal cupola.

The third temple is named for the Herculean-like warrior Bhima. It has a rectangular base and is surrounded by a partly colonnaded verandah held up by lions with a row of pavilions and a vaulted roof, a style borrowed from both Buddhist and secular architecture.

The Dharmaraja temple, linked to Yudhishthira, an extremely just and pious king, bears an inscription dating it to the reign of Narasimhavarman I (630-670 AD) who dedicated it to Shiva.

It is the highest of the group and rests on a particularly interesting base with a square

326 bottom left The ratha of the twin warriors Nahula and Sahadeva from the 7th century was built in the apsed "elephant's back" style.

326 bottom right Behind the lion, the mount of the goddess Durga, we can see the ratha of Draupadi consecrated to the goddess in effigies in the wall niches and that of Arjuna, the most famous of the five Pandava heroes. We still do not know whether the miniature temples were models or votive offerings.

327 left The Temple of the Bank, built on behalf of Narasimhavarman II, who reigned from 690 to 728, is dedicated to Shiva.

327 right The walls of the rathas incorporate many figures from the Hindu pantheon, framed by pillars. Two of these figures appear in the photograph.

328-329 Two of the five ratha – the Dharmaraja and the Bhima.

plan, preceded by a portico with lion columns.

Built on three floors, it is somewhat similar to the Arjuna model, with the same pyramid shaped structure with ledges separating the various levels and forming the base for rows of miniature pavilions. An octagonal cupola puts the final touch to the building. Statues of deities are found on the walls of the various floors.

The final temple is that of the warrior twins Nahula and Sahadeva. This is relatively small and has a portico held up by lions. The last great masterpiece of Mamallipuram

is *The Temple of the Bank*, erected on behalf of Marasimhavarman II Rajasimha who reigned between 690 and 728 AD. It stands alone on the beach and is dedicated to Shiva. This temple was known to sailors as a lighthouse and was mentioned by the Italian Gasparo Balbi in 1582. It was also written about in the 17th century by Nicolò Mannucci, but the first detailed description was in the book *Asiatic Researches*.

The temple, preceded by a small entrance, is divided into two square structures each topped by a pyramid shaped tower offering protection to the inner cells which later became typical of Dravidic architecture in southern India. The *vimana* has a triangular profile imitating the peaks of the soaring mountain, the mythical Mount Meru, the central axis around which the universe rotates in a well-ordered fashion.

The vimanas of the Temple of the Bank have three and four open floors each. The first and last of these are decorated with heraldic animals and have none of the rows of miniature pavilions that are found on the intermediate floors.

There are three inner sections although one is no longer covered. Shiva, his consort Uma and son Skanda occupy the first of these while in the second Vishnu rests on the primordial ocean.

A narrow passageway runs between the walls of the internal enclosure of the temple which is within a wider enclosure, surrounded by a low wall topped by various decorations including a statue of Durga riding a lion.

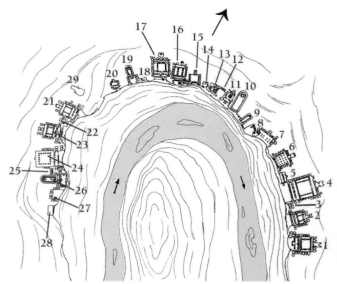

AJANTA,
THE GROTTOES OF THE BUDDHA

Ajanta is in the central Deccan, in the state of Maharashtra in India, 60 miles from the town of Jalgoan and about 110 from Aurangabad. It consists of a series of 30 caves excavated at various levels in a rocky amphitheater 80 yards high and facing the bed of the Waghora River. It has been a sacred place for thousands of years. It is considered one of the most idyllic settings in the world and was chosen by Buddhist monks as a place of retreat during the monsoon season when other places were uninhabitable. The grottoes extend for over half a mile. Each one was once connected to the river by stone or wooden steps and are now connected by a concrete path. The grottoes, or caves, have been numbered. Numbers 9, 10, 19, 26 and 29 are *chaityas* or places for worship, while the others are *viharas* or *sangharamas*, monasteries where the monks can live. The chaityas can be recognized by their imposing façades. These are always dominated by a gable which includes a horseshoe-shaped opening, called the *kudu*, above the entrance door. This sometimes has an arch with two columns supporting it in front of it.

330 left The chaitja of cave number 26, with three naves, the main one topped by a ribbed, vaulted ceiling, has columns close together ending in a figured capital upon which rests a rich entablature. In the apsed section, the stupa acts as a tabernacle. The design comes from the funeral mounds raised over the cremated remains of the Buddha, which later became a symbol of the cosmos with the Enlightened One as the center point that creates order.

330-331 The statue of Ajanta shows the Buddha in various postures related to important moments in his life. In cave number 26, which is used as a chaitya, the Enlightened One is shown at the point of transition. Aware that his earthly cycle is now ending, the Buddha lies down on his side between two trees, his head resting in his hand and pointing to the north. He is ready to accept nirvana, the state when the cycle of reincarnation and pain is over.

331 top left This is an overall view of the 30 grottoes of Ajanta, dug out of the rocky amphitheater created by the stream Waghora. The caves are partly chaityas, places of worship housing the stupa, the symbol of the Buddha and his doctrine, and partly vihara, the residences of the monks. The caves were dug out in two stages, first between the 2nd and 1st centuries BC and secondly, at the height of Ajanta's importance, in the second half of the 5th century AD.

331 top right One of the most significant examples of a chaitya is cave number 19, attributed to the second period of Ajanta. The entrance is preceded by an elegantly sculpted two-column portico, topped by a double cornice. The kudu, or horseshoe shaped opening, lights the interior. As well as the many figures of Buddha on the façade, there are other Buddhist figures, such as the two yakshas, the pot-bellied genies associated with the concept of fertility and wealth.

331 bottom right Cave number 1 shows the artistic maturity reached in the central stage of Ajanta. The verandah is decorated with splendid columns which have finely decorated stems and capitals crowded with figures. The diversity in the decoration of the pillars directs the eyes to the center of the face of the building, inviting the viewer to enter the antechamber. The sides of the verandah extend into two lateral, raised, colonnaded bodies leading to other areas.

332 The female figures are among the most fascinating motifs of Ajanta. They include servants, princesses and celestial nymphs, all with opulent sinuous richly jeweled forms. The half-closed, elongated eyes, full lips, bodies almost bent by the weight of the breasts, all suggest a sensuality which contrasts with the location, cave number 1, a 5th century AD vihara. And yet it is the attraction of the worldly t hat highlights the greatness of the ascetic choice.

332-333 In the first centuries of Buddhism, the so-called period of the Hinayana or the "small vehicle of salvation", the Buddha is represented only by symbols, never as a man. It is only with the advent of the Mahayana, "the great vehicle", which reinterprets the message of the Enlightened One in metaphysical and devotional terms, that the Buddha begins to be shown with human features. In Ajanta it is the Mahayana that gave the artists their greatest inspiration. In cave number 2 the image of the Thousand Buddhas in the teaching position offers a glorious dimension of the historic body of the Enlightened One and projects it into the infinite figures that every devotee creates of his Lord.

333 bottom Cave number 2, as well as containing splendid cycles of paintings, is one of the most important examples of a vihara. It consists of a great central hall with twelve pillars each with sixteen or thirty-two faces covered with a flat ceiling painted with beautiful circular motifs. This houses the cells of the monks alternating with sacristies. In the main hall, preceded by the vestibule of the Thousand Buddhas, is the image of the Enlightened One preaching as can be seen from his hands, which are placed against his chest with the rounded fingers of one touching the outstretched fingers of the other.

Façades from later periods will have figures of the Buddha in various positions and heights and other figures related to Buddhism. The interior is generally rectangular with three naves separated by purely decorative columns placed very close together.

The central nave is twice as wide as the other two, and has an apse and a reverse keel-shaped ceiling, while the side naves are lower and have either semi-vaulted or flat ceilings. The center of the apse, lit by light coming in from the kudu, is dominated by a stupa, a bell-shaped reliquary. This shape comes from the tumulus which was built on top of the remains from the cremation of the Buddha. This tumulus later became a major symbol in the religion, a place where a ritual procession called the *pradakshina*, in which the monks walked around it clockwise, took place. The *viharas*, or the residential buildings, consist of a large central hall with pillars covered by a flat, paneled ceiling. The monks' cells are placed along three sides of this. They are small openings dug out of the bare rock. In some cases there is a shrine with the stupa in the wall opposite the entrance. In the most recently built viharas there is often also a figure of the Buddha. The entrance to the hall may have a columned verandah opening onto the façade through one or two entrances which are richly decorated with interwoven patterns that imitate wood carvings.

The excavation of the stone that created these grottoes in Ajanta took place during two main periods, the first between the 2nd and 1st centuries BC and the second starting four hundred years later. Excavation initially stopped during the time of the local Vakataka dynasty with the second phase reaching its height in the latter half of the 5th century AD. The dates have been established by the study of the numerous inscriptions, the comparison of the statues and paintings with similar examples which had previously been dated, the study of the subjects depicted and their relationship with the development of Buddhism, and finally by analysis of the paintings and drawings using modern techniques. For over a thousand years the grottoes of Ajanta were forgotten by the world. They were only rediscovered in 1819 by John Smith, a British soldier who found

them while on a tiger hunt.

The first, rather clumsy attempts to restore the
grottoes, were carried out in 1875 using
yellow paint. Between 1930 and 1955 more
sophisticated work was done through the
archaeological center at Hyderabad.
Some rooms which are still uncompleted
make it possible to understand how the
grottoes were created. The work began from
the top and the ceiling was the first part to be
finished. Working without scaffolding, the
workers gradually removed the stone with
picks, leaving on the site the blocks that
would be used for the columns. These
columns are extremely sophisticated with
some of them having as many as sixty-four
sides. The floor was the last part to be
finished.

334 top This detail shows the great ability of the painter in depicting the emotions of lovers, including reluctance, passion, jealousy and cooling, shown with a subtle liveliness. The artists of Ajanta never indulged in pathos, agitation or any other emotion that could have disturbed the harmony. Desperation is softened into sadness, the exhaustion of life into melancholy. Although the painter shows these emotions in great detail he is not a realist and his main objective is to evoke a state of mind that leads to a spiritual dimension.

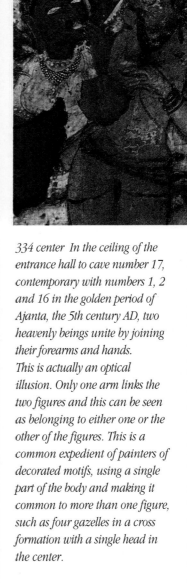

334 center In the ceiling of the entrance hall to cave number 17, contemporary with numbers 1, 2 and 16 in the golden period of Ajanta, the 5th century AD, two heavenly beings unite by joining their forearms and hands. This is actually an optical illusion. Only one arm links the two figures and this can be seen as belonging to either one or the other of the figures. This is a common expedient of painters of decorated motifs, using a single part of the body and making it common to more than one figure, such as four gazelles in a cross formation with a single head in the center.

It seems clear that several groups of craftsmen worked at the same time on finishing these caves, including the stucco work and the painting. The first part to be completed was the façade with the verandah when one was used, followed by the entrance hall, the main hall, the shrines and the cells.

Although the architecture and statues are of considerable importance, the grottoes of Ajanta are most famous for their wall paintings. By looking at grotto number 4, where the frescoes were left uncompleted, it is possible to understand the techniques used. The painting was applied after the wall had been made smooth with an inch or so layer of earth mixed with sand, shredded straw, other vegetable fibers and, in some cases, animal hair. This was left rough, apparently in order to give greater holding to the next layer,

334 bottom Another view of the splendid vihara number 17 which combines the sacred and the profane most impressively. In the frieze immediately above the architrave are shown pairs of lovers in various poses, while the figures of the Buddha above show detachment from earthly pleasures. The knowledge of a precise, subtle body language combining dance, statues and painting enables the artist to create postures suggesting the emotions of the couples while the hand gestures of the Buddhas, standing for specific inner attitudes, show in the two to the sides the position for meditation and in the center the position for teaching.

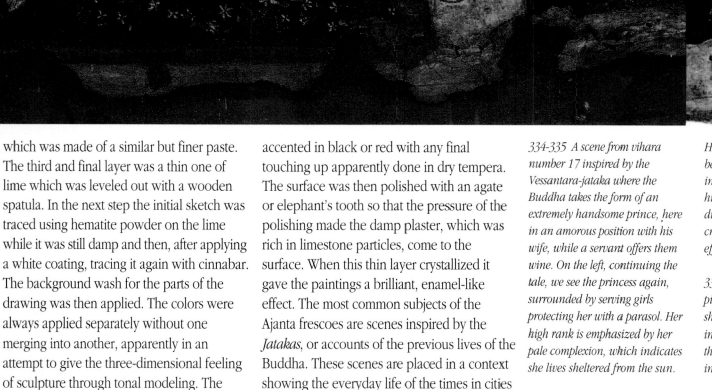

which was made of a similar but finer paste. The third and final layer was a thin one of lime which was leveled out with a wooden spatula. In the next step the initial sketch was traced using hematite powder on the lime while it was still damp and then, after applying a white coating, tracing it again with cinnabar. The background wash for the parts of the drawing was then applied. The colors were always applied separately without one merging into another, apparently in an attempt to give the three-dimensional feeling of sculpture through tonal modeling. The nearer parts are darkened while the smooth and distant features are lightened.

Five basic colors were used, all of either mineral or vegetable origin. They were ochre red, ochre yellow, smoky black, lapis lazuli blue and white. The free contours were accented in black or red with any final touching up apparently done in dry tempera. The surface was then polished with an agate or elephant's tooth so that the pressure of the polishing made the damp plaster, which was rich in limestone particles, come to the surface. When this thin layer crystallized it gave the paintings a brilliant, enamel-like effect. The most common subjects of the Ajanta frescoes are scenes inspired by the *Jatakas*, or accounts of the previous lives of the Buddha. These scenes are placed in a context showing the everyday life of the times in cities and villages, among both rich and poor. They show an amazing range of clothing, jewelry, objects, setting and characters which provide a rich source of both environmental and anthropological information about the times.

334-335 A scene from vihara number 17 inspired by the Vessantara-jataka where the Buddha takes the form of an extremely handsome prince, here in an amorous position with his wife, while a servant offers them wine. On the left, continuing the tale, we see the princess again, surrounded by serving girls protecting her with a parasol. Her high rank is emphasized by her pale complexion, which indicates she lives sheltered from the sun.

Her body is in the "triple bending" position with the head in line while the shoulders and hips arched in different directions, forming an S and creating a sensually sinuous effect.

336-337 and 338-339 The two pictures are of Grotto 17. They show the statue of the Buddha inside the sanctuary and one of the many refined paintings still in good condition.

PAGAN
BUDDHA'S KINGDOM

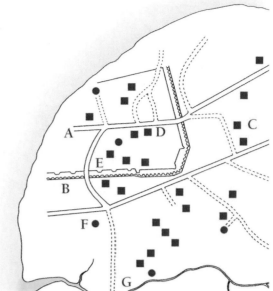

■ Temple
● *Stupa*

A Site of the walled town
B Walls
C Ananda
D Shwegugyi
E Pahtothamya
F Mingalazedi
G Minkaba Kubyaukgyi

340-341 The Thatbyinnyu or Temple of the Omniscent is perhaps the last great work produced under Sithu I, whose reign from 1113 to 1155 was one of the finest periods for Pagan, its so-called "golden age". The building spreads vertically over five floors, ending in a shikhara, which is a typical arched covering of Indian origin.

341 top Pagan, one of the most important archaeological sites in Asia, stretches over an area of 80 square miles and contains a huge range of Buddhist monuments. The date of the foundation of the city is usually given as 874 AD but its origins are older. Its period of greatest splendor covers just over two centuries, from the reign of Anawrahta (1044-1077) to the final destruction by the Shan princes in 1299.

Known in the past as Arimaddanapura, "The City of the Destroyers of Enemies", or Tambadipa, "The Land of Copper", this place in Burma (now Myanmar) was known as Pagan at least by the end of the 12th century AD.

One of the most important archaeological sites in all of Asia, it covers an area of about 60 square miles. The date of the city's founding is usually given as 874 AD but its origins are undoubtedly earlier. It was at its greatest importance in a period of just over two centuries, from the reign of Anawrahta (1044-77 AD) to the final destruction by the Shan princes in 1299.

Marco Polo was the first western explorer to mention this city, after the troops of Kublai Khan raided it in 1287. In 1795 an English diplomat, Michael Symer, briefly mentioned it, but it was not until 1855 that the Scottish engineer, Henry Yule, recognized its enormous importance. Following surveys by several archaeologists and the sacking by the Shans, the British, who had taken over Burma in 1886, established the first systematic archaeological work and began deciphering inscriptions.

The great pioneer in establishing the importance of Pagan and its architecture

341 center This is the Sulamani, the Crowning Jewel, a typical example of a gu, or cave-temple consisting of an inaccessible center section containing reliquaries or images used as a sacristy, a vestibule and a corridor. It was built under Sithu II who ruled from 1174 to 1211. The pyramid shaped structure, in brick with stone reinforcements, was completed by a shikhara which has been destroyed. A splendid decorated stucco covers the walls of the monument.

341 bottom The corridor of the Sulamani contains several late paintings which take their inspiration from the image of the Buddha and his disciples, central themes of the Theravada or Doctrine of the Ancients that was prevalent in Pagan.

was Gordon Hannington Luce who, although not officially connected with the British department covering archaeology worked with it for several years after 1912 and prevented Pagan from being bombed during World War II.

A terrible earthquake in 1975 seriously affected the area and brought UNESCO to the scene.

The total number of monuments at Pagan has been estimated at around five thousand, but those in good condition are about one thousand or so, some still in use. These are from three periods, the original period, or 850 AD to 1120 AD, the intermediate years, from 1120 AD to 1170 AD, and the later period, from 1170 AD to 1300 AD.

This city was once a green area on the banks of the Irrawaddy, thanks to a highly

influenced by the Theravada monk Shin Arahan and had close links with Sri Linka, the stronghold of Theravada.

The marriage of King Kyanzitha (1084-1113 AD) to Abeyadana, a Bengalese princess and a follower of Mahayana Buddhism brought a whole new group of religious symbols to Pagan.

Brahmins were a significant part of the population and this is a further indication of both the religious tolerance and eclecticism of the city. These individuals, who knew sacred Hindu science and were important in court ceremonies, also favored the belief that the king was an incarnation of Vishnu, the providential aspect of the divine in the Hindu world. Another splendid period in the history of Pagan came during the reign of Sithu II (1173-1210 AD).

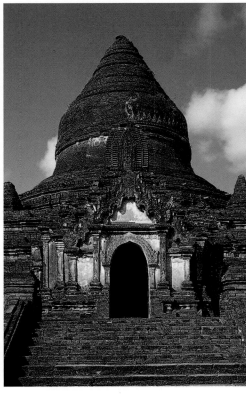

sophisticated irrigation system. Now it is one of the driest areas in Myanmar, or Burma.

None of the non-religious architecture remains as the houses and palaces and most of the monasteries and libraries were built in wood.

Chosen for its strategic position on the caravan routes between India and China, the city controlled a number of ports of tremendous commercial importance and was both famous and prosperous. When the Indian influence reached Indo-China, Pagan embraced Buddhism in the form of Theravada, or the so-called doctrine of the ancients.

This is the formula that is believed to be closest to the original message of the Buddha, sometimes called Hinayana which means "small vehicle of salvation."

The great King Anawrahta was highly

342 Local tradition tells that the king, who did not know which of his five sons to choose as his successor, placed the royal parasol, the hti, in the midst of them and this bent toward Nadaungmya, who reigned from that year, 1211, until 1230, under the name of Htilominlo. As a reminder of the event, he built a temple of the same name. The photograph shows the main entrance.

343 left The Htilominlo is the great temple of Pagan. The building, terminating in the shikhara, was originally painted white like all the temples of Pagan as this is the color of purity and transfiguration and then decorated with glazed green terra-cotta forms.

343 top right The Myinkaba Kubyaukgyi or Temple of Many Forms in the village of Myinkaba was built by Prince Rajakumar in 1113 to honor his father Kyanzittha. It contains the oldest paintings in Pagan and the famous Myazedi stone in four languages, Mon, Pali, Burmese and Pyu.

343 center The Indian model of the stupa can be seen in one of its most complex examples here in the Dhammayazika. Completed in 1196 by Sithu II, the building has a pentagonal plan and bears witness to the consolidation of the cult of Mettaya, the fifth Buddha and future savior of humanity, together with Siddhartha, the historic Buddha, and his three mythical predecessors.

343 bottom Built over two floors, the corridor of the Htilominlo has four niches facing the four compass points which house images of the Buddha. The one we see here is in The Gesture of Calling the Earth to Witness. The statue of the Enlightened One follows certain precise symbolic rules. For instance, the protuberance at the top of the head is the sign of the height of wisdom.

344 top The Dhammayangyi, in a Greek cross plan consisting of the central mass and the four access vestibules, takes the form of increasing upward flights of stairs connected by the terminal shikhara, now destroyed and underlined by the sturpa at the corners of the terraces, raised on a square base. The great ability of the builders can be seen in the joins of the bricks which are so perfect that not even a pin can be inserted in them.

344-345 On the plain of Pagan, once a fertile agricultural area and a prosperous trading center, there are about 5,000 monuments, a thousand of which are still in fairly good condition. Since the construction of a sacred building was considered the ideal way of building up spiritual merit the rulers set aside large sums not only for the buildings themselves but also for their maintenance.

345 left On a high base with elaborate moldings, the Buddha sits in the Gesture of Calling the Earth to Witness in the southern vestibule of the Chammayangyi,

considered one of the most mysterious temples of Pagan. Part of the interior is inexplicably bricked up, as are three of the four shrines in the central area, of which only the eastern one can be used.

345 right The western vestibule contains twin Buddhas which probably symbolize Siddhartha Guatama, the historic Buddha, meeting Mettaya, the Buddha of the future. The two figures evoke the dual aspect of the Buddhist doctrine of continuity and change, the old and the new, which determine the fertile dynamism of the religion.

At this time there was extensive building of monuments, probably brought on by the need to find suitable housing for sacred objects, the wish to create places of worship and celebrate the glory of the king, and the need to build the merits that give the right to reach Nirvana, the state of liberation from the continuous, painful return to life. There was another motive which is believed to explain this building frenzy.

This is the theory that a new Buddha would come to the Earth in the form of the savior Mettaya and it was important to be born when he was in the world.

Pagan has two basic architectural types: the *stupa* and the grotto-temple.

The Burmese stupa is mainly built from baked bricks which have been

origin symbolizing fertility and abundance in both material and spiritual terms.

The walls frequently have glazed, painted terra-cotta forms holding extracts from the *Jataka*, 550 stories telling about the previous lives of the Buddha. During the sacred procession known as the *pradakshina*, when the monument is always kept to the right of those in the procession, worshippers could reinforce their religious beliefs by reading these writings.

The access stairways to the highest points of the pilgrimage are placed at the four points of the compass.

The heart of the building is the reliquary contained in the sealed central chamber. There is no access to this after the construction of the zeidi.

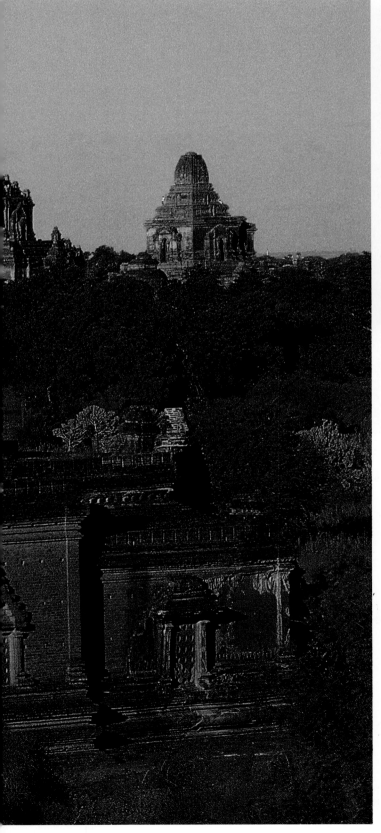

strengthened with sandstone and is known as a *zeidi*.

Derived from the Indian model it is seen as a burial mound built over the remains of the Buddha and therefore symbolizing the doctrine and presence of the Enlightened One, standing at the center of the universe.

It is generally made up of a square platform with a very high, many-sided plinth which holds the bell-shaped stupa itself. The structure is finished by a ringed spire with a sunshade.

There are many variations on this design, especially in the use of curves and the cupola-shaped body of the zeidi itself, and the division of the base into a series of terraces upon which it is possible to walk and which are designed to remind the viewer of the Indian cosmic mountain Meru, the center of the universe. At the corners of these terraces are miniature reproductions of the zeidi which were later replaced by water vases of Hindu

It houses the remains of holy figures, perhaps the Buddha himself or his closest disciples. If there are no such remains, it may contain fragments of sacred texts or statues that were particularly venerated by the Buddha.

The zeidi often contained more than one of these reliquaries as various sovereigns or dignitaries may have placed remains in the same monument over a period of time. At the later period in the development of this site, the interiors of these were maze-like, probably to discourage grave robbers. They were often protected by *dvarapalas*, typical Indian architectural figures placed alongside the doors like guards and other deities from the Hindu world. Buddhism and Hinduism were never in conflict.

When the building was completed it was covered with a thick layer of crude plaster made from sand and limestone and colored white, the color of purity and transfiguration.

346 top In Minnanthu, on the plain of Pagan, stands the Tayok-pye temple built by Narathihapati, the last sovereign, who ruled from 1256 to 1287, the year when the area was sacked by the Mongol armies of Kublai Khan. The stucco decoration frames the entrance portals with dramatic arches.

346 bottom The Tayok-pye is built on two levels and had a shikara which was either never completed or collapsed. The building is surrounded by huge walls with monumental entrances which incorporated wooden buildings for the temple's servants.

This was then decorated with multicolored motifs, sometimes garlands of lotus blossoms or almost frightening masks symbolizing the all-devouring nature of time.

The lotus-shaped cushion formed the base on which the pinnacle was inserted, a seven-disk stylized reproduction of the sunshades mentioned earlier. This was almost certainly made of copper, at first completed with a series of poles, later replaced by a crown of pendants and small bells. The zeidi is distinguished from the Indian stupa by its vertical sweep. The original bulbous shapes were gradually replaced by bell shapes, preferred in Pagan.

The other architectural shape in Pagan is the grotto-temple, called a *gu*, which is both more common than the zeidi and more suitable for ritual use.

Its structure, an artificial grotto, is ideal for meditation and worship and its gradual distribution of light is important to these purposes.

The contrast between the sun outside and the first shaded room, with windows placed to light wall paintings, as well as the angled slits that move the rays of light to the face of Buddha in the dark central part of the grotto, are aimed at creating this important emotional feeling in the viewer.

The gu was built facing either east or north and generally consists of an inaccessible central block containing remains or images and four niches housing the Buddha, each facing a different point on the compass. The images in these niches are usually made of plaster-coated bricks, sometimes reinforced with wood. The Buddha is shown with his hands in precise positions known as *mudras*, each representing a special moment in his path to enlightenment. Next to this central block is a vestibule with a corridor. Over the building is the typical arched covering of a northern Indian temple, topped by a reproduction of a zeidi. The Abeyadana temple is one of the finest examples of these.

During the intermediate period under Sithu I (1113-1155 AD) the design became less intimate and the symbols less important, with the accent placed on the ceremonies dedicated to Buddha, similar

346-347 As well as their fundamental religious function, the stupas also played a magic and protective role in the first period of Pagan and were therefore placed outside the walls at the four compass points. Those that marked the boundaries of the first capital of Anawrahta have been located. Later, as Pagan stretched further out, the defensive nature of these structures faded.

347 left A copy of the Indian Bodhgaya, the Mahabodhi, the temple of The Great Enlightenment, takes the vertical to extremes with its monumental shikhara.

347 right Built in the first period, the Nagayon temple is linked to an episode in the life of King Kyanzittha, who is said to have slept here protected by a naga, a part human, part serpent creature.

348-349 According to the legend, 4 million temples were built during the era of Pagan, of which only 2,000 have survived.

to the royal ceremonies in style.
The external architecture, and especially
the roofs of the temples, became of
particular importance.
The vaults, constructed using a special
technique of a radial arrangement of tiny
bricks forming interconnected flat arches,
were closed off at the top with a sandstone
slab. Some of the more massive structures
contain hidden vaulted corridors
apparently used to reduce the weight of the
materials and the loads exerted on the
walls, although these are generally very thick.
A combination of the terraced zeidi and the
temple with atrium led to the emergence of
another architectural type, a perfect
example of which is the *Thathbynnyu*.
Outstanding paintings can be seen in some
of the temples of Pagan. The outlines were

350 top left Six terraces, growing slimmer as they rise, go up from the central block of the Ananda, surmounted by a shikhara which, in turns, ends in a stupa. With its gilded hti (parasol) on the summit, the temple reaches a height of almost 182 feet. The four access doors to the two corridors are preceded by huge entrance arches, or toranas, which are repeated on the first and second terraces.

drawn in black or red on a white base and
then spread. Among the most important
zeidis are *Dhamayazika*, built by
Narapitisithu in 1196 and *Shweizigon*,
started under Anawrahta and completed by
Kyanzitta and Mingalazedi, around 1274.
This temple represents the cosmic
symbolism of the five Buddhas, including
Mettaya, and is therefore a pentagon with
five arched antechambers surrounded by

small, exquisite shikharas. There are three
terraces in front of the anda which is built
on a nine-sided base framed by miniature
zeidis. The Shweizigon is highly venerated
as it is believed to contain relics of the
Buddha. The anda rests on an octagonal
plinth on a three layered base with axially
mounted stairs and four pavilions covered
with shikharas to the front. The
Mingalazedi, also divided into three

terraces reached by steps, is on a circular
base, while the zeidi is bell-shaped and
ends in a conical spire. At the corners of the
terraces were originally miniature temples
which were later replaced by miniature
stupas on the top level.
The most famous gu is the *Ananda*, built
under Kyanzitta, a Greek cross construction
surrounded by six terraces topped by a
graceful shikhara and ending in a zeidi and

350 bottom left This figure of Buddha standing with his arms lowered and his cloak open, found in the niche of the sacristy in Ananda, is typical of Burma. The Enlightened One shows classic signs of beauty on his neck and earlobes which were lengthened by the heavy ornaments he wore when a prince. It is believed that the large earlobes show a capacity for compassionate listening.

350 top right The Ananda temple is part of a vast complex that also includes the Ok-kyaung, or residences of the monks. These could range in size from a single hut to a great monastery building containing many rooms. The monastery of Ananda, probably built in 1775, is frescoed with paintings in excellent condition.

gilded *hti*. At the four compass points are the entrance halls and inside there is a central pillar with four colossal Buddhas in the niches, around which there are two corridors with statues and precious decorations. Other important gus, as wall as Ananda, the most venerated, are the *Abeyadana*, which is famous for its paintings, and the *Thatbyinnyu* which combines convent and sanctuary styles.

350-351 A view of Pagan from the terraces of the Ananda, the most venerable temple in the area, built under Kyanzittha around 1105 at the request of a group of Indian monks. It was designed to look like the Himalayan cave which was their home. The plan of the gu with its central pillar and outer corridor was extended by a second corridor and four front wings.

351 top Anawrahta, the first great sovereign, who ruled from 1044 to 1077, ordered the building in 1057 of the massive Schuwehsandaw stupa to house a precious reliquary, a hair of the Buddha. The stupa is built on a five-terraced pyramid with staircases at the axes.

351 center Built in 1277 by King Narathihapati, the Mingalazeidi is one of the most elegant buildings in Pagan.

351 bottom The Manuha, a temple built in 1059 on behalf of the Mon king of Thaton of the same name who was defeated and taken as a prisoner to Pagan by King Anawrahta, houses huge statues of the Buddha.

BOROBUDUR MOUNTAIN OF THE MAHAYANA BUDDHA

352 Many of the statues of the Buddha looking into the court were lost or damaged through the years. Originally, there were 104 on the first level, 104 on the second, 88 on the third, 72 on the fourth and 54 on the upper circular terraces.

Boroburdur, the largest Buddhist temple in the world, is found in the heart of the island of Java. Built during the Sailendra dynasty, probably between 760 and 810 AD, it is situated in a plain surrounded by mountains and volcanoes, not far from the shores of the Indian Ocean. The temple is an important document about the kingdoms of Central Java on which there are almost no written documents or other materials to help us reconstruct this historic period.

Seeing these imposing centers of worship we realize that they could only have been built if there were also well-structured government run organizations able to produce surplus wealth which could be used for works on such a scale calling for a serious commitment. We do know that during this period some dynasties were competing with each other for the domination of Central Java, where highly populated settlements organized into often conflicting regimes had emerged centuries earlier, thanks mainly to the development of the agricultural method of growing rice in flooded fields.

The first traces of contacts with Indian culture date to the beginning of our age. Groups of Indian merchants, following after individuals from the higher castes including almost certainly the Brahmins, had reached the courts of the Indonesian kingdoms such as Srivijaya, Sumatra and Central Java by means of the maritime trading routes. It was primarily at the court level that the Indian religions of Buddhism and Hinduism began to spread. Between the end of the 8th century and the start of the 9th, the Buddhist Sailendra dynasty (also called Lords of the Mountains) probably took control from the rival groups and governed a great part of Java. This is the period when Borobudur began to take shape. It was not only a place for religious functions but also a place of celebration for the sovereigns of the period which was during the maximum development of the kingdom. The building of the complex required tremendous effort, especially if we take into account the techniques that were

available at the time. The structure, resting on a small hill, consists of over a million blocks of stone, each weighing over 200 pounds. These were brought to the site from the bed of a nearby river and were then cut, worked and decorated by the craftsmen. Hundreds of people must have been involved in this project, for a period of about 30 years, some time between 760 and 830 AD. The reign of the Sailendras must have been a time of great splendor to permit an effort of this scale. Some experts, in fact, believe that the decline of the country that followed this period was caused by over-extension during this time. A few decades after the completion of the work, in fact, the

A Square Terraces
B Circular Terraces
C Top *Stupa*

entire territory of Central Java fell into the most total obscurity, and the center of Javanese civilization shifted to the eastern part of the island. We still do not know why this area was abandoned, although various theories have been advanced. These include a volcanic eruption, an earthquake, a famine, or a combination of factors including the effort needed for the building of the major Central Java works, with the important Hindu complex of Prambanan, all of which could have been reasons for leaving the area. Boroburdur itself was forgotten, and it wasn't until the beginning of the 18th century that local information about it began to emerge. But the true rediscovery and valorization of the temple was the work of a European, Sir Thomas Stamford Raffles, who was British vice-governor at the start of the 19th century in this part of the world, usually controlled by the Dutch. The Dutch were, however, at the time busy fighting Napoleon and therefore had allowed the control of the

area to fall into the hands of the British. Raffles was young, efficient and knowledgeable, and enthusiastic about the history and civilizations of the countries where he worked. He commissioned a military explorer, Colin MacKenzie, who had spent many years in India and was familiar with Buddhist and Hindu art, to form a research group to investigate the remains of the ancient civilizations that had lived on the island. It was one of the members of this group, a Dutch engineer named H.C. Cornelius, who found the ruins of Borobudur in 1814, led to the site by local inhabitants. It took one and one-half months of work by 200 men to free the temple from the vegetation covering it. The first recovery work ended with the final surveys around 1870 but, ironically, this meant the beginning of the end for the building. The vegetation and ash from volcanic eruptions had not only hidden the structure but also protected it from harmful atmospheric agents.

352-353 Borobudur rests on a square base of 373 feet on each side. It is almost 150 feet high and built over five floors with a three mile route to the top. In this photograph we can clearly see the dual form of the stupa and the mandala.

353 According to legend, the building was designed by the religious architect Gunadharma, whose profile, it has been said, can be seen in the shapes of the Menoreh Hills which rise at the south side of the building itself. A great deal of the magical atmosphere that is so much a part of this area is due to the natural landscape into which the temple blends.

Consequently, when the sun, wind, rain and sudden changes in temperature started again to leave their mark on the building, it quickly began to decay. It was especially affected by very poor drainage during the periods of extremely heavy rain. In spite of this, a long period passed before the Dutch decided to embark on a first restoration and protection operation. This was carried out in 1907 but unfortunately it failed to solve the drainage problem. In the following years the deterioration continued, causing alarm among the administrators of the state of

role as a testimonial to a past of which we know so little. The only building which can be compared with Borobudur, and which may have to some extent inspired the architects, is the temple of Nandangarah, in northeast India. Both buildings can be interpreted as a plastic interpretation of the concept of the earth rotating around a center, as in the case of the Assyrian-Babylonian ziggurat and the layout of the imperial city of the Kings of Iran. If we look at Boroburdur from the air, it takes on the form of an immense *mandala*, a group of

354 The distant past may be far gone, but Borobudur recovers its importance as a major center of religion at least once a year. For Buddhists, a major festival takes place on the night of the full moon in April or May when Buddha's birthday is celebrated with his entrance into Nirvana.

355 top Depending on the side of the building and its position with regard to the terraces, the statues of Buddha take on different positions to express

different meanings. On the north is the abhaya mudra, to eliminate fear, on the east bhumisparsa mudra, the struggle against demons, to the south vara mudra, charity, and to the west dhyani mudra, meditation. Along the four sides of the row above the first balustrade are vitarka mudra, for prayer, and in the circular terraces dharmacakra mudra, the movement of the wheel of the doctrine, as in the statue in the photograph.

Indonesia, which had been formed during the period. In 1971, it was finally decided to start a serious program of restoration. This was completed in 1983 with the participation of various official bodies, including UNESCO. About one million of the stones of the building were removed, some treated and reshaped, and all were then put back in place in their original order. As a result of this operation it was possible to take a number of steps to stop the infiltration of water, and today the entire construction of Boroburdur has been restored completely, with about one million visitors coming to see it each year. Very few of these visitors are Buddhist pilgrims. Most are visitors who are attracted to the beauty of the building as an exceptional work of art, the fascinating religious aura that pervades the site, and its

geometric shapes marking out a sacred territory, with its most important part in the center and larger and larger areas developing out from that, with precise references to the four points of the compass. The main form of Buddhism in Java was Mahayana, or the Great Carriage, the form of Great Compassion, a religion that was very open toward the individual paths that the faithful could follow even in the course of a single life on their journey to Nirvana where they would be freed of the burden of continuing reincarnation. We know that between the 7th and 14th centuries there was a significant spreading of somewhat esoteric forms of Buddhism, such as Tantrism, which provided quicker paths toward enlightenment and Nirvana through various rites and practices. It is within this context that we have to see

355 bottom The numerous statues of the Buddha in niches look toward the outside of the building. These are on the eastern side, the holiest, and are the mudras, or positions representing the struggle against demons.

Borobudur, which eloquently expresses these conceptions of Buddhism. The temple consists of four square and three circular terraces, surmounted by the small *stupa* on top. In the course of the ritual procession in a clockwise direction, the pilgrim had to walk through the galleries of the first four terraces. These were richly decorated with panels facing inward and on the balustrade. As the first gallery was decorated with four series of panels and the others with two each, the pilgrim had to pass through these a total of ten times, observing and learning from the bas-reliefs, before being granted access to the circular terraces above. According to the cosmic symbolism of Mahayana Buddhism, at the center of the world is the sacred mountain, Mount Meru, around which the planets, skies and seas rotate. The path toward enlightenment metaphorically corresponds to the ascent of the mountain, here symbolized by Borobudur. The base of the temple stands for the material world, form and shape, the sphere of desires and the sufferings of life. The walls of the base, measuring about 380 feet on each side, are

356 top and bottom The image shows (top) a noble on horseback going into the forest with his followers to hunt. This figure can be found in the first gallery in the Avadana. In the bottom image festive musicians celebrate the birth of the Buddha.

356-357 The young Sudhana sits surrounded by wise teachers. This bas-relief is part of the series in the upper terraces, whose theme is taken from the Gandaviuha, the structure of the world compared to a bubble.

357 bottom The sailing vessel shown here is one of the most important sources for our knowledge of the shape and features of ancient Southeast Asian ships. This panel is part of the series of stories in the first gallery inspired by the Avadana episodes of self-sacrifice.

358-359 Two warriors armed with a sword can be seen in this detail from the decorated low-relief panels at Borobudur.

360-361 This elegant low relief shows an elephant preceding the young Siddhartha protected from the sun by a parasol.

almost entirely undecorated. For reasons that we still do not understand, the 160 decorated panels were covered by a wall and they were only discovered in 1885. Whatever the reason, whether to give the building greater stability or to hide the sections concerning worldly desire and passion from the devotees, a protective wall had been built around the base. After this was completely dismantled to photograph the decorations, it was rebuilt and today only four panels have been left, deliberately, uncovered. These show scenes from a Buddhist text, the *Mahakarmavibhangga*, on heaven and hell, sin and punishment, good deeds and rewards. In the middle of each side of the base there is a narrow stairway leading to the upper terrace. To follow the path correctly, this should be reached from the eastern side, which is considered the holiest. Seen from the outside, the temple shows no bas-reliefs, but there are numerous statues of Buddha. The building takes the form of an immense stupa, a typical Buddhist construction which originally contained the ashes of the historic Buddha, Siddhartha Gautama, and which later became one of the most important symbols of this religion. The stupa is as impenetrable as Borobudur, built on a hill and with no interior parts. To gain access to the teachings contained in the panels, we have to enter the upper galleries. The building is therefore very unusual in shape, inaccessible from the outside on first sight, and closed to those who do not want to enter the gallery and learn from the teachings, but continue on the path toward salvation. The first gallery has a shorter perimeter area, 200 feet per side at the base, with the walls of the upper levels becoming progressively shorter. The four square terraces stand for the Rupadhatu, the physical form of the Buddha. By walking through these the pilgrim has already set out on the path toward Nirvana, and finds himself in the phase of inner growth during which he has to learn the teachings, although he has already begun his process of detachment from the material life depicted on the base.

It is only after crossing all four galleries in the correct way that he can gain access to the final level of Arupadhatu, or non-form. Here we have the three circular terraces, with a series of stupas arranged concentrically, containing statues of Buddha which we can glimpse through small geometric openings. There are no icons. The phase of learning is complete and we can now reach the last great central stupa, which is absolutely impenetrable. The ascent of the sacred mountain, Mount Meru, is completed, we are in a state of non-form, in nothingness. Borobudur is therefore a building with many meanings, and its structure is highly complex. It can be seen in many different ways. It can be appreciated for its beauty and the artistic value of its decorations or as a historic testimony to a glorious past of which all traces have been lost.

However, its deepest meaning has to be interpreted in this threefold image of stupa, Mount Meru and *mandala*, three aspects of the same path which, in the intentions of the builders, would probably have enabled the pilgrims to achieve enlightenment and bring their spirits into contact with Buddha himself.

ANGKOR,
PALACES OF THE GODS

A Angkor Wat
B Phnom
  Bakheng
C Angkor Thom
D Bayon
E Preah Khan
F Neak Pean

G Eastern basin
H Ta Prohm
I Banteay Kdei
J Sras Srang
K Ta Som
L Eastern Mebon
M Prerup

The first strong but peaceful influence on what was once called Indochina took place in the first centuries of the Christian era. This influence came through the Brahmins, the Indian noble priestly caste, who were followed later by Buddhist missionaries. This is why the great temples at Angkor in what is now Campochia or Khmer or Cambodia are a testimony to a fascinating union of indigenous and imported elements. The local Khmer worship of ancestors and the sacred mountain blended in with the Hindu ideal of the universal cosmic mountain, the axis and ordered pivot around which the world itself revolves.

It was during the 9th century that a grandiose Brahmin rite held on the sacred mountain of Phnom Kulen on behalf of King Jayavarman II sanctioned the culture of devaraja, or the god-king, for the first time. Mythology tells the story of how the god Shiva, one of the most important deities in the Hindu religion, handed the king the lingham, the phallic stone symbolizing the god, and which from that moment became the tabernacle of the royal essence of *devaraja*, protector of the universe, whose place of residence was the temple-mountain.

As part of this tradition, each sovereign during his reign built a personal temple to house the lingam, symbol of both his royal power and divine being. At his death, this became his mausoleum. The most powerful devarajas went one step further. They also had sacred places built for their relatives. In this way the temple became not only an indication of a belief in an after-life but also a bridge between ancestors and descendants.

The Khmer empire had five centuries of splendor until, in 1431, it was destroyed by monarchs of the nearby area roughly similar to modern Thailand. Virtually all memory of the city was lost until a 19th century French naturalist, Henri Mouhot described Angkor for the first time is his book about his

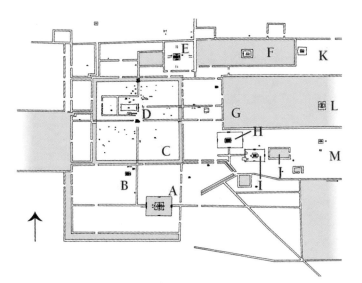

journey throughout the world, thus attracting the west toward the history of the Khmer civilization.

While this area was a French protectorate, the Ecole Française d'Extréme Orient, founded in 1900, began work recovering Angkor, cutting the monuments out from the jungle and restoring them. A specific organization, the *Conservation des Monuments d'Angkor*, with a succession of famous directors, was formed for this work in 1908.

In 1929 the Dutch developed a method of archeology called anastilosis, which involves the complete dismantling of a monument followed by its reconstruction, piece by piece, with reinforcements and this is the method used for the Khmer monuments, with outstanding results.

All Khmer architecture is inspired by the cosmic mountain and the square tower-sanctuary with its stepped pyramid is the oldest known Khmer design, in brick, sandstone or clay. The towers, or prasat, which were originally isolated but later grouped together in three or five on a single base were later developed within the complex of the temple-mountain into a five tower form, with one at each corner and the fifth in the middle, all connected by colonnaded galleries.

Hindu mythology of the origin of the world is the basis for these constructions with the

362 top *The fascination of the Khmer monuments is due not only to their great artistic value but also to their location in the wild, enveloping tangle of the jungle.*

362 bottom *Khmer architecture tends to transfigure the human body into the divine. The devatas, divinities with complex hairstyles and splendid jewelry, smile enigmatically from the walls of Angkor Wat, built by Suryavrman II between 1113 and 1150.*

363 *During the four middle centuries of the Khmer empire, between the 9th and 13th centuries AD, several capitals were built in Angkor, the last of which, Angkor Thom or Great City, displayed the constant motif of the Bodhisattva Lokeshvara, a central figure in Mahayana Buddhism.*

364-365 *The towers of Bayon, the central temple at Angkor Thom, are decorated with portraits of the famous king Jayavarman VII, the last and greatest Khmer builder.*

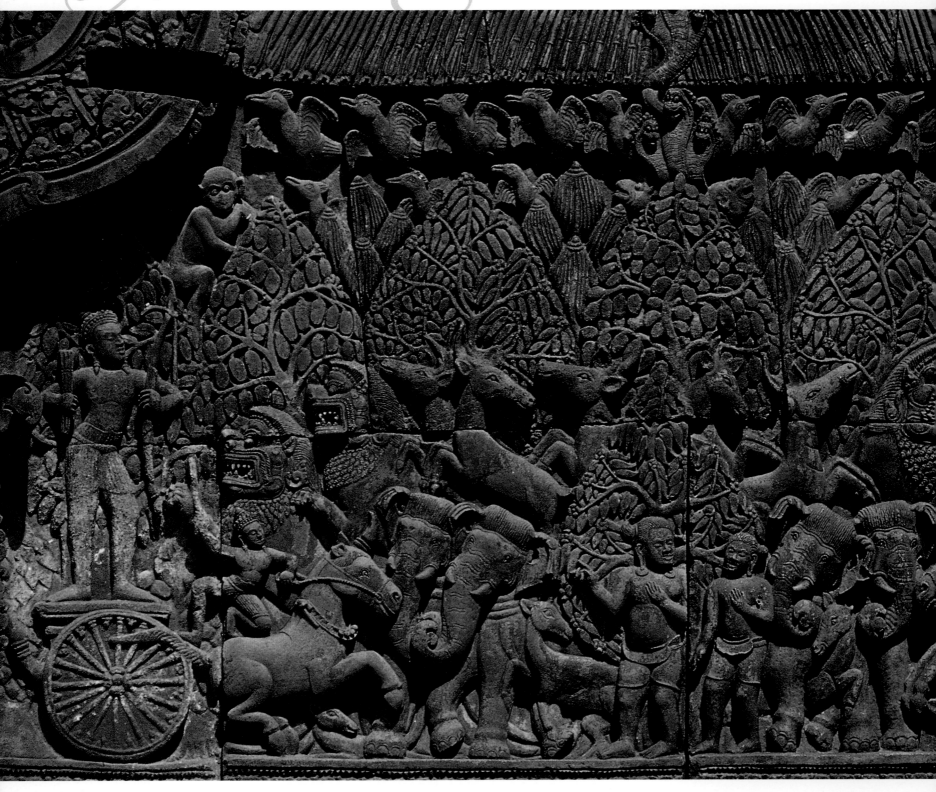

366-367 *Banteay Srei, a small temple complex 12 miles from Angkor, was built in 967 by the Brahman Yajinavaraha, spiritual advisor to Rajendravarman II and Jayavarman V. The reliefs show Khmer plastic art at its best. Here is shown a detail of the eastern front of the north library, centered around the adventures of Krishna, the incarnation of Vishnu, the providential version of the divine.*

366 bottom *The main figure on the eastern front of the south library of Banteay Srei is the thousand-headed demon Ravana, who is trying to uproot Mount Kailasa, the home of the god Shiva. He can be seen above with his wife Parvati who clings to him in terror. All the inhabitants of the sacred mountain, animals, ascetics and attendants, are terrified, but Shiva, unafraid, presses his foot to the ground so the mountain falls and the demon is crushed into the bowels of the earth.*

temple-mountain, rising from a base that symbolizes the cosmic ocean or the waters containing life waiting to be born. The importance of the baray which is the Khmer water base is fundamental to the building of religious centers as royal power not only is based on sacred precepts but also on the ability to use the waters for the rice fields. In this way the king became the source of life itself. The main body of the temple represents the mythical Mount Meru with its five peaks which, in the Hindu view, is at the center of the universe and symbolizes the original chaos in the world as we see it. The doors that jut outward in special pavilions from the constructions at the four corners symbolize the extension of royal power into the entire universe.

The bridge with its balustrade formed by *nagas*, serpents with five or seven heads, represents the rainbow uniting earth and sky and the rain the serpents bring.

As every sovereign had to carry out three fundamental duties which were his duty toward his subjects, with the construction of reservoirs and irrigation channels, toward his ancestors, with the building of a temple to commemorate them, and toward himself as devaraja with the building of a mountain-sanctuary, there are many monuments in the Angkor area.

This city extends over 60 square miles near the modern town of Sieam Reap in the northern part of the country.

One of the oldest settlements is near the modern village of Roluos, where the great king Indravarman placed his capital, Hariharalaya, digging out the great Indrataka and building the six-towered temple of

367 center right In addition to the mountain-temple, Khmer architecture also developed low buildings in which the main sacristy is flanked by other rooms and enclosed within a series of walls. Both types of building symbolize the inner pilgrimage in search of the sacred. In the case of the mountain temple the route moves upward, while in low buildings the movement is from the periphery to the center, from the outside inward.

367 bottom right The asuras or demons can be easily recognized in the reliefs. Their faces have distinctive features and round eyes, while the devas, or gods, have refined appearances and elongated, petal-shaped eyes. This relief is found on the steps of the Bakong, the mountain-temple built by Indravarman in 881 as the center of his capital, Hariharalaya, situated in the modern village of Roluos.

367 bottom left The Phnom Bakheng, from whose summit this photograph was taken, was built by Yashovarman I in 893 as the mountain-temple center of his new capital Yashodharapura.

367 top right The eastern Mebon, a mountain-temple built in 952 AD by Rajendravarman II, is a symbol of the cosmic mountain, the home of the god-king who is the guardian of earthly order.

368-369 *The Angkor Wat is seen as the masterpiece of Khmer art and marks the height of its brilliance. The building, surrounded by a huge trench, represents the Hindu myth of the cosmic mountain which emerges from the water of the primordial ocean. The construction of the water basins, one of the main activities of the rulers, performed the dual function of guaranteeing irrigation for the rice fields while symbolizing the role of the god-king as lord of the waters.*

368 bottom *Angkor Wat is enclosed in a double wall which follows the pyramid structure. It consists of three terraces, the last of which houses five towers in a cross formation like the five peaks of the cosmic mountain. It has been considered that the Khmer builders may have deliberately made the access alley nearly twice as long as the façade to provide a scenic relief.*

Preah Ko in 879 AD and the mountain-sanctuary of Bakong in 881. Roluos was inhabited from 882 but abandoned by Yashovarman (889-900 AD) who founded his capital Yashodhapura where it was fed by the enormous basin known as the Eastern Baray around the mountain-temple of Bakheng which housed the royal lingam. It is with Yashodhapura that the history of Angkor begins, a city which went on to act as the center of the Khmer empire for five centuries, except for a brief interlude from 921 to 941 AD, during which Jayavarman IV moved the capital to Koh Ker.

But it was not only the kings who built Khmer art. One of its masterpieces, the Banteay Srei, was constructed in 967 by two Brahmins, Yajnavaraha and his brother Vishnukumara about 20 miles northeast of Angkor.
Rectangular, with a series of buildings between the first and second wall and cross-shaped monumental edifices, known as *gopuras*, at the entrances to the third and fourth sections, the walls are accented with blind windows and small circular columns. The access road is flanked by two porticoes and the temple itself is divided into three

369 left Although the Thais sacked Angkor in 1431, thus bringing about the end of its great capital, Angkor Wat was never completely abandoned. Built for the Hindu king Suryavarman II, identified on his death as one of the forms of Vishnu, it became a Buddhist pilgrimage site as can be seen from the many statues of Buddha throughout.

369 top right The walls of the Angkor Wat are adorned with ranks of female deities wearing swirling skirts shown in elegant fabric. Their mysterious smiles are typical of the divine image of this period. Their serene but remote expression suggests the wide gap separating mortals from heavenly beings.

369 center right Nothing has survived of the residential buildings as only the temples were built from lasting materials. Since these were conceived as the home of a divine ruler they were meant to equal the heavenly pavilions of the gods. Eyes open in a vision or closed in meditation, the gods of Angkor Wat show the delights of paradise awaiting the monarch upon his transition.

369 bottom right The cross-shaped plan evokes the symbolism of the expansion from the one to the many and the spread of royal authority. It is the fundamental module used in Angkor Wat for both the towers and the access portals such as the one in the photograph.

370-371 This is Ankor Vat, the temple built by Suryavarman II between 1113 and 1150.

Angkor

small prasats on decorated bases with false doors on three sides beneath a covering of several floors that continue the construction in miniature.

Perhaps the most interesting features in Banteay Steis were the multi-lobed, mainly straight gables on the prasats with their waving profiles in the so-called "libraries" and in wooden imitation in the gopuras, which were frequently built over three floors to provide a telescoping effect, which is one of the typical features of Angkor Wat, the most famous monument.

This temple decoration is considered one of the most successful works in Khmer art because of the freshness and richness of the compositions.

Angkor Wat was built during the reign of Suryavarman II (1113-1150 AD). Restoration work, hampered by local warfare, has been taking place recently under the leadership of UNESCO.

The monument has had several names. Known at one time as Brah or Vrah Vishnuloka, the posthumous name of Suryavarman, its modern name of Angkor Wat means "royal residence which is also a monastery." There is still some confusion about the exact use of this monument, but the most popular theory is that Suryavarman had it built as his mausoleum.

The building measures about one-half square mile and is surrounded by a moat 600 feet wide with steps leading down to the water. The building faces west, rather than east, which seems to confirm that it was built as a tomb, and has two entrances at ground level where there are several interconnecting

372 left Suryavarman II was devoted to Vishnu, and the bas-reliefs of the outer gallery of Angkor Wat are inspired by the acts of this god and his incarnations of Rama and Krishna. The former, prototype of the just king, is celebrated in the Ramayana, and the latter in the Mahabharata, the two great Hindu epic poems whose battle scenes are shown in the upper

and lower panels. In the photograph in the center is a detail from the judgment of the dead, where several condemned, terrified, and emaciated individuals are beaten by the attendants while an elephant crushes others with its trunk. The function of Yama, god of the afterlife and supreme judge, is performed by Suryavarman II, who became divine after his death.

372 right The scenes, primarily crowded with figures, occasionally open to give emphasis to certain persons, such as this image of a victorious warrior contrasted with that of the enemy he has killed who is lying at his feet.

373 The frequent portrayal of war scenes can be understood by the fact that Suryavarman II was a soldier king and he was responsible for victories against the old enemies of the Khmer, including the Cham from nearby Champa, modern Vietnam. The adventures of Vishnu and his visits to earth, always in order to fight demons, were particularly suitable to express the overlap between kingly and godly deeds.

374-375 These two devata (female deities) are represented on a low relief on the walls of Angkor Vat. Their hair is adorned with garlands of flowers, diadems, pendants and plaits.

galleries. At the entrance to the building there is a paved entrance flanked by libraries, two artificial ponds and a cross-shaped platform leading up to the entrance to the temple itself. Angkor Wat is raised onto a three-terraced pyramid, with the first containing a cross-shaped cloister with three parallel galleries leading to three stairways to the upper terrace and a fourth, with three naves at right angles to the others, dividing the space into four ceremonial pools.

The second terrace repeats the same motifs as the first, with a surrounding gallery of *gopura* at the four points of the compass and cross-shaped pavilions at the corners. This also encloses two libraries connected by an elevated platform. Very steep stairways lead up to the third terrace which, in contrast to the other two terraces which are oblong, is completely square. This is

surrounded by a gallery with colonnaded windows, cross-shaped pavilions at the corners and the gopuras above the entrances facing the four compass points, imitating the cross-shaped plan of the cloister.

The monument is completed by outstanding decorations. The eight or sixteen-sided columns are divided into ten or twelve rings, making them seem both light and vibrant. The design of a flat interweaving of leaves creates a tapestry effect in which beautiful celestial nymphs are set.

Among the features of these nymphs are their elaborate hairstyles. In the gables, mythological scenes are repeated in the bas-reliefs of the galleries which run along the walls for about three hundred feet, almost

like manuscripts etched into stone. It seems likely that the technique was copied from painting, but no trace of that type of Khmer art remains. All the figures are from the Vishnu mythology so favored by Suryavarman II and refer to the two great Indian epics Mahabharata and Ramayana and to the myth of the shaking of the ocean which the gods and demons performed to extract ambrosia, the nectar of immortality and supreme knowledge.

Despite, from our viewpoint, certain basic constructional errors (weak foundation, insufficient use of iron tie-rods and joints and limited staggering in laying the stones), Angkor Wat is an architectural masterpiece of harmony and proportion.

377 center The parade of the army in motion against the enemy is an orderly one, with the infantry marching in two lines, the chariots, the imposing procession of the elephants mounted by the leaders, the band of musicians and the dancers. The army was followed by civilians with supplies and the soldiers' families. The expressions, clothing, weapons and details are shown with great care and dynamism.

377 bottom In the first gallery, on the southern face of the east side, the upper section shows fish and a crocodile biting the leg of a soldier who has fallen into the water of the river where the battle against the Cham is taking place, while the lower section with trees shows the bank of the river with life proceeding normally. The simplicity of the civil architecture and the essential objects of the time are the same as those of today.

The last and greatest of the builders was undoubtedly Jayavarman VII (1181-1201) who built without interruption for 30 years and with such speed that a huge brick tower was completed in 30 days. This haste and a lack of good quality sandstone as the best quarries were exhausted affected the quality of the building.

This king was a fervent Buddhist, particularly devoted to the bodhisattva of compassion, Lokeshvara.

The Lokeshvara motif is found in Bayon, a mysterious complex mountain-temple at the center of Angkor Thom, the "great city" which extends over almost three square miles and is surrounded by over 20 foot high

377 top Almost 4,000 feet of bas-reliefs decorate the galleries of Bayon, offering an incredible insight into the life of the period with scenes of day-to-day life beside views of the courts and battles. The images show many different scenes, the most important of which is a celebration of the great victory of Jayavarman VII in 1190 against the Cham, whose state was then annexed to the Khmer in revenge for the sacking of Angkor in 1177.

378-379 The Bayon, built at the start of the 13th century, is the most complex and mysterious construction in Khmer architecture and marks its decline.
A wild forest of towers which follows a certain logic despite undergoing many changes in the building, the temple expresses the complex and contradictory personality of Jayavarman VII and identifies him with the Bodhisattva Likeshvara, whose face can be seen on all the towers of the Bayon.

378 bottom Giant statues of the gods are lined up at the entrance to Angkor Thom. The walls of the town symbolize the chain of mountains that surrounded the universe and the moat refers to the cosmic ocean.
The temple of Bayon, in the center of Angkor Thom, stands for the same cosmic mountain that forms the base of the town. Under Jayavarman VII the esoteric meaning of the monuments reached their height.

379 top right The enormous central tower of the Bayon, dominated by the faces of Lokeshvara, unlike the other mountain-temples, has a circular plan, conforming to Buddhist symbolism. Jayavarman, follower of Mahayana Buddhism, closed the Hindu period, but not that of gigantic monuments that called for great expense in terms of costs and manpower.

walls with five gates, four at the points of the compass and the fifth north of the eastern gate and dominated at a height of 60 feet by four faces of Lokeshvara, clearly identified with Jayavarman as protector of the universe. In front of the gates are 54 gods with elongated eyes and 54 round-eyed demons, supporting a naga, and there is a clear reference to the shaking of the ocean when the mythical serpent Vasuki was used as a rope around the cosmic mountain, the temple of Bayon, to create the swirling needed for the mixing.

The city rotates around the Bayon, whose structures were modified over the years to the point that scholars had difficulty in dating it and determining its use prior to the discovery of the statue of Buddha.

In addition to the incredible impression that the great forest of towers creates on the visitor to this site, dozens and dozens of bas-reliefs on the walls of the galleries report the acts of Jayavarman VI, victorious over the Cham of the Champa kingdom, within the context of the everyday lives of the people. These reliefs, noted for their freshness and immediacy, are remarkable for the way in which the artists changed tone and design according to whether they were depicting the powerful, gods and kings, or ordinary people, so much like those of today.

379 bottom Angkor Thom, the Great City of Jayavarman VII, is inspired by a great Hindu myth, that of the Stirring of the Ocean by the gods and demons to extract ambrosia, a symbol of immortality and knowledge, with the cosmic mountain as a whip and the primordial serpent Vasuki as the cord. The gates of the town are preceded by 54 gods and the same number of demons (left) holding up a serpent.

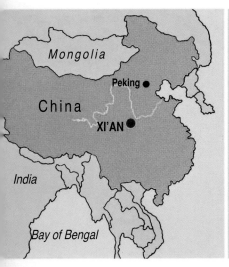

XI'AN, THE WARRIORS OF QIN SHIHUANG

In 1974 in the district of Lintong not far from the city of Xi'an, in the north of the Shaanxi region, 1400 yards east of the outer walls of the mausoleum of Qin Shihuang, the first emperor of China, a group of peasants made the chance discovery of an enormous trench containing terra-cotta figures of soldiers dating back to the Qin period (221-206 BC). During later excavation work, other trenches came to light.

The entire complex of the Qin Shihuang mausoleum, which was not completed when the emperor died in 210 BC, covers a surface of about 22 square miles.

The center of the burial complex is the burial mound beneath which the emperor's tomb has been identified although not yet opened for excavation.

Around this, over a radius of 10 miles, are the sacrificial trenches. In 1980, a ditch was found to the west of the mound containing two impressive bronze carriages, about half the size of real ones. Not far from there, 18 other trenches were found, containing wild birds and animals and 13 trenches with statues of slaves and servants, apparently symbolizing the hunting ground of the emperor.

Outside the tomb area, toward the east, 93 other trenches emerged. These contain pottery and iron tools and statues of charioteers, as well as a great number of skeletons of horses.

These were the imperial stables. Just over a mile to the east of the mound the four trenches containing the emperor's terra-cotta army were dug up.

These trenches are separated from each other by architectural structures and cover a total area of about 25,000 square yards. Inside there were 130 wooden war carts, more than 600 terra-cotta horses and well over 8,000 statues in the form of warriors of different kinds along with an enormous quantity of real bronze weapons.

All the trenches face east. Number one is on the south, two and three are east and west of one, trench four is between two and three. Excavation work is still taking place on this trench.

Inside trench one are over 6,000 statues of warriors and horses, arranged in rectangular formations of infantry and heavy carts. The front three rows have 210 soldiers, all facing east and not in uniform. They hold bows and crossbows and have quivers over their shoulders. At the ends and in the center of the row are three armored warriors, apparently officers.

Behind these three rows are 38 columns of soldiers, divided into eleven groups, six of which contain a war chariot with two standing soldiers. Each chariot is preceded by three lines of soldiers, each made up of four men with bronze lances.

On both sides of the 38 columns is a row of soldiers facing to the outside of the formation. Many of these are armed with bows and crossbows. At the end of the formation are three rows of soldiers, two looking toward the east and one looking toward the west.

In trench number two, nearly 1,000 statues of warriors were found together with over

A Outer wall
B Inner wall
C Trench of the bronze chariots
D Burial mound
E Trench 1
F Trench 2

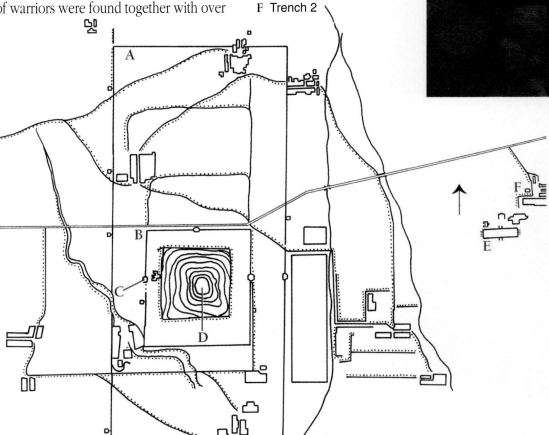

381 bottom and 382-383 An impressive view of the ranks of officers, infantry men and chariots with horses in the corridors of trend number 1. The organized mass of soldiers along the earth barriers shows the solidarity and compact nature of the army of China's first emperor.

400 horses and 89 war chariots in a pattern bringing the cavalry, infantry and chariots together protected by an armed vanguard. Trench number three appears to be the headquarters or the command post for the entire army. It contains a single war chariot and 68 apparently exceptional soldiers armed with bronze javelins.

The figures vary in size. The warriors are slightly taller than life size. The horses are about five feet tall and about six feet long. The soldiers and officers have full military equipment which could have actually been used in battle.

The weapons are made of the best quality materials and include lances, javelins, halberds, axes, hooks, swords and crossbows. The wooden carts and bridles of the horses are also suitable for real use. Some of the soldiers and horses have symbols etched or printed on their heads and bodies with stamps that apparently indicate the craftsmen who made them. The names of over 85 of these master craftsmen have been found, all of them highly skilled artisans who apparently employed numerous assistants and apprentices.

Scholars believe that each craftsman had about eighteen assistants.

In addition to the names of the sculptors, there are places where the names of other, apparently lower level, functionaries appear as well as inventories of the number of soldiers and horses.

In addition to the great number and imposing appearance of these statues the most striking thing is the extreme realism and precise details these craftsmen gave this army. The finishing and shapes of the chariots reflect the customs of the time while the horses, including blinders, bridles, bits and saddles are absolutely realistic.

The same precision can be found in the

stature, bearing, clothing and hairstyles of the warriors, but it is most of all the features of the faces which have the greatest impact on the viewer.

These even show the ethnic characteristics of the various parts of the empire from which the emperor's army were recruited. Therefore, some of the statues have elongated profiles, large mouths, fleshy lips, high foreheads, and wide cheekbones, typical of people from the central valley of the River Wei, while others have the round

384 A young junior officer, whose rank we can identify by the simple helmet and combat uniform covered by square-plated armor, shows both expressive bravery and austerity.

384-385 The shape and appearance of the lined up infantry show the real situation of the great army of the state of Qin. The officers can be recognized by their more elaborate hairstyles and the braid on their shoulders. The infantrymen show simpler hairstyles covered with hoods. Every face is different, expressing its own personality in these statues which are masterpieces of ancient Chinese sculpture.

385 bottom Here are stable boys from the first rows. The seriousness and determination in the faces of these servicemen contrasts with the inferiority of their condition, which we can see in the simplicity of their clothing and hairstyles.

or oval face and prominent chin of the inhabitants of modern Szechuan. Each figure has a truly realistic expression and its own individual features which differ from the other figures.

While the lines and modeling of the bodies of the statues are fairly simple, the heads are highly detailed. The eyebrows are treated with great care. The hair, usually in a topknot beneath a helmet or simple hood, is realistically styled as are the mustaches of many of the soldier. The bodies of the statues have a certain uniformity in styling, apparently due to the fact that they were usually hand-made on the spot, while the heads were designed from an initial sketch, to which the features of the face and expression were added later.

The statues represent different builds, ages, personalities and moods. Each figure seems to have his own character.

Traces of color on some of the statues indicate that after being baked in furnaces at a temperature of around 1,000 degrees Celsius the statues were painted with a variety of colors.

Although most of this color has been lost a few statues still have all their original coloring.

The statues represent not only the high

In this way, King Zheng intended his rule to mark the beginning of a new era and for this reason he placed the character for "shi", which means the first, in front of his title. He was therefore the first Huangdi in a dynasty which he viewed as lasting for 10,000 generations.

This did not, however, turn out to be the case. Instead, he reigned for only twenty years or so and was replaced by the much stronger Han dynasty (206-220 AD) although the reforms he introduced influenced Chinese history for over two thousand years. His fundamental objectives were the political and military unification of the whole of China and the centralization of power. He believed that the base of the united state rests on the fa, or law.

This meant that the base of the united state was the adoption of a very strict code of laws throughout the country, to guide the government of the ruler. This was an exceptionally modern concept.

Confucians believe that the ideal good ruler is a man with all the virtues.

Taoists believe the ideal ruler is one who did not rule. For the fa school the king would not apply his own will in an arbitrary way, but had the precise task of controlling the correct and fair application of the law.

The code of Qin, founded on the principle of

386 and 387 right A crossbow man is kneeling, about to shoot. As his body had to sustain the shock of enemy attacks, he was issued with heavy armor, leggings and square-toed shoes. The position of his hands on his right side show that original he held a real crossbow.

387 left A horseman and his mount. The braided hair covered with a hood, the simplicity of the armor and the single combat tunic shows this warrior was of a low rank. The bit and bridle are copper plate, standard in the state of Qin.

artistic levels and maturity reached by Chinese sculpture during the Qin period, but also establish a style which was to transform the sculpture of the period and develop as typical of Chinese plastic arts in later ages.

The warriors, horses, chariots and weapons in the trenches form a complete army, emphasizing the power and size of the force with which Qin Shihuang was able to bring about the unification of the empire.

In 221 BC King Zheng of the state of Qin took on the new title of Huangdi, which is usually translated as "August Emperor", a term which previously had been used only of sovereigns in the far distant past who, according to tradition, had contributed to the founding of Chinese civilization.

collective responsibility, was imposed throughout the empire to establish principles to which future rulers would adhere with the certainty that the law would protect subjects from the whims of the rulers.

Qin Shihuang's work of unification included the adoption of a set of measures of weight, capacity and length applicable throughout the empire as well as the

in today's cultural unity in China.
In addition, this leader put into effect a unification measure throughout the territory which created a single axle width for carts based on the measurements used in the state of Qin. It was probably these accomplishments that justified this emperor, despite his relatively short reign, being accompanied in death with his own powerful army.

388 bottom left This is an army charioteer as can be told from his helmet. He wears a breastplate above his combat uniform, leggings and square-toed shoes. The position of the right hand suggests that this figure originally held a real weapon, possibly a sword.

distribution of the circular coins used under his rule which became the only legal tender.

Another measure of unimaginable importance for the future of China was the unification of the writing system.

The letters used during the first period of Zhou (1066-221 BC), in the style called the Great Seal, had changed tremendously over time throughout the country so that scripts were significantly different from each other. Under the central government, the characters were simplified and rationalized to the style used in Qin, called the Little Seal, so that there was a single style of script throughout the empire.

This uniformity of writing despite different dialects in speech is a determining factor

In addition, of course, to illustrating the power of this great ruler, accompanied as so many rulers were into the afterlife with his own servants, the findings of this army illustrate once again the amazingly almost haphazard way in which many of our great archaeological finds are discovered. No one remembered that at one time a great terra-cotta army had been created and buried with a great emperor. It was just, as so often has been the case, chance that ordinary peasants at their ordinary work made a discovery that astonished the world.

388 right A cart horse with shaved mane and handsome tail. The horse has such a realistic expression it seems as if it is about to neigh.

389 The distinct features and elongated face of this figure show all the dignity of an officer, looking proudly to the front. Note the highly elaborate headgear with knotted ribbon under the chin. The armor and the ribbons on the breastplate show signs of high military rank.

390-391 and 392-393 Two perfectly equipped bronze chariots were found in perfect condition.

LUOYANG, THE CAVES OF LONGMEN

394-395 A partial front view of the complex of the caves of Longmen. In the foreground is the cave-temple of Fengxian, with an enormous statue of Buddha Amithaba in the center, accompanied by a bodhisattva. On the walls of the great hall and dug from the rock that form the central complex of the temple are two imposing figures of celestial guardians. The cave is reached by a ramp of stairs which winds through a series of niches dug at the edges of the main temples. On all the rocks of the Longmen complex, next to the main temples, numerous small sanctuaries were built on behalf of single donors.

395 top left On the right is standing one of the two great statues of the celestial guardians, 30 feet high. Giants with ferocious expressions are found in many Buddhist temples. Their role was to protect the Buddha from evil spirits. Next to this statue is that of the King of the Celestial Guardians, standing over a dwarf and holding a model of a stupa in his left hand. It was customary to place such guardians at the sides of the entrances to important houses.

About 10 miles south of the city of Luoyang in Henan in China is the cave-temple complex of Longmen. Work on the construction began in 494 AD, during the Northern Wei dynasty (386-534 AD) making use of the original rock clefts, and continued for over 400 years, under various dynasties. The complex extends for over a mile along the rock walls on the banks of the River Yi which is rich in a compact gray limestone particularly suitable for precise, detailed carving.

Over 97,000 statues of Buddha and *bodhisattva* were sculptured out of these walls in various sizes. The largest is over 60 feet high, the smallest is less than an inch. There are also 1,325 large and small caves, 750 niches, and 40 pagodas which together provide the most dramatic and significant evidence of the importance of devotion to Buddha in medieval China.

Buddhism emerged in China during the 3rd century BC. It is unlikely that any images of the Buddha were produced before this date. Research indicates that there was a flourishing Buddhist community in Luoyang by the end of the 2nd century AD and this community later became the center for Buddhism in the country. It was this community that drew up the first monastic rules and the construction of the Longmen complex can therefore be seen as a sign of the importance that the priesthood had acquired.

The construction of the grottoes can be divided into two stages. In the first, which lasted from the start of the Northern Wei to the Sui dynasty (581-618), there are still certain archaic elements in the sculpture. Since three-dimensional sculpture had not yet been developed the figures are all seen against a background so that they are seen in a front view only. The interiors of the grottoes are decorated with images along all the walls on a rich background with almost no space left uncovered. Endless rows of figures are shown with various degrees of realism, with long, angular bodies, thin waists, drooping shoulders, extremely long necks and narrow heads. The faces of the

395 bottom left The central statue of the Buddha in the Fengxian cave. The enormous size of the figure, almost 60 feet high, is softened by the face which is lit up with the hint of a smile, suggesting the sense of well-being typical of believers in the Buddha. The expression is intensified by the arched eyebrows above the eloquent eyes. The figure of the Buddha, seated in the traditional lotus position, blends in with the images of the bodhisattva that accompany it, presumably Avalokitesvara and Makasthamaprapta, making it one of the finest examples of Buddhist sculpture from the Tang period.

395 top right Detail of the wall with celestial guardians in the Fengxian cave, with images of Buddha dug from the rock. The small figures show a certain uniformity in their clothes and hairstyles but are distinguished from each other by their hand gestures.

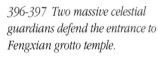

396-397 Two massive celestial guardians defend the entrance to Fengxian grotto temple.

398 top left A figure of a bodhisattva in the left wall of the Fengxian cave. The statue, 35 feet high, is an example of the Indian style in the Buddhist art of Longmen, with its rich drapes and precious pendants. The fixed nature of the standing position is softened by the movement of the folded right arm and the gesture of the hand.

statues have small mouths, eyes which are only narrow slits, high arched protruding eyebrows and earlobes, stretched as was the custom, at the side of pointed chins. The overall impression is of a light, almost fleeting beauty, innocence and an infantile purity that runs through all Chinese Buddhist sculpture of this period.

Typical of this first stage is the great halo, or nimbus, in the form of a leaf that forms the background to the seated or standing images of Buddha and bodhisattva. The most common images are of the historical Buddha, Sakyamuni, but as a result of the spread of the Mahayana Buddhist doctrine, according to which everyone can reach the condition of Buddha with the help of the bodhisattvas, beings who stop on their path toward enlightenment to assist common mortals along the same path, there are also thousands of bodhisattvas shown on the walls of the grottoes along with the various Buddhas in scenes illustrating the sacred writings.

With the spreading of the best-known of the *Sutras*, the story of the Lotus of the True Law, the figure of Bodhisattva Avalokitesvara was introduced to Longmen. In China this takes on the form of the only female figure from popular Chinese religion, Guanyin, the Buddha of Piety, often shown with a thousand eyes or arms. There are also many images of Buddha Amithaba, whose worship in China dates back to 386 AD. The second building stage began with the Sui dynasty and marks a true step forward in the history of Chinese Buddhist sculpture. It is in this period that isolated stone statues, treated in individual styles and showing a new degree of sensitivity, reflecting a more direct contact with the Indian style, appear. The body of the Buddha clad only in a light

398 bottom left Detail of the King of the Celestial Guardians in the right wall of the Fengxian cave. Unlike the figure of the assistant guardian alongside, this Celestial King shows full awareness of his function as defender of the Buddha in the severe but not unkind expression of his face and the dignity of his rank in the regal gesture of his left hand, which holds a stupa, symbol of the Buddhist faith.

drapery is undecorated except for a delicately carved circular halo with a luxurious leaf motif inside it. The bodhisattvas, also surrounded by a floral wreath influenced by the luxurious Indian styles, are shown wearing heavy jeweled ornaments, crowns, necklaces and pendants, symbolizing the gifts of rich donors. Along the bank of the river the first grotto, called Qian Xi, contains the Buddha Amithaba with two disciples, two bodhisattvas and the guardians. The three following grottoes, known as Binyang, were probably completed in 523 AD and are perhaps the most important examples of the mature rock sculptures of Longmen. The shrine, 25 feet long and 20 wide, is clearly designed with the main statue of Buddha, sculpted from the rock, against the 12 foot

398 right The Indian influence, showing a trace of Greek styling, can be seen in the precious diadem and refinement of the hairstyle framing the face of this contemplative bodhisattva.

399 The face of the assistant to the Celestial Guardian King, on the right wall of the Fengxian cave, is outstanding. Note the ferocious expression of the eyes, without pupils which, together with the hollow cheeks, makes this a fear-inducing mask. The left hand is raised in warning.

Luoyang

400 top left In the grotto of the Guyang, built in the reign of the emperor Xiaoming (488-528) of the Wei, various niches were dug which contain scenes of the day-to-day life of the Buddha and a number of bodhisattvas with their hands in significant gestures. The age of this grotto can be seen from both the archaic style of the figures which are typical of the first stage of Buddhist rock sculptures in China and the way in which the images overlap.

400 bottom left A detail of the north wall of the Guyang grotto. The repeated statues of Buddha in a variety of positions along the vault of the cave demonstrates intense devotion, expressed in a somewhat archaic way.

400-401 Here in the small niches in the southern wall of the Guyang cave episodes from the daily life of the Buddha are shown. They are enclosed in an architectural structure in Han style, which are enriched with festoons separating them from each other. Images of devotees worshipping the Buddha are also sculpted into the walls.

401 top right In the north wall of the Lianhua cave and in larger caves containing statues of the Buddha in various postures a number of small niches, holding figures of the Buddha alone or with two seated bodhisattvas, have been sculpted. The damaged faces of most of these show the hostility to Buddhism that is part of various periods in Chinese history.

401 bottom right The statue of the Buddha flanked by two bodhisattvas, standing on a lotus-shaped platform, is sculpted in the southern wall of the central grotto in the Binyang group and gives some idea of the artistic maturity of the Longmen sculptures. The central figures of the Buddha expresses the synthesis between the Chinese and Indian styles.

Tzi, the found of Taoism.

Following is the grotto of Fengxian Si, a large chamber dug from the rock which it is believed originally held a wooden temple of which no trace remains.

Inside there is a large Buddha with bodhisattvas off to the sides, still in excellent condition. Two heavenly guards, giants with ferocious expressions, are on the walls. These are found in many Buddhist temples and their role is to keep spirits hostile to Buddha away. Further south is the grotto of Wanfo Dong, excavated during the Tang

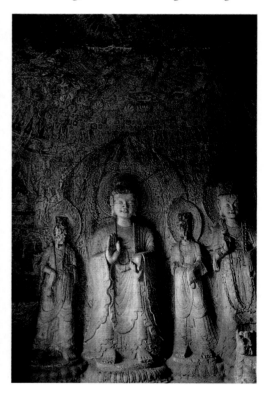

wide rear wall. Buddha is seated cross-legged on a step which is nearly 20 feet wide and is accompanied by statues of his disciples who are flanked by two enormous standing bodhisattvas. Against the side walls is a standing Buddha assisted by two bodhisattvas. The space in between, bordered by almond designs and haloes, is filled by rows of worshipping figures. On the opposite wall, at the sides of the door, is an almost life-sized effigy of the emperor to the left and the empress to the right along with a group of courtesans who represent donors to

this combination cave-temple.

The grotto of Lianhua Dong, which means "Lotus Flower", is distinguished by the lotus-shaped roof vault with the whirling movement of the apsaras, or heavenly dancers.

The Guyang cave is the oldest. On the side walls with their many niches we can see scenes from the everyday life of Buddha and the various bodhisattvas with their hands in various significant gestures. The most outstanding statue is that of the Buddha Maitreya which is believed to have been altered in the 17th century to look like Lao

period (618-907 AD) for the Empress Wu Tsetian. The name of this cave, "Ten Thousand Buddhas", comes from the fact that innumerable small statues of Buddha have been carved from the rock. There is also an image of Amithaba on a lotus-shaped pedestal supported by four giants, protectors of Buddhism.

Following the Tang dynasty little was added to this complex. Followers of Buddhism frequently suffered from persecution and the classes which had supported this religion turned away from it.

these houses. One of the best conserved, site number 117, consists of a large room with a central hearth and an antechamber for access and ventilation.

The mud and straw roof was held up by four robust wooden beams and was pierced to allow smoke to escape. From 850 AD onwards, in the Pueblo I phase, the Anastasi changed their living habits. They did not completely abandon the trench houses, but started to build houses above ground on the mesa. These new houses consisted of several rooms with a square floor plan. Originally they were built of dried clay and straw and later with regularly shaped baked bricks. As time passed, the number of rooms in these houses increased and they took on a complex structure, expanding to form villages later called pueblos by the Spanish. The economy and skills of the inhabitants of Mesa Verde, originally based

have been identified in Chapin Mesa, and not far from there was what must have been a type of reservoir in ancient times, today known as Mummy Lake.

According to some experts, however, this was not a lake at all, but a huge kiva used by the whole community for dancing and ceremonial purposes.

Evidence shows that in many cases the kivas were connected to structures similar to towers, whose purpose has still not been discovered. Among these are the Tower of the Cedar and a monumental complex with a double surrounding wall, perhaps a temple or mausoleum, known as the Temple of the Sun. However, the most impressive site in Mesa Verde is without doubt the Cliff Palace, an immense building built around 1200 AD in a sheltered area under the rock, containing 220 rooms and 23 kivas, and clearly housing several

412 This photograph shows a view of Cliff Palace, one of the biggest and most surprising rock villages in Mesa Verde. The houses are built over several floors among the rock walls. Many of the rooms have painted decorations.

413 left This photograph shows the rock village called Spruce Tree House. Its ideal position gave sun and light in the winter and many hours of shade in the summer.

on agriculture, grew thanks to trade. Pottery production reached high quality levels. In the course of the centuries the villages were transformed into towns, and around 1100 AD there was an enormous increase in the population of the Colorado Plateau. In the Mesa Verde National Park, most of the sites are distributed over two high plains separated by deep canyons. These are the Chapin Mesa and the Wetherill Mesa. Chapin Mesa had a large rural community, which led to the construction of twenty or so villages, made up of houses on several floors with a large number of rooms.

In spite of this change in dwelling habits, the Indians of the high plains never abandoned the trench huts completely. Instead, they transformed them into *kivas*, huge circular underground structures for ceremonial and religious use. Five kivas

hundred people.

Among the various cliff houses built by the Anastasi inside rock cavities, with their towers on square or circular bases, Cliff Palace is without doubt the most remarkable, and the first sight of it amazed the first explorers who reached the area at the end of the 19th century.

These fabled palaces, the many houses built on the rocky spurs, the towers and the kivas were completely abandoned after 1300 AD. We can only assume that the Anastasi were forced to leave by long years of drought and famine, but there is no clear evidence of this. Today, Mesa Verde with its 4,000 archaeological sites is a world heritage center of incalculable value where, according to the Indians, you can still hear the echoes of the dances and prayers of the ancestors.

413 top right The decoration on this beautiful vase with its rope motif dates to around 1100 AD and shows the heritage of the Anastasi of the Basket-making tradition.

413 bottom right Spruce Tree House is a village from the Pueblo III culture, inhabited between 1200

and 1300 AD. Probably the best preserved village in Mesa Verde, it contains 114 rooms and 8 kivas. In contrast to other sites, many roofs and terraces still remain today and the walls are decorated with painted plaster work.

414-415 The Anasazi rock village of Mesa Verde.

TEOTIHUACAN, THE CITY OF THE GODS

416-417 This photograph shows an impressive overall view of Teolihuacan, the huge city that dominated the high plain of Mexico and neighboring regions. It is not yet known what people built this city or developed its civilization. Imposing pyramid buildings, palaces and platforms flank the main street of the town, known as the Avenue of the Dead. The Aztecs told the European conquerors of the existence of Teotihuacan, or the City of the Gods.

416 bottom The Pyramid of the Moon, seen here, stands at the northern end of the long road known as the Avenue of the Dead and faces onto a large square, known as the Square of the Moon. This was the name given to the pyramid by the Aztecs, but it is not known for certain to which god it had been dedicated by the inhabitants of Teotihuacan.

The European conquerors who took control of the Aztec empire and its capital Teochtitlán in the 16th century learned of the existence of a mysterious ancient city, known by the local inhabitants as Teotihuacan, which means "the city of the gods". At the beginning of the colonial period several Spanish explorers visited the ruins of this city, which had probably been abandoned many centuries earlier. The Aztecs themselves considered Teotihuacan to be a mythical place, linked to the existence of ancestral cults. Friar Bernardino of Shagán relates in his chronicles that, according to the traditional stories of the people of the Mexican plateau the Fifth Era, or the period in which they found themselves living, began in Teotihuacan and many people visited the pyramids there which were dedicated to the Sun and Moon to take part in ceremonies and offer sacrifices. Later, other chroniclers went to the site, attracted by the aura of mystery that surrounded the ruins of the ancient city. The first excavations took place as early as 1617 under the leadership of the Mexican scholar Carlos Siguenza y Gángora. In 1865, Don Antonio Garcia Cubas carried out the first topographical survey of the

Teotihuacan area, and at the end of the 19th century the archaeologist Eduard Seler dedicated himself to the in-depth study of the art and architecture of the city, as well as to the religious iconography to be found on the wall paintings. A series of systematic excavation which was begun in 1917 and is continuing today revealed the enormity and architectural richness of Teotihuacan and its basic features but failed to solve its fundamental mysteries. We still do not know who built this great place, nobody knows in whose honor the great pyramids were built and how they were able to transform the original small ceremonial center into a metropolis that dominated the Mexican plateau for centuries and exerted its cultural influence on the rest of Indo-America.

The history of Teotihuacan began in the Pre-Classical period. The oldest archaeological layers, which date back to 150 BC, show evidence of the existence of a primitive trading center and a rural village in an excellent geographical position. The valley, surrounded by mountain chains and extensive plains, is rich in fertile land, lakes, wildlife and waterways. Beneath the main temple of Teotihuacan, the Temple of the Sun, an underground spring was found. In remote times it is believed this gave rise to a cult which linked to water and the caves, which were frequented throughout the centuries that followed. Around 100 BC, a terrible volcanic eruption destroyed the village of Cuicuilco, several hundred miles away and

417 bottom One of the most interesting artistic forms from Teotihuacan is the burial masks made in hard stone, like the one shown here. The eyes and teeth are made of bone, giving a considerable sense of realism to the object.

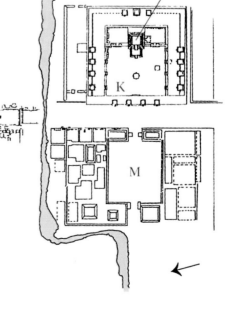

A Pyramid of the Moon
B Altar building
C Square of the Moon
D Palace of Quetzalpapalotl
E Avenue of the Dead
F Palace of the Sun
G Pyramid of the Sun

H Patio of the Four Small Temples
I Priest's Palace
J Viking Group
K Citadel
L Pyramid of Quetzalcoatl
M Gran Conjunto

418 top left Here can be seen a view of the patio inside one of the most distinctive buildings of Teotihuacan, the Palace of Quetzalpapalotl. The name literally means Quetzal Butterfly (a quetzal is a brilliantly colored bird) and refers to a god. Bas-reliefs of this god can be seen on the pillars of the courtyard.

it is believed that the survivors took refuge in Teotihuacan. This new ethnic and cultural influence gave considerable energy to the small agricultural center which was gradually transformed into a town. From 100 BC onward various monumental buildings were erected and Teotihuacan took on a role of major importance on the Mexican plateau and in the surrounding areas.

Today's visitor to the archaeological site,

418 bottom left The massive square-based pillars that support the central portico of the Palace of Quetzalpapalotl still have traces of the original painted decoration. The bas-reliefs on the stone slabs covering the columns have geometric motifs associated with the mysterious hybrid bird-butterfly god.

which is only 30 miles from Mexico city, will be struck by the huge size and imposing nature of it. It definitely deserves its title of "City of the Gods". As it appears today the city of Teotihuacan reveals how it appeared in the years between 200 and 650 AD, the centuries of its greatest splendor, during which it reached an area of almost ten square miles and had a population of 125,000. From the impressive stone structures and the terraces of the pyramid-shaped platforms which once supported temple buildings we can see how

Teotihuacan had been planned to satisfy all the requirements of the ruling classes as well as those of the common people and the way in which the town was laid out so that religious buildings existed side by side with state and civil ones. Two main streets divided the city into four square areas. One of these, the Avenue of the Dead, ran from south to north, ending in a huge square dominated by the famous Pyramid of the Moon, surrounded by stepped platforms. Not far away was the great Pyramid of the Sun, the biggest building in all of this part of the world after the pyramid of Cholula. The Avenue of the Dead intersected with the east-west axis, which was flanked by an architectural complex containing a number of buildings and known as the Citadel. A network of streets and avenues intersecting with each other at right angles divided up the various quarters which were originally made up of buildings of several stories. The inhabitants had constant running water, thanks to an efficient drainage system. The smaller pyramids were a new feature also found among other civilizations in this area, with one panel at a slope followed by another in oblique slab formation, known as *talud* and *tablero*. The citadel includes several interesting buildings, especially the Temple of Quetzalcoatl.

The outer walls of the pyramid are decorated with sculptures showing alternating monstrous creatures. These sculptures are of the Plumed Serpent, known as Quetzalcoatl by the Post-Classical populations of Mexico and Tlaloc, the God of Water and Fertility, with his long trunk-like nose. How important were these images in Teotihuacan? The presence of the Plumed Serpent gives an idea of the existence and age of this cult, later taken

418 top right This photograph shows another fine example of a Teotihuacan stone burial mask. Note that the features of the face, especially the mouth, show strong similarities with those on Olmec masks. These masks were placed over the faces of the high-ranking dead, to accompany and protect them on their final journey.

418 bottom right In this detail of one of the decorative panels on the patio of Quetzalpapalotl, we can see the bizarre imagery of the hybrid god, both bird and butterfly, which was worshipped here. Other mythological creatures, linked with maritime and fertility cults, can be found on the wall frescoes.

419 This photograph shows another detail of the Palace of Quetzalpapalotl. What we see is one of the almenas, a type of battlement at the top of the wall which contained the calendar symbol for the year.

Palenque

434 top The photograph shows a detail of the architectural complex of Palenque called the Palace although no one actually knows its original function. It takes the form of an inner courtyard, a four-sided patio reached by short staircases.

not been destroyed by fire or earthquake as had been believed by some earlier viewers but rather abandoned by its inhabitants and overgrown by vegetation. A few years later, in 1789, the king of Spain, Carlos III, sent Antonio del Rio, a soldier of fortune, to study these mysterious ruins in the jungle of Chiapas on his behalf. This expedition can be considered, in a sense, the start of archaeological surveys of the pre-Columbian world.

Later, the successor to the Spanish throne, Carlos IV, sent a certain Colonel DuPaix and the Mexican Luciano Castaneda on a mission to explore Palenque. In 1805 and 1806 these travelers visited the ruins and drew the main architectural features, drawings which were later published in Paris as *Antiquités Américaines*. During the 19th century, interest in the remains of Palenque spread throughout the Americas and Europe through the reports of several other respected explorers, including John Stephens and Frederick Catherwood. The main monuments in this ancient Mayan city are covered with inscriptions which have only recently been deciphered, enabling us to solve many of the mysteries that previously surrounded Palenque's history and that of its people. The results of these archaeological surveys show that the site of Palenque was occupied as early as the late Pre-Classic Period, between 150 and 250 AD. However, the city rose to its greatest cultural and architectural heights between 615 and 800 AD, when the most important monuments were built and the historic texts produced which contain the names and acts of the sovereigns who reigned over the city.

Today's visitors travel along a road which starts at the northern part of the urban area and leads to the Main Square, which is believed to be the heart of the ceremonial center. On the eastern side, this huge open space is dominated by what is called the Palace, a huge monumental complex. It is generally believed that the buildings forming this complex had some kind of a civic function, either housing the ruling elite or as an administrative center. This, of course, is by no means proven. The Palace consists of a high platform measuring about 250 feet long and about 200 feet wide topped by a complex of porticoed galleries. These galleries have false vaulted ceilings arranged around three larger interior courtyards. On the square pillars and the surfaces of the roofs we can see traces of the original bas-relief decoration, which was covered by multicolored stucco. The entire complex is dominated by a four-story tower. Some experts have suggested that this may have

434 bottom The structures that make up the Palace of Palenque consist primarily of porticoed galleries, whose outer walls were decorated with elegant bas-reliefs. This photograph shows one of the galleries with a false-vaulted ceiling. These areas may have been used for religious ceremonies.

434-435 This unusual
photograph shows an overall
view of the Palace of Palenque,
situated in the heart of the
ceremonial center surrounded
by the luxurious vegetation of
the jungle. The purpose of this
architectural complex is still a
mystery. It may have been used
for religious rituals. The Tower
is believed to have been an
astronomical observatory.

435 left This plaster tablet was
found in the central courtyard of
the Palace. It contains a graphic
symbol in Mayan script in the
form of a human head.

435 right This table, like the
previous one, was found in the
courtyard of the Palace of
Palenque. It contains four signs
from the Mayan script of the
Classical period, most of which
has now been deciphered.

*436 top This photograph shows an aerial view of a religious architectural complex at the northern end of the ceremonial center of Palenque, the so-called Northern Group.
It is a stepped platform topped by three sanctuaries.*

436 bottom This picture shows the top of one of the most important buildings in Palenque, the Temple of the Sun, built by the son of Pacal, Chan Balam, in 690 AD. Traces of the plaster bas-reliefs that adorned the roof lining and imposing top still remain.

been a watchtower but the most widely accepted theory at present is that it was an astronomical observatory.

On the southern side of the square, down from a hill still covered in dense tropical vegetation, is the most imposing sacred building of Palenque, the Pyramid of the Inscriptions, which is 120 feet high and formed by nine overlapping bodies. Three stone panels placed inside the upper temple and completely covered in sculpted hieroglyphs, forming one of the longest Mayan inscriptions found so far, gives the Pyramid its name.

A narrow staircase gives access to the temple which is at the top of the building. It is topped by a crest which is a typical architectural feature of the Classical period

in the Usumacinta Valley. In 1952, the Mexican archaeologist Alberto Ruz Lhuillier discovered a long staircase covered by a false vaulted ceiling. Starting at the sanctuary this led down to an underground crypt which was concealed just below the level of the square in front of the pyramid. This secret chamber, which had been completely unsuspected, even by the archaeologist himself and his assistants, contained a large stone sarcophagus with the remains of what had obviously been a high ranking figure.

Years later, following the deciphering of the Mayan texts, it was discovered that the remains were those of King Pacal, who ruled the city of Palenque from 615 to 683 AD, the year he died. The sarcophagus was

Palenque

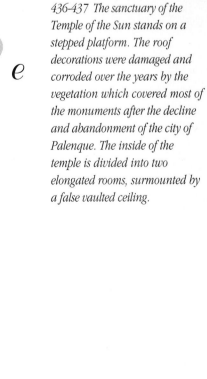

436-437 The sanctuary of the Temple of the Sun stands on a stepped platform. The roof decorations were damaged and corroded over the years by the vegetation which covered most of the monuments after the decline and abandonment of the city of Palenque. The inside of the temple is divided into two elongated rooms, surmounted by a false vaulted ceiling.

437 bottom One of the religious buildings of Palenque is Temple 18, with its typical terraced structure. Today, only some of the city's monuments have been freed from the spread of the tropical jungle.

438-439 The three sanctuaries in the 'North Group' rise above the vegetation at Palenque.

440 left The Temple of the Inscriptions is hidden almost in the thick tropical vegetation. A step staircase leads to the sanctuary at the top, where a porticoed entrance gives access to the vestibule and religious center. At the bottom of the staircase is a stone disk held up by four cylindrical supports which was a sacrificial altar.

440 top right The most important king of the city, King Pacal, Shield of Sun, was buried in a crypt beneath the floor of the Temple of the Inscriptions. The crypt was discovered in 1952 by the Mexican archaeologist Alberto Ruz. The stone sarcophagus that contained the remains of the dead king was covered with a slab weighing five and one-half tons.

440 bottom right In this photograph can be seen the steep narrow staircase inside the Pyramid of the Inscriptions, leading to the crypt in which King Pacal was buried in 682 AD. The ceiling has a typical false vaulted structure.

441 This beautiful stucco head, executed with great skill and found in the burial chamber of Pacal, is almost certainly a portrait of the sovereign as a young man. Inscriptions said that Pacal ruled over the city of Palenque for about 70 years and was an enlightened ruler.

closed by a slab of stone which weighed well over five tons. The stone itself was decorated by an elaborate bas-relief. At the center of the scene is the figure of the dead king, shown as he fell into Xibalbá, kingdom of the deceased, symbolized by the Terrestrial Monster. Behind him is the Tree of Life whose branches take the form of serpents' heads. A two-headed snake with wide open jaws and a fantastic bird with the features of a reptile is perched on the top. Included in the sarcophagus were jewels and ornaments and the fragments of a fabulous jade mask which had apparently been placed over the face of Pacal. It was later patched together. Two stucco heads that were found in the burial chamber give us a portrait of Pacal, the most famous and honored sovereign of Palenque.

This discovery, of course, was important not only for itself but also because it proved that the Mayan pyramids in the Classic Period were not only used as temples but also were funeral monuments for the ruling class.

In addition to the Palace and the Pyramid of the Inscriptions, the ceremonial center of Palenque contains other groups of buildings of importance, such as the Northern Group, the Temple of the Count, and the stadium used for the ritual ball game. A basic role is played by the so-called Group of the Cross. This is formed by three temple buildings which are smaller in size than the Pyramid of the Inscriptions. They have been given the names of the Temple of the Cross, the Temple of the Leafy Cross and the Temple of the Sun. These buildings were built between 672 and 692 for the sovereign Chan Bahlum, "Jaguar Serpent", the son of and successor to Pacal. They are located down from the hill below the Palace. All these are pyramids with their upper sections covered with an attic roof topped by a complex crest which was originally decorated in modeled, multicolored stucco. The modern names of the three monuments come from the iconographic designs on the friezes which run along the walls. These are linked to Mayan cosmological themes which were largely misinterpreted by the first explorers of Palenque. The Temple of the Sun and the

Temple of the Leafy Cross contain a number of interesting inscriptions on the dedicatory rites of Chan Bahlum, who deliberately chose a time when the moon, Saturn, Jupiter and Mars were in conjunction and in an unusual position in relationship to the constellation Scorpio for the consecration of the temples. Although Palenque is a major tourist attraction in Mexico, a great part of it remains to be brought to light. It can be assumed that in the future many more extraordinary discoveries will be made here, raising new questions and answering old ones concerning Mayan civilization.

TIKAL, PYRAMIDS IN THE FOREST

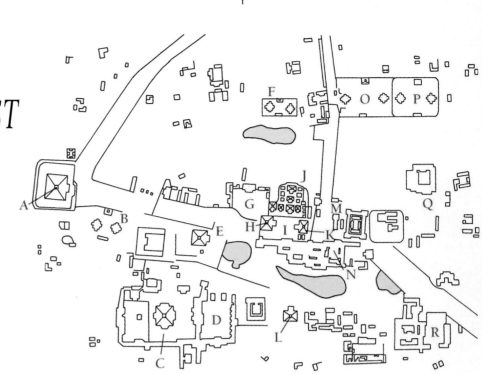

A Temple IV
B Complex N
C Southern Acropolis
D Square of the Seven Temples
E Temple III

F Complex O
G Western Square
H Temple II
I Great Square
J Northern Acropolis
K Temple I

L Temple V
M Eastern Square
N Central Acropolis
O Complex R
P Complex Q
Q Group F
R Group G

At the end of the 19th century, Alfred Maudslay and Teodor Maler photographed the main monuments of a Mayan city found in the tropical forest of Petán, a region of modern Guatemala. This was Tikal. At the start of the 20th century, work was begun on tracing out the plan of the site and examining its mysterious inscriptions. In the 1950s, the University of Pennsylvania began the first excavations. Even though only part of the city has been brought to light, the remains of Tikal are extremely impressive for their huge size and the dizzying heights of the pyramids, unique in the Mayan area. These surprising constructions, the latest archaeological survey indicates, were erected based on the architectural models of Cerros and Uaxactun, where the oldest Mayan pyramids are located, dating back to the Late Pre-Classical Period.

The recent deciphering of the inscriptions on Tikal's many stone columns has revealed significant aspects of the history and ruling dynasties of this city, which is located in a strategic position among important roads and waterways. The oldest stone column in Takal, number 29 and considered to be the

442 top left The Pyramid of the Lost World has an imposing, massive structure similar to the ancient pyramids of the Pre-Classical Period.

442 bottom left This temple, which is between the Pyramid of the Lost World and the group of Seven Temples, has a large crescent on top, typical of the architecture of Tikal.

442 top right This incense holder with its image of a priest or a god holding a skull was found in a tomb.

442 bottom right Four steep staircases lead to the top of the great Pyramid of the Lost World, which stands at the southern end of the ceremonial center of Tikal.

443 From the endless stretch of tropical forest emerge, in all solemnity, the Pyramid of the Lost World and Temple IV.

444 top This photograph shows a view of the Great Square, heart of the ceremonial center of Tikal, dominated by the imposing structure of Temple I. The area is scattered with stones, rich in bas-reliefs and inscriptions. Many of the texts on these have been deciphered.

444 center Here is a view of the ceremonial center of Tikal. In the foreground is the architectural complex of the Central Acropolis and, in the background, Temple I and the Square. The archaeological site of Tikal, one of the largest in Meso-America, contains about 3,000 monuments, built at various times.

Tikal
Tikal

oldest in the entire Mayan area, has been dated to 292 AD, the start of the Classical Period. The most recent, number 11, is dated at 869 AD. We now know that at the end of the 9th century the Mayan cities of the low-lying plains were suddenly and rapidly abandoned and the period between these two dates corresponds to the height of Tikal's political and cultural importance. In recent studies, German archaeologists have shown that Tikal, along with Calakmul, ruled over the other Mayan city-states. The columns scattered throughout the ceremonial center were erected roughly every 20 years, and have passed down to us the names and bas-relief portraits of the rulers who contributed to the political, economic and cultural growth of Tikal. Among these are rulers given the names of Jaguar's Paw, Stormy Sky and Mr. Cocoa. The texts tell us that these rulers conquered many enemies, took control of neighboring territories and formed diplomatic alliances based on the payments of tributes and the arrangement of marriages. Leida's Plate, a tiny jadeite jewel found in the city, contains an inscription referring to a ruler, Bird Zero Moon, whose image is etched on the other side. In Tikal, as in Palenque, the pyramids served as supports for the temple buildings

444 bottom The huge complex of the Central Acropolis, seen here, is made up of a series of terraced platforms used to support the religious buildings. It faces onto the Square, in front of the Northern Acropolis, and is flanked by the large Twin Pyramids.

444-445 Temple I stands near the Central Acropolis and is about 165 feet high. A steep staircase leads to the sanctuary whose center is divided into three rooms with false vaulted ceilings. The summit of the temple is decorated with a dizzying crescent, a typical element in Tikal architecture.

446-447 This is the Central Acropolis at Tikal.

and the cemetery, a sacred site containing the burial chambers of the ruling elite. Like the tomb of Pacal, the burial sites of Tikal also contained precious burial treasures including painted pottery, masks and jade jewels. These objects are precious evidence of the prestige enjoyed by the ruling classes as well as the extremely high levels of skill displayed by the craftsmen working at the court. The part of the ceremonial center which has been freed from the jungle and brought into the light occupies an area of more than six square miles and contains about 3,000 monuments. It had at least two huge reservoirs which contained the city's water supply. One of the oldest buildings is the one known as "of the Lost World" which is located in the southern part of the city. Its huge structure is similar to others from the

Late Pre-Classical Period. Most of the buildings date from 400 to 800 AD, the period of Tikal's greatest splendor. What is most surprising, perhaps, about this town is the height of the pyramids. Temple IV reaches a height of over 200 feet and its summit can be seen emerging from the green canopy of the jungle from quite a distance away. Here more than ever the Mayans attributed the role of "artificial mountain" to the pyramids, which made them a way for man to draw nearer to the gods. In the photographs taken at the start of the 19th century, the pyramids appear to be completely covered in earth, vegetation and rubble. Temple IV is similar in structure to the twin temples I and II which are situated at opposite sides of the Great Central Square. They are step pyramids with a long, steep

staircase in the façade, which leads directly to the sanctuary. The sanctuary consists of a simple central section with a false vault which is topped by an impressive crescent. The cultural influence of Teotihuacan is often present in the use of the architectural modules of the talud and tablero. The Square, believed to be the heart of the ceremonial center, is surrounded by numerous architectural structures, including terraced platforms which originally supported the religious buildings, spacious courtyards, groups of palaces used as the residences and ceremonial centers of the ruling classes, and more modest residences for the common people. The most famous terraced platforms are undoubtedly the Central Acropolis and the Northern Acropolis. In the 9th century AD, when Tikal was abandoned, this gigantic platform, 300 feet

448 top The scene painted on this multicolored vase from Tikal shows a high ranking figure with an elaborate feathered headdress seated comfortably on a type of sofa. A number of signs which make up a text are near the mouth.

448 bottom This vase too is decorated with a painted scene showing the life at court. A figure kneels obsequiously before a dignitary, perhaps a king, seated on a throne. It is interesting to notice the contrast between the soberness of the clothing and the elaborate, plumed multicolored headdresses. In the top left are a number of graphic signs.

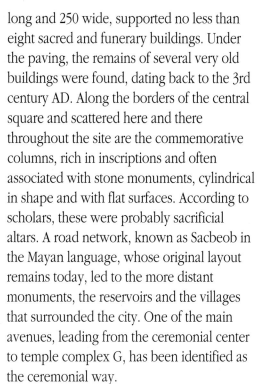

long and 250 wide, supported no less than eight sacred and funerary buildings. Under the paving, the remains of several very old buildings were found, dating back to the 3rd century AD. Along the borders of the central square and scattered here and there throughout the site are the commemorative columns, rich in inscriptions and often associated with stone monuments, cylindrical in shape and with flat surfaces. According to scholars, these were probably sacrificial altars. A road network, known as Sacbeob in the Mayan language, whose original layout remains today, led to the more distant monuments, the reservoirs and the villages that surrounded the city. One of the main avenues, leading from the ceremonial center to temple complex G, has been identified as the ceremonial way.

During the Late Classical Period, Tikal probably had a population in the region of 10,000, making it the largest of the Mayan city-states, and it is not difficult to believe that it reigned supreme over the other urban centers, which were probably smaller and less wealthy. The bas-relief portraits of the rulers, usually in profile, as well as the inscriptions and the rich burial treasures, give us an idea of what these aggressive, powerful people were like. The inscriptions describe sacrifices of enemies defeated in battle and self-mutilation by rulers and priests who, after reaching a trance through taking hallucinogenic substances, stabbed various part of their bodies to let the blood flow out. The purpose of this type of rite was to bring the individual into contact with the gods and to offer the gods gifts of human blood, the

448-449 Temple II, opposite its twin, Temple I, on the square, has a three-level pyramid structure and a high crescent on top, as do the other temples of Tikal.

449 top This photograph shows one of the many stones in the Square of Tikal. The high ranking figure is shown in bas-relief, unlike in Copán, where the stones were sculpted in three dimensions.

vital blood which satisfied and nourished them. From the images, we can see the clothing, jewelry, weapons and head-dresses of kings and warriors. Female figures are extremely rare, appearing only in references to marriage contracts. For as yet unknown reasons, no columns were found that date after 869 AD. This great metropolis that flourished in the luxuriant, fertile region of Petán began a rapid decline and was abandoned, although the reason why remains a mystery. No traces of violent destruction, for instance, have been found. Perhaps there was a sudden decline in trade, impoverishing the city and its surrounding villages. Or, more probably, the absolute power exerted by the monarchy over the people and the inhabitants of the other centers was destroyed by military rebellions or internal civil war. Tikal, like other Mayan centers of the low-lying plains, disappeared from the history of Indo-America, until its pyramids were rediscovered, covered in rubble and overgrown with vegetation.

449 center Pyramid Q is one of the many stepped structures with temple functions in the religious area of Tikal. In the foreground are a group of memorial stones.

449 bottom The Northern Acropolis gives an overall architectural effect that is symmetrical and organic, despite the fact that it has structures built at different times, often on top of older buildings.

449

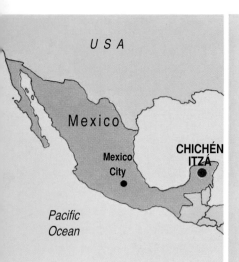

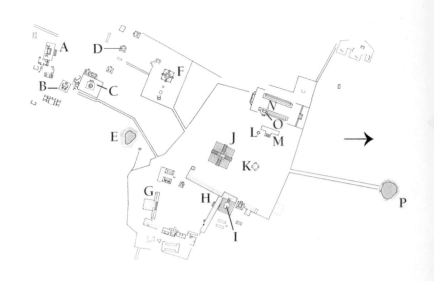

CHICHÉN ITZÁ,
THE CITY OF THE GREAT WELL

A House of the Nuns
B Temple of the Painted Reliefs
C Caracol (Observatory)
D Casa Colorada
E Cenote
F Tomb of the High Priest
G Covered market
H Group of the Thousand Columns
I Temple of the Warriors
J Castillo
K Platform of Venus
L Platform of the Eagles
M Tzompatli
N Great ball game Court
O Temple of the Jaguars
P Sacred Cenote

In the 16th century, the Spanish bishop Diego de Landa, who had been given the task of converting to Christianity the Mayan peoples of the Yucatán in what is now Mexico, learned that these people regularly made pilgrimages to their own sacred place. Here, near the ruins of an ancient city was a huge natural cavity which apparently had been worshipped by the local inhabitants for centuries. In his report, De Landa wrote with horror that this was a place of human sacrifice. Here people were thrown alive into the deep dark waters of this cavity, which was called cenote, or deep rock pool, by the Spaniards, a word which was a corruption of the Mayan word dzonot.

The bishop discovered that these human sacrifices were made as part of an extremely ancient cult linking water and fertility. The ruins that were around the well belonged to one of the ancient Mayan cities which had not been entirely abandoned and forgotten. This city is Chichén Itzá which, in the Yucatán language, means Cenote of the Itzá and the Itzá were the people who had inhabited the area for many centuries. In 1814 the explorers John Stephens and Frederick Catherwood visited the area and after drawing the most spectacular buildings began the first archaeological surveys. American scholars continued the surveys and, in 1900, Edward Thompson, one of the best-known archaeologists, continued this work, even going so far as to dive into the sacred pool.

460-461 This photograph shows two famous temples in Chichén Itzá. On the left is the Temple of the Jaguars and on the right the Pyramid of the Castillo. In the foreground is a large serpent's head.

461 top This stone disk is set in a wall of the playing field area. The bas-relief skull expresses the concept of death and sacrifice that were part of the ritual ball game.

461 top center The Temple of the Jaguars in Chichén Itzá contains a porticoed hall with an elegant statue of a jaguar, a sacred animal for the Mayans.

461 bottom center Inside the temple at the summit of the Castillo are two stone monuments typical of the Post-Classical Period, the Chac Mool, in the foreground, which was used as a sacrificial altar, and the Throne of the Jaguars, at the rear of the building.

461 bottom The field for the ball game in Chichén Itzá is the largest in Indo-America. On the eastern side it is overlooked by the structure of the Temple of the Jaguars.

462-463 The Castillo is one of the most famous Mesoamerican pyramids.

Regular excavations, begun in the 1920s by Sylvanus Morley, revealed numbers of amazingly grandiose buildings which were rescued from the advancing vegetation of the forest.

Today, although Chichén Itzá has still not revealed all its secrets, it is one of the most famous archaeological sites in the Yucatán and the Mayan world.

It's important to take a look at this city's history before viewing its remains. It is situated between the modern cities of Merida and Cancún. At the end of the Classic Period, between 800 and 950 AD, when the Mayan cities of the low plains of Mexico fell into a stage of decay and abandonment, a group of Mayan peoples known as the Itzá or Chontál, who were strongly influenced by the culture of Northern Mexico, established a town of modest size whose importance rested on the cult of the sacred Cenote. According to the data which has come from the various archaeological investigations and what

historical information is available, a new group of people, the Toltecs, arrived in Chichén Itzá at the end of the 10th century AD.

These invaders came from Tula, the city that had ruled over the Mexican plateau for several centuries following the fall of Teotihuacan. Several Toltec histories state that around 987 AD, under the leadership of the ruler Ce Acatl Topilzin, who had been removed from his throne by his brother Tezcatlipoca, a group of inhabitants left Tula and, after a long journey through Mexico, reached the Yucatán. Here they settled in Chichén Itzá which became a new capital and where magnificent buildings were built. Both sources and historical tradition linked Ce Acatl Topilzin with Quetxalcoatl, the mythical Plumed Serpent whose worship and iconography permeate the monuments of Chichén Itzá. The Maya of the Yucatán were persuaded to worship this new god which had been brought to them by the Toltec colonists, and this religion took over from the ancient cult of ancestor worship. The new religion was called Kukulkán, a word meaning Quetzal-feathered serpent. (A quetzal is a vividly feathered South American bird.)

The oral history of the flight of Ce Acatl from Tula, sent into exile by his brother with his followers, is borne out by what has been discovered through archaeology. It seems that around 1000 AD Chichén Itzá was transformed into a very large urban center, rich in monuments which clearly illustrate the combining of the Mayan culture of the late Classic Period with that of the Toltecs. A strong militaristic influence in the ruling class can be seen in the local artistic expressions, in contrast to that of the Mayan cities of the low plains

465 top *This photograph gives us an idea of the great size of the Temple of the Warriors in Chichén Itzá. The staircase, preceded by the colonnade, is overlooked by the somewhat disturbing Chac Mool.*

retain its own cultural identity. Archaeological information seems to indicate that the rulers of Chimu allowed the various urban centers to enjoy a certain economic independence, although the administrative power was centralized. The main reason for this centralization was probably to handle the distribution of water and consequently the agricultural system which, together with fishing and crafts, was the most important economic resource. Accounts tell us that in spite of both Incan and Spanish conquests the Chimu dynasty remained in existence until 1602.

At the height of its splendor, from 1300 AD onward, the kings of the Chimu appointed the town of Chan Chan the capital. They transformed what had been a modest town, dating back to the late Wari period, into a genuine metropolis. Its ruins, which cover an area of almost eight square miles, would

brick walls decorated with niches and stuccoed friezes, many of which were frescoed, showing fish, birds, half human-half animal figures and geometric motifs, undoubtedly symbols of religious ideology. Although the remains of the area of Chan Chan leaves much to be desired as it was robbed and despoiled many times over the centuries, no visitor can help being impressed by the originality of the architectural style and the elegance of the decorations, similar to arabesques, an element that is quite unique in the Pre-Columbian world. Here, just as in Nazca, Tiahuanaco and other sites, a variety of different and often quite contradictory theories have been developed to explain the remains, especially in the case of the question of the function of the nine citadels, gigantic and isolated from each other. Perhaps a dignitary, known as a curaca in

platforms, one 14 feet high and the other 10 feet high. The structure takes its name from the bas-reliefs on the walls. At the center is a two-headed serpent, perhaps a symbol of water and fertility, associated with other serpent-shaped creatures which have yet to be finally interpreted. The style is similar to the stuccoed friezes that decorate the walls in the citadels of Chan Chan, and the symbols are very similar to those seen on the fabrics, the simple pottery and the gold and silver vessels. The Chimu craftsmen were highly skilled in the working of precious metals, producing items of extraordinary quality. At the end of the 15th century, when Chan Chan was despoiled and abandoned by the Inca army, the sovereigns of Cusco forced the most highly skilled goldsmiths and metallurgists to continue their work at the court, where they continued to work until the Spanish conquest.

suggest that it was the largest city in Pre-Columbian America. The structure of the town was extremely complex and quite original. Nine walled areas have been identified, considered by some scholars to have been citadels, surrounded by walls up to almost 24 feet high and just a little less than a mile long. Other experts use the term palaces rather than citadels to describe these areas, with the terms understood in the broadest sense as referring to buildings similar to medieval courts. Each of these fortified units contained streets, residential quarters, perfectly irrigated gardens, cemeteries, reservoirs, temples and small cell-like areas for purposes that have yet to be identified.

The most important state or ceremonial buildings can be recognized by their elegant architectures. These buildings have adobe

the local language, was at the head of each of these, as a representative of the king. But there is another theory which suggests that each citadel may have been the headquarters of the members of a specific social class, none of whom were allowed to mix with the others, so that they were forced to live their lives separated from each other by these solid walls. Near the urban complex of Chan Chan, other important structures have been found which are unique to the Chimu civilization. These include artificial platforms known as Huacas, a word which comes from the Spanish for "sacred", due to their original function as places of worship. The most famous of these are the Huaca Esmeralda and the Dragón, which was restored in the 1960s. This is a structure consisting of a surrounding wall within which there are two superimposed

472 The thick adobe walls of the Tshudi citadel have diamond-shaped niches and bas-relief decorations.

472-473 and 473 top left Not far from Chan Chan are the impressive ruins of the Huaca del Dragon decorated with complicated scenes of warriors and mythical creatures.

473 top right This splendid golden mask shows the most important god worshipped in the coastal area of northern Peru during the 2nd Intermediate Period.

It is Nylamp, the deified hero from the sea, with the eyes of a bird. There are various examples of this type of mask, most from the ceremonial center of Batan Grande.

474-475 The picture shows in detail the unusual anthropomorphic low-relief decorations in the clay of the 'Huaca of the Dragon'.

OLLANTAYTAMBO, STRONGHOLD OF THE INCAS

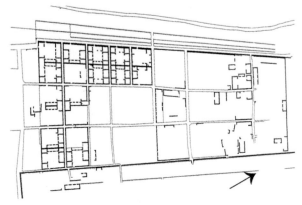

Plan of the grill-pattern road layout of the town. The remains of the houses are in black.

482-483 As in Sacsayuaman and Pisac, at Ollantaytambo, too, one of the famous Fortified Sites of the empire of Tahuantisuyu with vast walls and temple structures, built at a height of almost 10,000 feet, forms a spectacular architectural complex that dominates the valley below.

482 top This photograph shows a wall of the Main Temple, formed of enormous blocks perfectly cut and fitted together. In the center is an unfinished double-pillared portal.

483 top On the back wall of this room big shelves, carved from rock, can be seen. They once held the roof beams.

483 top center These imposing walls, formed from pink stone blocks, are the remains of the Main Temple, one of the religious buildings of Ollantaytambo.

483 bottom center One of the architectural features unique to Ollantaytambo can be seen in the remains of the Temple of the Sun, a group of six pink porphyry rectangular monoliths joined together with stone wedges to form a huge wall. On the stone are decorations similar to the staircase motif of Tiahuanaco.

483 bottom This unusual architectural structure which is near the Ollantaytambo is called the Bath of Nusta. It is a fountain, probably used in ritual bathing, cut out of a single block of stone four feet high and eight feet wide. Note the elegant cornice cut from the rock, decorated with the staircase motif.

Sacsayuaman is not the only massive fortress in the Cuzco area. There are other similar sites, always with their own air of mystery. One of the most famous of these is Ollantaytambo, on a slope at the entrance to the Sacred Valley, a couple of dozen miles from the Inca capital. The Spaniards wrote that Ollantaytambo, together with Pisac, was one of the strategic places from which it was possible to control the main road to Cuzco. Here, too, the imposing nature of the structures and their enigmatic appearance amazes the beholder. The lowest part of the site contained an urban settlement organized in the same Inca style that we can see in Cuzco and elsewhere, with a series of neighboring kanchas occupying a huge four-sided area on the low flood plain of the river. Above this, at the top of a rocky spur, are the remains of massive walls, whose construction was probably interrupted by the arrival of the Europeans. These walls consist of six monoliths in red porphyry, over 12 feet high, connected by very thin vertical plates in the same material. The façades of these monoliths show strange protuberances whose meaning is still unknown. On the central one is a bas-relief showing the staircase motif, similar to the one found on the stones in the site of Tiahuanaco. Here, too, it is impossible to say for certain whether or not the building is a fortress. As in Sacsayuaman, it has been suggested that the site was occupied by a temple dedicated to the sun and protected by surrounding walls. These remains, like many others from the Inca civilization, show that these were a people with a rich material culture, a wealth of knowledge and a set of religious beliefs, all of which was brusquely interrupted. Understanding and true knowledge of this people, despite the efforts of experts in many fields, may continue to elude modern man. In his writings, Garcilazo de la Vega, one of the most important witnesses to life in the court of the last of the Incas, describes some of the magical and esoteric aspects that filled this place, whose name means "The Place of

484-485 *One of the dominant features of Ollantaytambo is the terracing and staircases that climb the steep slopes. The photograph shows the remains of houses, originally covered with sloping roofs.*

484 bottom *In Quechua, Ollantaytambo means "The Place to Rest". As in Sacsayuaman, this monumental complex was a fortified religious center rather than a military outpost.*

Ollantaytambo

485 left The great trapezoidal door shown here, a typical feature of Incan architecture, is the entrance to the Main Temple. Many of the buildings at the summit of the archaeological site are unfinished, as they were abandoned when the Spaniards arrived in 1536.

485 right Another photograph of the Main Temple.

486-487 The cyclopic walls are made from perfectly cut and set blocks that reveal the high architectural and technical skills achieved by the Inca people. These are also seen in other centers in Ollantaytambo, such as Pisac and Sacsahuaman.

the Rest". It would appear, for example, that the inner organs of the dead rulers were buried at Ollantaytambo once these had been extracted from the embalmed body. And according to tradition a golden statue was built in memory of each sovereign after his death. At the time of the Conquest, there was an important war. In 1536, the king Manco Inca succeeded in not only fleeing from the army of Francisco Pizarro at Ollantaytambo but also in defeating it during his attempt to reconquer the empire and his power, after withdrawing from the city of Cuzco. Access to the fortress is by a steep stone staircase built into the incline. To the right, we can admire sixteen terraces, while on the other side there is a series of huge walls which enclose most unusual structures, some of which have been described by scholars as

Terrace-Observatories.
In the highest sectors of the Alacenas is the so-called Chincana, an enclosure built with large stone blocks, which probably reached a number of underground galleries. Today, archaeologists who have worked on this remarkable group of structures and who have studied the building techniques used to construct them tend to believe that the quarry from which the stone was taken was on the opposite bank of the River Vilcanota, about five miles from the village of Cachiquata. This theory assumes that the people of the time had both the knowledge and the high technological level necessary for the movement of large blocks up and down rocky inclines and across the river. There is one theory that the course of the river was perhaps diverted to make the work easier.

MACCHU PICCHU, THE LOST CITY

Among the many outstanding remains that tell us of the power of the last Indian civilization of the Andes, the Incas, the most amazing are those of Macchu Picchu, which is situated in an area that is almost inaccessible and virtually impossible to enter.

While the town of Cuzco, of which only a few fragments of walls and foundations survived the Spanish conquest, is known to have been the capital of the empire, mystery still surrounds Macchu Picchu and we know neither when its massive constructions were built nor what functions they served. The site was forgotten for four centuries, and only rediscovered in 1911 by the American architect Hiram Bingham. The ruins of Macchu Picchu are about 70 miles northwest of Cuzco at a height of over 9,000 feet, between two Andean peaks, known as the Young Peak (Huayna Picchu) and the Old Peak (Macchu Picchu). When we visit this site, we can recognize the imperial style of the other Incan centers, although here the surroundings are very different as it is set among the luscious vegetation irrigated by the River Urubamba that thunders through the valley below. For many years scholars have searched for explanations as to why the Inca rulers would build such a majestic complex in this hot, humid area at the edge of the Amazon rain forest.

Perhaps it was to protect the inhabitants of Cuzco from the pressure of the warlike peoples who lived in these regions, in which case it would have been built as a fortress, a strategic center with a truly eccentric structure.

Another theory is that Macchu Picchu was a kind of giant convent used to house the Virgins of the Sun, young foreign women whose purpose was to satisfy the desires of the Inca ruler.

Others believe the complex was built to

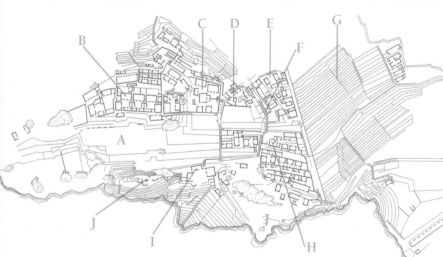

A Main Square
B Sector of the Three Doors
C Sector of the Stonemasons
D Sector of the Prisons
E Sector of the People
F Stairway of the Fountains
G Terraces
H Sector of the Torreón
I Temple of the Three Windows
J Intihuatana

hide King Manco, who was placed on the throne by the Spaniards as a puppet ruler after the betrayal and death of Atahualpa. In 1536 Manco rose up against the conquistadors and was forced to flee. Many legends handed down to modern times speak of the Last City of the Incas which may refer to Macchu Picchu or another fortress, hidden forever in the tropical forest.

Recent studies have led to some interesting new hypotheses about the function of the site, such as as a place of worship linked to

488

488 left This unusual altar, unique to the Inca world, bears witness to the skill of this people in the art of stone cutting.

488 right Walls, houses and staircases leading from one terrace to another are among the outstanding features of Macchu Picchu, an Inca site whose purpose is still not known.

488-489 The famous site of Macchu Picchu stretches over a mountain ridge linking "Old Peak" (Macchu Picchu) to "Young Peak" (Huayna Picchu). Its splendid location and extraordinary architecture, blending in perfectly with the landscape, make it the most fascinating archaeological site in Peru.

489 bottom The many terraced levels over which the outer sector of Macchu Picchu extends were probably used for agriculture. Some experts, however, believe the structure has other meanings which are not yet known.

490-491 This is an unusual view of Machu Picchu.

492 top This photograph shows a view of the huge non-urban structure of Macchu Picchu, considered to be the agricultural sector, with a number of terraces stretching along the slope.

492 bottom The religious sector of the town of Macchu Picchu contains buildings for worship including the Temple of the Three Windows, the Main Temple and the Intihuatana Monument (in the picture).

the observation of the stars. For the moment both clues and theories are limited, but research continues.

The architecture of Macchu Picchu shows the extraordinary way in which the human settlement adapted to the natural features of the site.

There are no more than 200 buildings, arranged on spacious parallel terraces and organized around a vast central square, which is also divided into various levels and oriented east-west, dividing the city into two sectors, each on a natural summit. The quarters, known as kancha in Quechua, are narrow in shape, elongated and divided in such a way as to take maximum advantage of the space offered by the terraces.

These, outside the inhabited areas, were used for agriculture and we can presume that there were also rural huts and settlements there, now vanished as they would have been built from perishable materials.

Sophisticated irrigation channels kept the crops watered and various stone staircases on the sides of the walls led to different levels of the structures. The two sectors of Macchu Picchu presumably had residential and ceremonial-religious functions respectively.

In the ceremonial western section, one structure that stands out is El Torreón, a massive semi-circular tower with windows, similar to the lookout towers that can be seen all through Europe.

Another famous example of a building of this kind from the Inca period was the Coricancha of Cuzco, which contained the Temple of the Sun and the Golden Garden, upon whose walls the modern Santo Domingo is built. The rock that supports the Torreón has been dug out and has the appearance of a burial chamber. For this reason, the place was called the Royal Mausoleum, even though there is nothing to prove that a person of high rank is buried there.

Another ceremonial building was probably the Temple of the Three Windows, so-called because of the three great trapezoid niches built into it.

An even bigger sacred complex is the Intihuatana, a word meaning "The place where the sun is kept prisoner". At the top of this group of buildings, at the center of a kind of patio, is a granite monolith, considered by some to be simply an usnu, the sacrificial altar to be seen in all the Inca centers, while others believe it to be a sundial, a theory that supports the belief that Macchu Picchu was the site of an important astronomical observatory connected with the cult of the Sun God, but once again it is impossible to say anything with mathematical certainty.

If we cross the great square, leaving the ceremonial part of the city behind, we reach the northeastern section, believed to have been the residential quarter.

Each quarter has been given a different name, according to the functions it is believed it performed from the architectural elements found there. So we have the quarters of the Three Doors, the Stonemasons and the Prisons. Wandering up and down the narrow streets is an impressive experience. Most of the houses were of one story only, had sloping roofs and were fitted with four-sided doors and windows that narrowed toward the top, probably to create a kind of balance with the weight of the architecture.
The structure of these modest buildings

492-493 The imposing, circular building, known in Spanish as the Torreón, reminds us of the lookout towers seen on European castles. Here, however, some experts believe it may be an astronomical observatory or a temple dedicated to the cult of the Sun.

493 bottom The so-called Sector of the Stonemasons is a group of small, modest houses with windows, believed to be the town's crafts center.

494 top left In the eastern quarter of Macchu Picchu, near an unusual building at the top of a spur of rock, is what some experts believe is a small fountain cut out of the rock. Other experts believe, however, that it is an altar on which a stylized condor head is sculpted.

494 center left No one knows for certain what the original role of the various sections of Macchu Picchu was. Archaeologists have suggested various theories, in accordance with the architectural features or the archaeological elements found in the specific areas. This photograph shows a view of the Temple of the Condor in the Prison Quarter.

494 bottom left Archaeologists have given different names to the different quarters into which the urban area of Macchu Picchu is divided. This photograph shows a view of the Central Sector with the Sacred Sector, which stretches to the summit of a spur of rock from which it dominates the center of the town, shown in the background.

494 top right In the heart of the town, near the Sector of the Torreón and the Royal Cemetery, is the long Stairway of the Fountains, shown here. This and the Central Stairway link various residential areas.

495 A long staircase leads from the Temple of the Three Windows and the Main Temple to another sacred structure on the summit of a rocky spur, the monolith called Inithuatana.

496-497 These are the substructure walls that run along the slope of Machu Picchu.

consists of blocks of crude granite joined together with a clay-based cement. However, here too, as in Cuzco, Pisac, Ollantaytambo and other centers built by the Incas, the surprising feature for experts and tourists alike is the enormity of the surrounding walls, made out of gigantic blocks of granite, using the technique typically applied to the most important ceremonial buildings. The Incas, like the other Andean peoples, had neither the wheel nor iron tools, and this makes their ability to work with and transport masses of granite weighing several tons even more amazing. Research has shown that the blocks were simply cut out from the quarries and that the finishing work took place on the building sites, to which the blocks were apparently taken by rolling

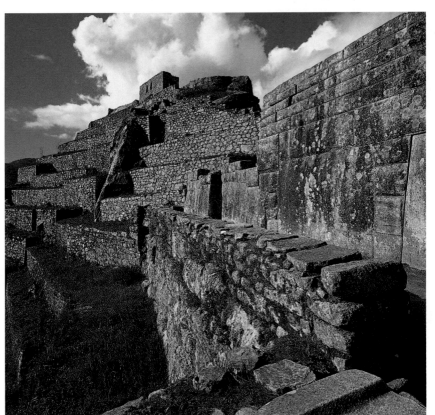

them on tree trunks. In spite of the popularly held belief that the blocks were fitted together using a dry stone technique, they were nearly always joined together using a kind of mortar which is no longer visible today.

Archaeologists have discussed widely the question of whether the Incas were the inventors of these building techniques or if they followed pre-existing models. Although many believe they invented them, it seems probable that they actually got their inspiration from the much earlier constructions of Tiahuanaco. The agricultural system of terraced cultivation, particularly impressive and applied to perfection in Macchu Picchu with the aid of ingenious systems of irrigation canals, was certainly nothing new, but a continuation of a tradition in the Andes that goes back to the First Intermediate Period. It has been confirmed, in fact, that on the northern coast of Peru the Moche people had created aqueducts and systems of canals several centuries before the 1st millennium which enabled them to grow excellent crops on artificial terraces. The Incas, skilled and ingenious, took these and other ancient ideas and modernized them, adapting them to their own special architectural and town planning requirements, giving birth to one of the most unusual and mysterious civilizations found on the American continent.

TIAHUANACO, GODS OF THE SCEPTERS

A Palace
B Gate of the Sun
C Kalasasaya
D Inner wall
E Eastern Temple
F Kantatayita
G Akapana

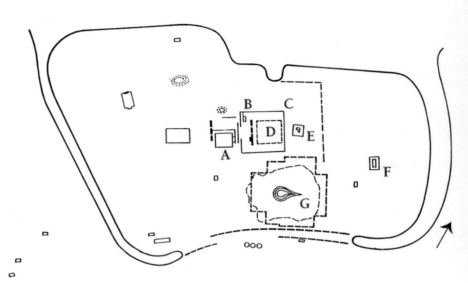

On the shores of Lake Titiaca on the Bolivian plateau are the monumental remains of an ancient civilization, undoubtedly linked with the Andean cultures of Pre-Columbian Peru, but rich in stylistic expressions of its own. The archaeologists named it the civilization of Tiahuanaco, and it was the first pre-Inca civilization of the Andes that the Europeans discovered. The Conquistadores of the 16th century learned from local legends that the royal blood of the Incas had its origins in the sacred places around Lake Titicaca, and a number of them went to visit the mysterious ruins of settlements long before abandoned. The 16th century Spanish chronicler Pedro Cieza de León described the remains of Tiahuanaco as "A sight worthy of admiration" and believed they belonged to Antigualla, "the oldest city in all Peru." Some scholars, including Arthur Posnanski, fascinated by the many unresolved problems surrounding the site of Tiahuanaco, reached the conclusion after years of research that its origins were very ancient, that it perhaps even dated back as far as 10,000 years ago. More orthodox archaeologists, however, were unwilling to accept this hypothesis and identified a number of chronological stages in the history of the site, from 100 BC to 1000 AD, based above all on the information obtained from the developments in pottery production. Along the basins of the rivers flowing into Lake Titicaca evidence was found for the existence of an older civilization than that of Tiahuanaco, known as Pukará, including its architecture, pottery and monumental sculpture, even though there are still many unresolved mysteries surrounding the type of settlement it was and the origins of its symbols and motifs. The archaeological site of Tiahuanaco

498 left The mysterious geometric shapes carved in these stone monuments at Tiahuanaco include the stair design which is found throughout Peruvian culture.

498 right Among the ruins scattered throughout Tiahuanaco, north of the Calasaya, is the architectural complex known as Pumapuncu. Here a series of cut sandstone

blocks form a platform on whose eastern side a series of "seats" are cut from the rock. Some experts believe this monument is the remains of an ancient pyramid.

occupies an area of roughly 600 square yards, and is located at over 11,000 feet above sea level. The various architectural structures, some of which are extraordinarily large, were built at different times. Some would appear to be unfinished, as if something had suddenly brought this civilization to an end. The monumental appearance of the buildings has led many archaeologists to consider Tiahuanaco as a vast, flamboyant trading

ceremonial center, where gods were worshipped and cults linked to the observation of the stars were practiced. It is believed that for many centuries it was a place of pilgrimage for the Andean peoples, but no one has yet succeeded in attributing an undoubted, definite role to the site. For the construction of the monuments, great blocks and slabs of basalt and sandstone were used, squared off and smoothed with great technical

498-499 *The Gate of the Sun was originally in a different section of the Calasaya. It has been estimated that the entire structure weighs about 12 tons. The great crossbeam is decorated with a frieze made up of four rows of winged figures with the god of the Arc in the center, a being that has been identified with the mythical Wirs Cocha.*

499 bottom *This photograph shows the remains of one of the most distinctive monuments in Tiahuanaco, the Calasasaya. The monolithic walls surrounding it are reminiscent of the megalithic stone monuments in the Old World.*

skill. These blocks were then fitted to each other using T-shaped copper or bronze joints. The quarries were several hundred miles from the site. One of the most important structures is known as Akapana. This is a flat-topped pyramid formed by superimposed platforms, square in plan and about 50 feet high, oriented from east to west. The name of the monument, perhaps one of the oldest in the ceremonial center, means "Artificial Rise" and is believed to have been a kind of temple. To the north of the Akapana is a most unusual complex, once believed to have a connection with the megalithic stone circles of Europe such as Stonehenge.

The name of the site, Kalasasaya, means Straight Stone, and clearly comes from the peculiar nature of the structure. A series of monolithic plates, not unlike menhirs,

with virtual certainty is that this is the same being as that of the Stelae Raimondi of Chavin de Huantar, dating back to around 1000 BC. There is therefore a definite connection between the cult of the Gate of the Sun in Tiahuanaco and the ancient cult of the cat and serpent-shaped figures worshipped by the civilization of Chavin, which many experts now believe to be the parent of the later cultures of pre-Columbian Peru. The God of the Arch remains a fascinating mystery still to be resolved. Equally enigmatic and unusual are the other two human-like sculptures of the Kalasaya, the Fraile, which is Spanish for "friar" and the Ponce, named after its discoverer.

Rather than sculptures in the true sense of the word, these are massive pillars on which the figures and other details are etched or sculpted in bas-relief.

500 center This photograph highlights the monoliths standing at the center of the sacred area of the Semi-Underground Temple. In the background is the access staircase to the Calasasaya and, at the center of the portal, the Ponce monolith.

500 bottom This photograph shows another example of a sculpture of a human head, this one with a square, stylized face, inserted in the wall of the Semi-Underground Temple. The style of this head is very similar to that found in the monoliths, such as the Faile and the Ponce.

500 top This delightful silver statuette comes from Tiahuanaco and was certainly part of the votive remains found at the site of a temple. Silver carving was a major and ancient skill in the Andean cultures.

form a circle enclosing a low, square platform, at the center of which is a partly-buried square, a kind of patio facing the east. Inside the Kalasaya are a number of stone monuments whose current location, after restoration work, is different from their original position.

The most spectacular of these is the Gate of the Sun, which is now the symbol of Tiahuanaco. As well as the massive structure of the whole, weighing ten tons, it owes its fame to the friezes that decorate its architrave. These show a series of supernatural-looking winged creatures converging on a center figure of a man with his head crowned with feathers who is holding a serpent shaped stick in both hands. Countless theories have been put forward to explain this divinity, commonly known as the God of the Arch or the God of the Sticks. The only thing we can say

There are two other temple buildings, to the east and west of Kalasasaya, the semi-underground temple and the great complex known as Pumapunku, the remains of a sandstone pyramid structure. Not far from this are the remains of the Palacio and the so-called Gate of the Moon.

A large quantity of pottery items was found in the area of the ceremonial center. By means of comparisons between the decorations on these and those of the monoliths and the fabrics, the specialists are continuing in their difficult task of putting together the fragments of the puzzle that will lead to a final understanding of the many obscure aspects of this civilization, which built great monuments near the banks of Lake Titicaca, in the cold of the Andean Plateau.

500-501 *The Semi-Underground Temple is a small building to the east of the walls of Calasasaya. In this photograph small head-shaped sculptures, inserted in the walls, can be seen.*

501 top left *This large human-shaped monolith, almost 10 feet high, is known as the Ponce. Like the other sculptures of Tiahuanaco, it has highly stylized features and a square face. Some scholars believe these monuments represent priests.*

501 top right *One of the most important monolithic sculptures of Tiahuanaco is the Fraile, shown here. Like the others of its kind, the features are rigid and stylized, the arms are folded over the breast and the hands are holding a number of objects. The sculpture is called the Fraile from the Spanish word for Friar, but there is no sure knowledge of what it represents.*

EASTER ISLAND,
LAND OF THE MOAI

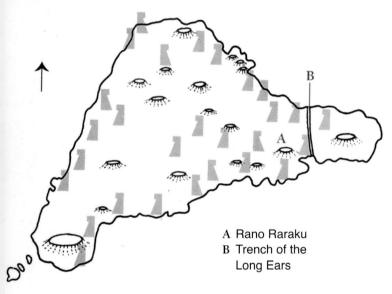

A Rano Raraku
B Trench of the
   Long Ears

502 The moai, mainly sculpted in the rock of the volcano Rano Raraku, were erected on the ahus, one beside the other. Their number apparently varied according to the importance and wealth of the family that commissioned the monument. It is believed that the ahus were sanctuaries honoring the deified ancestors of the noble families and political and religious centers. The moai were erected along the coast, turning their backs to the sea, perhaps to watch over the plains used for meeting places and celebrations.

503 Recent research seems to indicate that some moai were erected according to an astronomical pattern. The inconsistent nature of this apparently deliberate arrangement has complicated even more attempts to understand Easter Island. One of the few certainties is that the construction and transport of these stone giants must have cost enormous energy in a civilization without metals. There must have been a sophisticated social system to keep teams of workers together for entire seasons.

The fact that Easter Island was an unusual place was clear at once to the first westerners who, by pure chance, discovered this isolated strip of land in the middle of the Pacific Ocean, almost 2500 miles from the coast of South America and 1200 from the nearest atolls of Polynesia. The Dutch admiral Jacob Roggeveen landed there on Sunday, April 5, 1722, during his search for what was called Davis Land which had been seen by a passing English corsair 40 years earlier. The island Roggeveen found needed a name and April 5 was Easter Sunday, so he gave it the name Easter Island.

The captain noted in his log that the natives seemed less surprised by the strange meeting than his crew, and that they showed great interest in the three ships as if they had never seen such things before. The Dutch, on the other hand, were surprised by the monolithic statues scattered around the island, before which the natives prostrated themselves every sunrise. Unfortunately, Roggeveen did not have time to look into the matter in greater detail as the relationship with the islanders quickly deteriorated and shots were fired. On April 10th the ships sailed away. Forty years later, the islanders had another encounter with Europeans when in 1770 two Spanish ships commanded by Don Felipe Gonzales y Haedo, who stayed for six days, arrived. He drew a map of the island and took possession of it in the name of the King of Spain. Again, the visitors were amazed by the great statues. Gonzales reported that they were about 30 feet high and many had a circular red stone on their heads. On March 11, 1774, the famous English navigator, Captain James Cook, came to the island as he wanted to see for himself how true the accounts of this totally isolated island were. Like his predecessors, Cook said it was a windswept, totally treeless land, clearly of volcanic origin and inhabited by modest people with nothing savage at all about them. The natives

seemed to belong to the Polynesian race, lived in large huts made of rushes and wattles in a society based on agriculture and fishing. The Englishman also described the statues with interest, saying that there were hundreds of them all over the island but also noticing that many of them were overturned. As such large statues, solidly implanted in the ground, were unlikely to be moved by the wind or even by earthquakes, they must have been knocked over intentionally. But why? Even more difficult to explain was how the islanders had been able to erect such colossal structures in the first place, as there was not a single tree anywhere on the island, which meant they could not do it by using trees to roll them. In 1786 the Frenchman Jean-François De La Perouse, landed on the island and drew pictures of some of the stone giants. He too noted that the islanders were unable to explain the origins of the statues nor did he discover why all the statues faced away from the sea. In 1804, a Captain Lisjanski, commandant of a Russian ship, reached the island and he wrote that many of the statues that had still been standing when Cook visited were now lying on the ground. Twelve years later, the captain of another Russian ship, the Kotzebue, said that he found only two statues still standing on their bases. When the first Christian missionaries came to the island all the monoliths had been knocked over. Clearly, a fierce war among the island tribes had been raging since time immemorial and after every battle the victors humiliated the defeated party by knocking over the most sacred monuments. But worse was to come. In 1805 the captain of a U.S. vessel had captured some of the islanders to make slaves of them. This naturally angered the islanders who massacred many missionaries as soon as they set food on the island. Then, between 1859 and 1863 over a thousand men and women were captured by the Peruvians and taken to the island of Chincha where they

were forced to dig up the guano from the local mines. The vast majority of these slaves died of deprivations suffered during their work and when the hundred or so survivors were returned to Easter Island following pressure from several foreign governments they brought with them a terrible heritage. Only 15 men survived the return voyage and they brought with them smallpox and tuberculosis to their native island. These terrible diseases ravaged the population, so that only 111 inhabitants remained alive in 1877. Naturally, the missionaries did their best to change the lives of the few survivors by canceling out their traditions, customs and history while other westerners introduced alcohol and venereal diseases. Since experts estimate the maximum population of the island at

15,000 to 20,000, and there were at least 4,000 people on the island when the first Europeans arrived, the tragic figures speak for themselves. Unfortunately, the destruction and the cultural crises that followed the attempt by the westerners to "civilize" the islanders meant that the confused history of the place was totally unknown to the few survivors, who only rarely told credible legends and beliefs. It should not therefore be surprising that no one has ever been able to trace the various stages of the island's history with any certainty and the origins of its inhabitants remain obscure. All we can do, then, is set out the few known facts and a few of the more believable hypotheses. Easter Island is a triangle of volcanic rock with a surface area of about 70 square miles. The natives,

who were so isolated that they knew of no existence of any other land, called it Rapa Nui, meaning "The Center of the World". There are some who believe that the first settlers came from the Marquis Islands, 2400 miles away, about 500 AD, and that once they had settled they developed a completely independent culture based on their Polynesian roots. This theory is backed up by a local legend that tells of a ruler who abandoned an island named Hiva in the remote past on two long vessels and reached the new land after a long and tiring voyage, naming his new home Hotu Matua. Here, his people, beginning in the 10th century BC, started to build large statues, known as moai, aligned on monumental platforms called ahu. These statues were dedicated to the gods and to deified

504 and 505 *Various moai have been carefully restored in recent years, such as these at Tahai (left) and Anakena (center). They stand in what are believed to be their original positions, their heads once again* *adorned with the pukao in red volcanic rock, their eyes once, it is believed, made from coral now replaced with white plaster. The fact that the moai were knocked over bears out the theory that they were effigies of* *the leading members of the most important families, in which case their destruction would make sense if anarchy swept the island. Unfortunately, the true history of Easter Island is still unknown.*

ancestors. Unfortunately, after an initial period of splendor a long period of tribal war followed, lasting from the 17th century until the start of the 19th, and this led to both the destruction of the moai and the society itself. This idea offers as proof the fact that the name Hiva is very widespread on the Marquis Islands, and there are also linguistic affinities between the language of Rapa Nui and the ancient Polynesian languages. Finally, an examination of the DNA on some human bones found on the island has shown a close similarity with the DNA of the Polynesians. That would be the end of the story and would discredit the theory of colonists from Peru put forward in the 1940s by Thor Heyerdahl, the Norwegian explorer who succeeded in reaching the Polynesian islands from the

coast of South America on board the Kontiki, a fragile balsam wood raft. But there's a second legend that complicates things further. This legend tells that the ruler Hotu Matua came from the Marquis Islands with his people in the 12th century, and found the island already inhabited by a fairer-skinned people. The two ethnic groups lived together in peace and merged into a single race. All went well until a third group suddenly appeared, this time from the east. They were so robust they were called the Hanau Eepe which means "Strong Race". Since they also had ears with highly developed earlobes they were also nicknamed "The Big Ears" with the more established residents calling themselves "The Small Ears". There are several elements that favor this theory, too, such as the

ABACUS: square or rectangular tablet-shaped element between the capital and the architrave.

ACROPOLIS: highest part of the city, often defended by walls and containing temples.

AMALAKA: architectural element that takes its name from the fruit of the same name. It terminates the oval structure above the cell in the temples of Northern India.

ANDA: central body of the *stupa*, semi-circular in shape.

APSARA: celestial nymph.

ASURA: powers of the darkness, demons.

BARAY: artificial basin for the collection of rainwater in the Khmer towns.

BODHISATTVA: venerable Buddhist figures who, in spite of being enlightened and therefore deserving to go to Nirvana, remain in the world to succour suffering humanity.

CHAC MOOL: stone sacrificial altar showing a semi-reclining man resting on his elbows, with his head to one side. Introduced to Meso-America by the Toltecs. The most famous chac mools are in Tula, Chichén Itzá and Tenochtitlan.

CHAITYA: places of worship, especially Buddhist, consisting of a naved, apsed structure.

CHATTRAVALI: the final pillar of the *stupa* that holds up one or more parasols.

COMB: ornamental structure at the top of the Mayan temples from the Early Classical Period onwards. During the Post-Classical Period, the combs were covered with modelled, painted plaster decorations showing masks of the gods, serpents, jaguars and high ranking figures.

DEVA: powers of light, gods.

DEVARAJA: the Khmer ruler, considered as being a god.

DEVATA: diviniy.

DHARMA: in the Hindu world, the cosmic order that regulates the phenomena of the universe and the moral law that inspires men. In the Buddhist world the doctrine preached by the Buddha.

DYPHTHERON: temple surrounded by a double row of columns.

DROMOS: corridor leading to the entrance of a monumental tomb, or a kind of avenue that leads to the entrance to a temple.

DVARAPALA: armed figures that guard the entrance doors of Hindu temples.

ENNEASTYLE: exceptional type of classical temple with nine columns at the short sides.

ENTABLATURE: in classical archaeological orders, it is the structure lying on the columns, composed by the architrave, the frieze and the cornice.

HEXASTYLE: classical temple with six columns at the short sides.

FALSE VAULT OR SHELVED VAULT: architectural element used by the Maya, who knew nothing of the use of the arch of the true vault. The shelved vault is obtained by building two walls that jut out progressively upwards until they meet.

GABLE: triangular architectural element placed in the façade as the crown of a temple or other classical monumental buildings.

GANDHARVA: genie of the air and celestial attendant of the gods.

GYMNASIUM: in Ancient Greece, school for the moral and intellectual education of young boys.

GLYPH: graphic symbol (from the Greek glifein, "to write") in Zapotec and Mayan writing. It appears closed in a kind of cartouche and may serve as an ideogram, phonetic or mixed.

GOPURAM: monumental structures above the entrances to the temple surrounds in South India.

GU: "grotto", term used to define the temples at Pagan.

HARMIKA: enclosed structure at the top of the *stupa*, from which the pillar with parasols emerges.

HTI: a kind of hanging parasol with small bells above the *zeidi*.

HYPOSTYLE HALL: a room whose ceiling is held up by columns or pillars, very common in Egyptian religious or funerary buildings.

KALASHA: the water vase at the end of the Hindu temples which evokes the origins of the universe from the primordial waters and symbolizes fertility and abundance.

KINNARA: partly animal celestial musicians.

KIRTIMUKHA: the "face of glory", a grotesque mask symbolising all-transforming, all-devouring time.

KUDU: small horseshoe-shaped arch.

LINGA: phallic stone symbolising the god Shiva.

MAKARA: mythical sea creature.

MANDAPA: colonnaded hall or pavilion.

MASTABA: Arabic word for the four-sided bench with slightly tapering sides, built in bare brick covered in plaster and found in front of the houses in Egyptian villages. The term is used to refer to the Egyptian tombs, which are similar in shape.

MEDHI: the base of the *stupa*.

MUDRA: hand gestures expressing the most important moments in the spiritual experience.

NAGA: half human half serpent creatures connected with water, fertility and knowledge

NAGINI: the female companions of the nagas

NIRVANA: the state of liberation from the continuous, painful return to worldly existence.

NYMPHEON: building with niches and central fountain, often with apse.

OPISTODOME: the rear part of a temple, opposite the pronaos, used as a storage area for the treasure.

PERIPHTHERON: building or temple surrounded by a row of columns.

PERISTASIS: the colonnade that surrounds the cell of the periphtheral temple or, more rarely, a building of varying type.

PERISTYLE: in sanctuaries and Greek houses - and later in Roman ones - courtyard surrounded by a colonnaded portico.

PRADAKSHINA: a rite of procession with the object to be venerated always to the right of the walkers.

PRASAT: the sanctuary towers in Khmer architecture.

PRONAOS: in Greek and Roman temples, the space between the cell and the colonnade of the façade.

PYLON: monumental entrance to the Egyptian temples, formed by massive towers of trapezoid shape, alongside the portal.

RATHA: wooden carriage that contains the images of the gods when these are taken in procession outside the temple.

RYTHON: drinking vessel in the form of a curved horn, often terminating in the head of an animal.

SALABHANJIKA: nymph of the trees.

SANGHA: monastic community.

SANGHARAMA: residence of monks, see "vihara".

SHIKHARA: oval tower above the cell in the temples of North India. The term also defines certain domed structures in the architecture of the south of the country.

STUPA: bell-shaped reliquary deriving from the burial mounds built on the remains of the cremation of Buddha, later becoming cosmic symbol.

STYLOBATE: base of the columns in classical temples.

TABENA: the reliquary in the central sealed chamber of the *zeidi*.

TALUD-TABLERO: architectural element originating in Teotihuacan, and found in many other areas of Meso-America. It consists of a vertical panel, or *tablero*, above an oblique part, or *talud*. The dimensions of the two parts vary, creating a wide range of architectural compositions.

DOWNSTREAM TEMPLE: building connected to the funerary temple annexed to the pyramid with a descending covered ramp, in which the mummification and purification rites of the body of the ruler take place. In front of the entrance, there was usually a boarding stage connected to the Nile by an artificial channel.

THOLOS: temple, building or part of a building, with circular plan, bounded by a row of columns and usually terminating in a dome or conical roof.

TYMPANUM: in classical temples, the triangular part of the façade bounded by the two projections and the architrave, usually adorned with groups of sculptures.

TORANA: access portal to the surrounding enclosure of the *stupa*.

TRIRATNA: the "triple jewel", or the Buddha, his doctrine and the community of monks.

TZOMPANTLI: stone monument reproducing a wooden rack to which the skulls of the sacrificial victims or decapitated enemies were attached, brought to Mesoamerica by the Toltecs in the Post-Classical Period.

VARAHA: the "wild boar", one of the *avataras*, or earthly forms, of the god Vishnu who took this form to set the goddess Earth free from the muddy depth of the ocean.

VEDIKA: the enclosure surrounding sacred buildings.

VIHARA: monastery.

VIMANA: terraced pyramid structure used to cover the cell and other important buildings in the temples of South India.

YAKSHA: pot-bellied genie of the trees.

YAKSHI OR YAKSHINI: dryads, nymphs of the trees and woods.

ZEIDI: Burmese term used for the *stupa*.

BIBLIOGRAPHY

Abu Simbel
-L. A. Christophe, *Abou-Simbel et l'épopée de sa découverte*, Brussels 1965.
-Chr. Desroches-Noblecourt and Ch. Kuentz, *Le petit temple d'Abou Simbel: "Nofretari pour qui se lève le dieu- soleil"*, Cairo 1968.
-Various authors, *The Salvage of the Abu Simbel Temples*. Concluding Report, Stockholm 1971.
-H. el-Achirie and J. Jacquet, *Grand temple d'Abou Simbel* vol. I: Architecture, Cairo 1984.

Ajanta
-S.P.M. Mackenzie and M. Taeda, *Ajanta. I monasteri rupestri dell'India*, Milan 1982.
-Philip Rawson, *La pittura indiana*, Milan 1964.
-Debala Mitra, *Ajanta, Archaelogical Survey of India*, New Delhi 1983.
-Jayanta Chakrabarti, *Techniques in Indian mural painting*, Calcutta 1980.

Angkor
-D. Mazzeo and C. Silvi Antonini, *Khmer Civilisations*, in *"Le grandi civiltà"*, Milan 1972.
-B. Dagens, *Angkor, la foresta di pietra*, Trieste 1995.
-J. Boisselier, Le Cambodge, in *"Manuel d'archéologie d'Extrême Orient, Asie du sud-est, Tome I"*, Paris 1966.
-G. Coedès, *Angkor, an introduction*, London 1963.

Athens
-C. Tiberi, *Mnesicle, l'architetto dei Propilei*, Rome 1964.
-A. Giuliano, *Urbanistica delle città greche*, Milan 1966.
-H.A. Thompson and R.E. Wycherley, *The Agora of Athens*, Princeton 1972.
-E. La Rocca, *L'esperimento della perfezione. Arte e società nell'Atene di Pericle*, Milan 1988.

Babylon
-H. Frankfort, *Arte e Architettura dell'antico Oriente*, Turin 1970.
-J. C. Margueron, *Mesopotamia*, in *Enciclopedia Archeologica*, Geneva 1976.
-M. Liverani, *Antico Oriente, Storia Società Economia*, Rome-Bari 1988.
-N. Roaf, *Cultural Atlas of Mesopotamia and the Ancient Near East*, Oxford 1990.

Borobudur
- Lucilla Saccà, *Borobudur Mandala de Pierre*, Milan 1983.
- John Miksic, *Borobudur - Golden Tales of the Buddhas*, Singapore 1990.
- Jacques Dumarcay, *The Temples of Java*, Singapore 1992.
- Pietro Scarduelli, *Lo specchio del cosmo*, Turin 1992.

Carnac
-Pierre-Roland Giot, *I menhir allineati di Carnac*, Rennes 1992.

Chan Chan
-A. Lapiner, *Pre-Columbian Art of South America*, New York 1976.
-D. Bonavia, *Perù. Hombre y Historia*, Lima 1991.
-Various authors, *Inca-Perù*, Rito, Magia, Mistero, Rome 1992.

Chichén Itzá
-M.E. Miller, *The Art of Mesoamerica*, New York 1986.
-M.E. Miller and K. Taube, *The Gods and Symbols of Ancient Mexico and the Maya*, London-New York 1992.
-S. Morley and G. Brainerd, *I Maya*, Rome 1984.

Cuzco, Sacsahuaman and Ollantaytambo
-H. Favre, *Les Incas*, Paris 1972.
-D. Lavallée and L.G. Lumbreras, *Les Andes. De la Prehistorie aux Incas*, Paris 1985.
-Various authors, Inca. Perù, *3000 Ans d'Histoire*, Ghent 1990.
-F. Kauffman Doig, *Perù*, Venice 1995.

Easter Island
-G. della Ragione, *L'Isola di Pasqua*, in *Atlante di archeologia*, Turin 1996.
-A.G. Drusini, *Rapa Nui. L'ultima terra*, Milan 1991.
-T. Heyerdahl, *Archaeology of Easter Island*, Santa Fe 1961.
-M.C. Laroche, *Ile de Pâque*, Paris 1981.

Ephesus
-W. Alzinger, *Alt Efesos topographie und architectur*, Berlin-Vienna 1967.
-W. Alzinger, *Die ruinen von Efesos*, Berlin-Vienna 1972.
-E. Akurgal, *Ancient Civilisations and Ruins of Turkey*, Istanbul 1983.
-H. Lauter, *Die Architektur des Hellenismus*, Darmstadt 1986.

Hadrian's Villa

-S. Aurigemma, *Villa Adriana*, Rome 1962.
-F. Coarelli, *Lazio*, Bari 1982.
-H. Kähler, *Villa Adriana*, in *Enciclopedia dell'Arte Antica*, Rome 1961.
-F. Rakob, *Villa Adriana*, in *Enciclopedia dell'Arte Antica*, Rome 1994.
-H. Stierlin, *Roman Empire. From the Etruscans to the Decline of Roman Empire*, Cologne 1996.

Herodion
-V. Corbo, *Herodium: gli edifici della reggia-fortezza*, Jerusalem 1989.
-Y. Netzer, *Herodium: an Archaeological Guide*, Jerusalem 1997.

Karnak and Luxor
-P. Barguet, *Le Temple d'Amon-Rê à Karnak. Essai d'Exegese*, Cairo 1962.
-H. Brunner, *Die Südlichen Räume des Tempels von Luxor*, Mainz 1977.
-A Roccati, *Karnak e Luxor*, Novara 1981.

Knossos
-A. Evans, *The Palace of Minos at Knossos*, London 1921-1935.
-S. Hood, *The Mynoans*, London 1971.
-S. Hood and D. Smith, *Archaeological Survey of Knossos*, London 1981.

Lascaux
-A. Leroi-Gourhan and J. Allain, *Lascaux inconnu*, Paris 1979.
-L.R. Nougier, *La Preistoria*, Turin 1982.
-L.R. Nougier, *Lascaux*, in *Atlante di Archeologia*, Turin 1996.

Leptis Magna
-P. Romanelli, *Storia delle province romane dell'Africa*, Rome 1959.
-P. Romanelli, *Leptis Magna*, in *Enciclopedia dell'Arte Antica*, Rome 1961.
-J.B. Ward Perkins, *Leptis Magna* in *The Princeton Encyclopedia of Classical Sites*, Princeton 1976.

Luoyang
-L. Sickman and A. Soper, *L'arte e l'architettura cinesi*, Einaudi, Turin 1969.
-W. Willets, *L'arte cinese*, Sansoni, Florence 1963.
-Various authors, *Longmen Shiku*, Wenwu, Beijing 1980.
-Various authors, *Luoyang Longmen Shuangku*, in Kaogu Xuebao no.1, Beijing 1988.

Macchu Picchu
-C. Bernand, *Gli Incas. Figli del Sole*, Milan 1994.
-L.G. Lumbreras, *Arqueología de la América Andina*, Lima 1981.
-Various authors, *I Regni Preincaici e il Mondo Inca*, Milan 1992.

Mamallipuram
-Stella Kramrisch, *The Hindu Temple*, Delhi 1980.
-Christopher Tadgell, *The History of Architecture in India*, Hong Kong 1990.
-A Volwahsen, *Architettura indiana*, Milan 1968.

Masada

-Y. Netzer, *The Buildings, Stratigraphy and Architecture (Masada III)*, Jerusalem 1991.
-Y. Yadin, *Masada*, London 1966.

Mesa Verde
-J.J. Brody, *Beauty from the Earth*, Philadelphia 1990.
-M.D. Coe, D. Snow and E. Benson (eds.), *Atlante dell'Antica America*, Novara 1987.

Monte Albán
-I. Bernal and M. Simoni Abbat, *Il Messico dalle Origini agli Aztechi*, Milan 1992.
-A. Caso, *El tresoro de Monte Albán*, Mexico City 1969.
-R. Pina Chan, Olmechi. *La Cultura Madre*, Milan 1989.

Mycenae
-S.E. Iakovidis, *Late Helladic Citadels on Mainland Greece*, Leyden 1983.
-G.E. Mylonas, *Ancient Mycenae*, London 1957.
-W. Taylour, *The Mycenaeans*, London 1964.

Nemrut Dagh
-S. Sahin, *Watchful Stones*, in *Atlas Travel Magazine*, Ankara 1996.
-F.K. Dörner, *Nemrut Dagh*, in *Enciclopedia dell'Arte Antica*, Rome 1961.

Nubian Temples
-J. Baines and J. Málek, *Atlante dell'Antico Egitto*, Novara 1985
-S. Curto, *Nubia*, Turin 1966.
-Various Authors, *Topographical Bibliography of Ancient Egyptian Hieroglyphic Texts, Reliefs and Paintings*, Vol.VII: *Nubia, the Desert and Outside Egypt*, Oxford 1952.

Paestum
-E. Greco and D. Theodorescu, *Poseidonia - Paestum I*, Rome 1980.
-E. Greco and D. Theodorescu, *Poseidonia - Paestum II*, Rome 1983.
-D. Mertens, *Der alte Heratempel in Paestum und die archaische baukunst in Unteritalien*, Mainz 1993.

Pagan
-Mario Bussagli, *Architettura orientale*, Venice 1981.
-Thein Sein, *The Pagodas and Monuments of Pagan*, Rangoon 1995.
-Paul Strachan, *Pagan, Art and Architecture of Old Bhurma*, Singapore 1989.

Palenque
-C. Baudez and S. Picasso, *Les Cités perdues des Mayas*, Paris 1987.
-L. Shele and D. Friedel, *A Forest of Kings: the Untold Story of the Ancient Maya*, New York 1990.
-Various authors, *Mondo Maya*, Milan 1996.

Palmira
-M. Harari, *Palmira*, in *Atlante di Archeologia*, Turin 1996.
-K. Michalowski, *Palmira*, in *Enciclopedia*

dell'Arte Antica, Rome 1961.
-M. Rostovtzeff, *Città Carovaniere*, Bari 1971.

Persepolis
-M. Liverani, *Antico Oriente, Storia Società Economia*, Rome-Bari 1988.
-M. Roaf, *Cultural Atlas of Mesopotamia and the Ancient Near East*, Oxford 1990.

Petra
-M. Avi-Yonah, *Petra*, in *Enciclopedia dell'Arte Antica*, Rome 1961.
-F. Bourbon, *Yesterday and Today, The Holy Land, Lithographs and Diaries by David Roberts, R.A.*, Bnei-Brak 1994.
-H. Keiser, *Petra dei Nabatei*, Turin 1972.
-M. Rostovtzeff, *Città Carovaniere*, Bari 1971.

Pompeii
-A De Franciscis, *The Buried Cities: Pompeii and Herculaneum*, New York 1978.
-E. La Rocca, A. de Vos and M. de Vos, *Pompei*, Milan 1994.
-A. Maiuri, *Pompei ed Ercolano fra case e abitanti*, Milan 1959.
-P. Zanker, Pompei. *Società, immagini urbane e forme dell'abitare*, Turin 1993.

Philae
-G. Haeny, *A Short Architectural History of Philae*, BIFAO 85, 1985.
-E. Vassilika, *Ptolemaic Philae*, OLA 34, Leuven 1989.
-A. Roccati - A. Giammarusti, *File, storia e vita di un santuario egizio*, Novara 1980.

Rome
-J. P. Adam, *La construction romaine. Materiaux et techniques*, Paris 1984.
-M. Brizzi, *Roma, i monumenti antichi*, Rome 1973.
-F. Coarelli, *Roma*, Milan 1971.
-A.M. Liberati and F.Bourbon, *Roma Antica, Storia di una civiltà che conquistò il mondo*, Vercelli 1996.
-U. E. Paoli, *Vita romana, usi, costumi, istituzioni, tradizioni*, Florence 1962.
-Various authors, *Vita quotidiana nell'Italia Antica*, Verona 1993.

Sanchi
-Michel Delahoutre, *Arte indiana*, Milan 1996.
-Debala Mitra, *Sanchi*, New Delhi 1978.
-Calambur Sivaramamurti, *India, Ceylon, Nepal, Tibet*, Turin 1988.
-Maurizio Taddei, *India antica*, Milan 1982.

Saqqara and Giza
-M.Z. Goneim, *Horus Sekhemkhet*, Cairo 1957.
-S. Hassan, *Excavations at Giza*, 10 Vols., Oxford 1932-1960
-J.P. Lauer, *The Royal Cemetery of Memphis*, London 1979.
-E. Leospo, *Saqqara e Giza*, Novara 1982.
-C.M. Zivie, *Giza au deuxième Millénaire*, Cairo 1976.

Stonhenge
-R.J.C. Atkinson, *Stonehenge and Avebury*, Exeter 1974.
-J Dyer, *Southern England: an Archaeological Guide*, London 1973.
-W. Schreiber, *Stonehenge*, in *Atlante di Archeologia*, Turin 1996.

Tarquinia
-M. Torelli, *Elogia Tarquinensia*, Florence 1975.
-Various authors *Gli Etruschi di Tarquinia, catalogo della mostra*, Modena 1986.
-Various authors, *Studia Tarquinensia*, Rome 1988.

Teotihuacan
-I. Bernal and M. Simoni Abbat, *Il Messico dalle Origini agli Aztechi*, Milan 1992.
-E. Matos Moctezuma, *Teotihuacan, La Metropoli degli Dèi*, Milan 1990.

Tiahuanaco
-P. Cieza de Leon, *La Cronica del Perù* (1553), Lima 1973.
-F. Kauffman Doig, *Perù*, Venice 1995.
-A. Posnanski, *Tihauanaco y la Civilización Prehistórica en el Altiplano Andino*, La Paz 1911.

Tikal
-M. Grulich, *L'Art Precolombien. La Mesoamerique*, Paris 1992.
-H. Stierlin, *The Maya Palaces and Pyramids in the Rainforest*, Cologne 1997.

Ur
-H. Frankfort, *Arte e Architettura dell'antico Oriente*, Turin 1970.
-M. Liverani, *L'origine della città*, Rome 1986.
-M. Liverani, *Antico Oriente, Storia Società Economia*, Rome-Bari 1988.

Uxmal
-C. Baudez and P. Becquelin, *I Maya*, Milan 1985.
-P. Gendrop and D. Heyden, *Architettura Mesoamericana*, Milan 1980.
-Various authors, *Mondo Maya*, Milan 1996.

Western Thebes
-E. Edwards, *Tutankhamon, la tomba e i tesori*, Milan 1980.
-B. Porter and R. Moss, *Topographical Bibliography*, Vol. I, *Theban Necropolis*, Oxford 1960.
-B. Porter and R. Moss, *Topographical Bibliography*, Vol. II, *Theban Temples*, Oxford 1972.
-N. Reeves and R. Wilkinson, *The Complete Valley of the Kings*, London 1996.

Xi'An
-X. Nai, *Sanshi Nian Lai De Zhongguo Kaoguxue*, in *Kaogu*, Beijing 1979.
-W. Willets, *Origini dell'Arte Cinese*, Florence 1965.
-Various authors, *Settemila anni di Cina*, Milan 1983.

ILLUSTRATION CREDITS

Introduction
Antonio Attini/Archivio White Star: page 12 top right.
Marcello Bertinetti/Archivio White Star: pages 6-7, 9 bottom, 12-13, 20-21.
Marcello Bertinetti/Archivio White Star: "Concessione S.M.A. N.325 del 01-09-1995" pages 4-5.
Massimo Borchi/Archivio White Star: pages 10-11, 12 top left, 16-17, 18-19.
Giulio Veggi/Archivio White Star: pages 2-3, 21 top right.
Christophe Boisivieux: pages 14-15.
Giovanni Dagli Orti: pages 1, 10 top, 10 bottom, 20 left.
Alison Wright: pages 8, 9.
Giancarlo Zuin: page 12 bottom.

EUROPE
Marcello Bertinetti/Archivio White Star: pages 24-25, 26-27.

Lascaux
Woodfin Camp: page 30 top.
Chatellier/Sipa/Grazia Neri: page 28 right top.
François Ducasse/Ag. Top: pages 28 left, 28 right bottom, 28-29, 29 top, 30-31.
Shelly Grossmann/Grazia Neri: pages 28 right center, 30 bottom.
Pierre Vauthey/Corbis Sygma/Contrasto: 32-33.

Carnac
Damien de Bronac/Ag. Top: page 34 right.
Hervé Champollion/Ag. Top: pages 34 left, 35.

Stonehenge
David Parker/Science Photolibrary: pages 36-37.
Photobank: pages 36, 37 top.

Knossos
Antonio Attini/Archivio White Star: pages 38 center, 38 bottom, 38-39, 40-41, 43 bottom left.
Christophe Boisivieux: page 43 top left.
Giovanni Dagli Orti: pages 38 top, 41 top, 41 bottom, 42 top, 42 bottom, 42-43, 44 bottom, 44-

45, 45 bottom right, 46-47.

Mycenae
Archivio Scala: page 48 left.
Guido Alberto Rossi/The Image Bank: pages 48-49, 51.
Giulio Veggi/Archivio White Star: pages 49 top, 49 bottom, 50 top left, 50 top right, 50 bottom, 52-53.
Giovanni Dagli Orti: pages 50 top right, 54 left top, 54 left bottom, 54 right.
AKG: page 55.

Athens
Antonio Attini/Archivio White Star: page 59 bottom.
Giulio Veggi/Archivio White Star: pages 57 left top, 60 center, 60 bottom, 61 bottom, 62-63.
Archivio Scala: pages 57 right top, 60-61.
Marco Casiraghi: page 57 bottom.
Giovanni Dagli Orti: pages 56-57, 57 right center, 58 top, 58-59, 59 top, 62 top left, 62 bottom left, 62 bottom right, 63 bottom left, 63 bottom right.
Guido Alberto Rossi/The Image Bank: page 62 center left.

Paestum
Marcello Bertinetti/Archivio White Star: pages 70-71.
Livio Bourbon/Archivio White Star: pages 62 bottom.
Giulio Veggi/Archivio White Star: pages 64-65, 65 bottom right, 66-67, 68 top, 69 center.
Archivio Scala: pages 64 bottom left, 64 bottom center, 72 top right.
Giovanni Dagli Orti: pages 69 top left, 72 top left, 72-73, 72 bottom, 73 top.
Guido Alberto Rossi/The Image Bank: pages 64 bottom right, 65 center right.
Alberto Nardi/Modern Times:/The Image Bank: pages 68-69.
Luciano Pedicini/Archivio Dell'arte: pages 65 top left, 69 top right.

Tarquinia
Archivio Scala: pages 74 bottom, 74-75, 75 top, 76-77, 77 top, 77 bottom.
Giovanni Dagli Orti: page 77 center.
Marco Mairani: page 75 bottom.

Luciano Pedicini/Archivio Dell'Arte: page 74 top.
Pompeii
Antonio Attini/Archivio White Star: pages 80-81
Araldo De Luca/Archivio White Star: pages 90-91, 92-93.
Giulio Veggi/Archivio White Star: pages 78 top, 78 center, 82, 83, 84 center, 84 bottom, 85 bottom, 88 top.
Archivio Scala: pages 86, 87, 89 bottom right, 94 bottom, 94-95, 95 top.
Giovanni Dagli Orti: pages 79, 84-85, 85 right.
Luciano Pedicini/Archivio Dell'Arte: pages 88 bottom, 88-89, 89 bottom left, 94 top.
Guido Rossi/The Image Bank: "Concessione S.M.A N.01-337 del 03-09-1996" pages 78 bottom, 84 top.
Rome
Marcello Bertinetti/Archivio White Star: "Concessione S.M.A. N.325 del 01-09-1995" pages 96-97, 102 bottom, 102-103, 104-105, 108 top, 108 center, 108-109, 109 bottom, 110-111, 112-113, 113 top, 113 bottom right
"Concessione S.M.A. N.316 del 18-08-1995" pages 110 center, 112 bottom.
Giulio Veggi/Archivio White Star: pages 96, 97 right, 100, 101, 102 top, 103 bottom left, 103 bottom right, 106-107, 108 bottom left, 110 top, 110 bottom, 111 bottom, 112 top, 112 center, 113 bottom left.
Archivio Scala: pages 104 top, 104 bottom, 105 top, 105 bottom.
Araldo De Luca: pages 97 bottom, 98-99, 108 bottom right.
Hadrian's Villa-Tivoli
Marcello Bertinetti/Archivio White Star: "Concessione S.M.A. N.316 del 18-08-1995" pages 114 top, 114-115, 116-117, 119.
Giulio Veggi/Archivio White Star: pages 114 center, 114 bottom, 117 bottom, 118 top.
Giovanni Dagli Orti: page 117 top.
Araldo De Luca: page 118 bottom.
Archivio Scala: page 115 bottom.
AFRICA
Antonio Attini/Archivio White Star: pages 120-121.
Araldo De Luca/Archivio White Star: pages 124-125.
Alfio Garozzo/Archivio White Star: pages 126-127.
Giulio Veggi/Archivio White Star: page 121 bottom.
Alberto Novelli/The Image Bank: pages 120 bottom left, 120 bottom right.
Alberto Siliotti/Archivio Geodia: page 120 top.
Saqqara
Antonio Attini/Archivio White Star: page 137 top.
Marcello Bertinetti/Archivio White Star: pages 128-129, 129, 130-131, 136 top right, 136-137, 138-139, 141 top right, 141 center right.
Araldo De Luca/Archivio White Star: pages 134-135, 136 top left, 140, 141 top left, 141 bottom.
Giulio Veggi/Archivio White Star: pages 132 top, 132 top right, 137 center, 137 bottom.
Giulio Andreini: page 132 top right.
AKG Photo: page 142 bottom.
Giovanni Dagli Orti: page 128 top.
Claudio Concina/Realy Easy Star: page 132 bottom right.
Werner Forman Archive: pages 133, 142 top, 142-143, 143 bottom.
Karnak
Antonio Attini/Archivio White Star: pages 144 right, 155 bottom left, 155 bottom right.
Marcello Bertinetti/Archivio White Star: pages 144 left, 146-147, 148-149, 150 top, 150 bottom left, 150 bottom right, 150-151, 152-153, 154 top left, 154 top right, 154-155, 155 top, 156-157, 157.
Giulio Veggi/Archivio White Star: pages 145 bottom, 151 top, 154 bottom, 156.
Anne Conway: pages 144-145.
Luxor
Antonio Attini/Archivio White Star: page 163 top.
Marcello Bertinetti/Archivio White Star: pages 158-159, 159 bottom, 160-161, 164-165.
Giulio Veggi/Archivio White Star: pages 158, 162, 162-163, 163 bottom.
Valley of the Kings
Antonio Attini/Archivio White Star: pages 166 top, 168 center top, 168 center bottom, 173 center, 180-181.
Marcello Bertinetti/Archivio White Star: pages 166 bottom left, 166-167, 167 top, 168 top, 168-169, 170-171, 172-173, 172, 173 top, 173 bottom, 174-175.
Araldo De Luca/Archivio White Star: pages 178-179, 184-185, 188-189, 190-191.
Giulio Veggi/Archivio White Star: pages 166 center, 169 bottom, 176 top left.
Hervé Champollion: page 182 bottom.
Christophe Boisivieux: pages 182 top left, 182 top right.
Giovanni Dagli Orti: page 183 top.
Archivio White Star: pages 183 center, 183 bottom.
Damm/Bildagentur Huber/Sime: 186-187, 186 bottom right, 186 top left.
Araldo De Luca/Archivio White Star: pages 166 bottom right, 176 top right, 176 bottom left, 176 bottom right, 177.
Bertrand Gardel/Ag. Hemispheres: page 168 bottom.
Andrea Iemolo: pages 182 center, 182-182, 187 top right, 187 bottom left.
Charles Lenars: pages 186 bottom left, 187 bottom right.
Nubian Temples
Antonio Attini/Archivio White Star: pages 192, 193, 199 top, 199 bottom left.
Marcello Bertinetti/Archivio White Star: pages 194-195, 196-197.
Giulio Veggi/Archivio White Star: pages 198-199.
Hervé Champollion: page 199 bottom right.
Enrico Martino: page 198 bottom.
Sandro Vannini/Ag.Franca Speranza: page 198 top.
Abu Simbel
Antonio Attini/Archivio White Star: pages 200 top, 200 bottom, 200-201.
Marcello Bertinetti/Archivio White Star: pages 206-207.
Giulio Veggi/Archivio White Star: pages 200 center right, 201 bottom, 202-203, 203, 204, 205.
Enrico Martino: page 200 center left.
Philae
Antonio Attini/Archivio White Star: pages 208, 210-211, 212 bottom.
Giulio Veggi/Archivio White Star: pages 209, 212-213, 212, 214-215.
Guido Rossi/The Image Bank: pages 208-209.
Leptis Magna
Marcello Bertinetti/Archivio White Star: pages 224-225.
Araldo De Luca/Archivio White Star: pages 222-223.
Cesare Galli: pages 216, 216-217, 218, 219, 220-221, 221 top, 221 center.
T. Mosconi/Panda Photo: pages 226-227.
Giancarlo Zuin: page 221 bottom.
ASIA
Marco Casiraghi: pages 228-229.
Photobank: page 228 top right.
Alison Wright: page 228 left.
Livio Bourbon/Archivio White Star: pages 232-233, 234-235.
Nemrut Dagh
Massimo Brochi/Archivio White Star: pages 236-237, 237, 238-239, 240, 241, 243, 243, 244-245.
Ephesus
Antonio Attini/Archivio White Star: pages 246, 247, 250, 251, 252, 253.
Livio Bourbon/Archivio White Star: pages 248-249, 254-255.
Herodion
Marcello Bertinetti/Archivio White Star: pages 256-257, 258-259.
Itamar Grinberg: page 257 right.
Charles Lenars: page 257 left.
Masada
Antonio Attini/Archivio White Star: pages 261 top, 261 center, 263 center top, 263 right top.
Marcello Bertinetti/Archivio White Star: pages 260 top, 260-261, 262-263, 263 left, 264-265.
Itamar Grinberg: page 263 center bottom.
Petra
Antonio Attini/Archivio White Star: page 267.
Massimo Borchi/Archivio White Star: pages 266, 268, 269, 272, 273, 274, 275, 276, 277.
Giulio Veggi/Archivio White Star: pages 270-271.
Palmyra
Felipe Alcoceba: pages 278 top, 282 bottom, 287 top.
Giovanni Dagli Orti: pages 278 bottom, 285 top, 285 bottom left.
Suzanne Held: page 281 bottom.
Franck Lechenet/Ag. Hemispères: pages 278-279, 282-283, 286-287.
Robert Tixador/Ag. Top: pages 279 bottom, 280-281, 282 top, 282 center, 287 bottom.
Angelo Tondini/Focus Team: pages 281 top, 284, 285 bottom right.
Babylon
Bildarchiv Kulturbesitz: page 290-291.
Giovanni Dagli Orti: pages 289 center, 291 left top, 291 right.
Charles Lenars: page 289 bottom right.
R.M.N.: pages 290 top, 291 left bottom.
Henri Stierlin: page 289 top.
Robert Tixador/Ag. Top: pages 288 top, 288-289, 289 bottom left.
Ur
Giovanni Dagli Orti: pages 294 bottom, 295 top.
Henri Stierlin: pages 292 top, 293.
The Ancient Art & Architecture Collection: pages 294-295, 295 bottom.
Robert Tixador/Ag. Top: pages 292-293.
Persepolis
Aisa: pages 306-307.
Christophe Boisivieux: pages 308 bottom, 309 bottom, 310-311, 311 top.
E. Boubat/Ag. Top: page 303 top.
Marco Casiraghi: pages 298 bottom, 300 bottom, 300-301, 302-303, 308-309.
Giovanni Dagli Orti: page 305 right top.
Duclos-Gaillarde/Ag. Gamma: pages 298 center, 304, 305 center.
Suzanne Held: pages 296 left, 296-297, 297 bottom, 298 top, 301 bottom, 302 left, 303 bottom, 305 left, 305 bottom, 310 bottom, 311 bottom.
Henri Stierlin: pages 296 bottom, 300 top, 301 top, 308 top.
Minnella/Overseas: pages 298-299.
Sanchi
Marcello Bertinetti/Archivio White Star: pages 312-313, 315.
Livio Bourbon/Archivio White Star: pages 316-317.
Suzanne Held: pages 312 left, 313 bottom.
Enrico Martino: page 313 top.
Photobank: pages 313 center, 314, 318, 319.
Mamallipuram
Antonio Attini/Archivio White Star: pages 322-323, 328-329.
Photobank: pages 320, 321, 324 top, 324 center top, 324 bottom, 324-325, 325 bottom, 326-327, 326 bottom left, 327.
Robert Tixador/Ag. Top: page 324 center bottom.
Cesare Galli: page 326 bottom right.
Ajanta
Massimo Borchi/Archivio White Star: pages 336-337, 338-339.
Charles Lenars: page 332.
Photobank: pages 330, 330-331, 331 top left, 331 top right, 332-333, 333 bottom, 334, 335.
The Ancient Art & Architecture Collection: pages 331 center right, 331 bottom right.
Pagan
Christophe Boisivieux: pages 340-341, 341 top, 341 bottom, 342, 343 bottom, 344, 344-345, 345 left, 346, 346-347, 350 top right, 350-351, 351 top.
Francois Lochon/Corbis/Contrasto: pages 348-349
Photobank: pages 341 center, 343 left, 343 center, 347, 350 top left, 350 bottom left, 351 center, 351 bottom.
Alison Wright: page 345 right.
Borobudur
Marcello Bertinetti/Archivio White Star: pages 353, 354, 355, 356, 357, 358-359, 360-361.
Charles Lenars: page 352.
Photobank: pages 352-353.
Angkor
Livio Bourbon/Archivio White Star: pages 364-365, 370-371, 374-375.
Patrick Aventurier/Ag. Gamma: page 366 bottom.
Christophe Boisivieux: pages 362 top, 367 bottom right, 368-369, 368 bottom, 369 center left, 372 center top left, 377, 378 bottom, 379 top, 379 bottom right.
Marco Casiraghi: pages 363, 372 top left, 372 center bottom left, 376-377, 379 bottom left.
B. Harsford/Fotograff: pages 369 center right, 372 bottom right.
A. Lanzellotto/The Image Bank: pages 366-367.
Photobank: pages 362 bottom, 369 top, 372 bottom left, 378-379.
Ben Simmons/The Stock House: page 373.
Alison Wright: pages 367 top, 367 center, 367 bottom left, 369 bottom, 376.
Xi'an
Araldo De Luca/Archivio White Star: pages 382-383, 390-391, 392-393.
Brissaud/Ag. Gamma: page 381 bottom.
Giovanni Dagli Orti: pages 384-385, 386, 387, 388, 389.
Nigel Hicks/Woodfall Wild Images: page 385 bottom.
H.LLoyd/SIE: pages 380-381.
Angelo Tondini/Focus Team: page 384.
Luoyang
Suzanne Held: pages 400 bottom, 401 top.
Brian A. Vikander/Corbis/Contrasto: pages 396-397.
Christian Viojard/Ag. Gamma: pages 398, 399, 400-401, 401 bottom.
Werner Forman Archive: page 400 top.
AMERICAS AND OCEANIA
Angelo Tondini/Focus Team: page 402 left.
Massimo Borchi/Archivio White Star: pages 402-403 sullo sfondo, 402-403 center, 403 right, 406-407, 408-409.
Mesa Verde
Antonio Attini/Archivio White Star: pages 414-415.
Christophe Boisivieux: pages 410 bottom center, 413 left, 413 right bottom.
Jerry Jacka: page 413 right top.
Guido Rossi/The Image Bank: pages 410 bottom right, 411 bottom, 412.
Simon Wilkinson/The Image Bank: pages 410-411.
Teotihuacan
Antonio Attini/Archivio White Star: pages 416, 417, 418, 419, 420, 421, 422-423.
Monte Alban
Antonio Attini/Archivio White Star: pages 424, 425, 426, 427, 428, 429.
Palenque
Antonio Attini/Archivio White Star: page 441.
Massimo Borchi/Archivio White Star: pages 430, 431, 432-433, 434, 435, 436, 437, 438-439, 440.
Giovanni Dagli Orti: page 430.
Tikal
Massimo Borchi/Archivio White Star: pages 442, 443, 444, 445, 446-447, 448, 449.
Uxmal
Massimo Borchi/Archivio White Star: pages 450, 451, 452-453, 454, 455 left top, 455 right top, 455 center, 455 bottom, 456-457, 458-459, 458 bottom, 459 top, 459 bottom.
Chichén Itzá
Massimo Borchi/Archivio White Star: pages 460, 461, 462-463, 464, 465, 466 center, 466 bottom, 466-467, 468, 469.
Giovanni Dagli Orti: page 466 left top.
Chan Chan
Massimo Borchi/Archivio White Star: pages 470-471, 471 right top, 471 right center, 471 right bottom, 474-475.
Giovanni Dagli Orti: pages 472, 472-473, 473 left top.
Charles Lenars: pages 471 left top, 473 right top.
Cuzco
Antonio Attini/Archivio White Star: pages 476, 477, 478-479, 479 top, 479 center.
Yann Arthus Bertrand/Corbis/Contrasto: 480-481.
Giovanni Dagli Orti: page 479 bottom.
Ollantaitambo
Antonio Attini/Archivio White Star: pages 482, 483 top, 484, 485, 486-487.
Macchu Picchu
Marcello Bertinetti/Archivio White Star: pages 493 bottom, 494 left top.
Antonio Attini/Archivio White Star: pages 488, 489, 492, 492-493, 494 left center, 494 left bottom, 494 left top, 495, 496-497.
Massimo Borchi/Archivio White Star: pages 490-491.
Tiahuanaco
Antonio Attini/Archivio White Star: pages 498, 498-499, 500, 500-501, 501 left top.
Massimo Borchi/Atlantide: pages 499 bottom, 501 right top.
Giovanni Dagli Orti: page 501 top.
Easter Island
Bruno Barbier/Ag. Hemisperes: page 505 center.
Massimo Borchi/Atlantide: pages 504-505.
B.S.P.I./Corbis/Contrasto: 508-509
Guido Cozzi/Atlantide: pages 506 top, 507 top, 507 bottom.
The Image Bank: pages 502 top, 503.
Angelo Tondini/Focus Team: page 505 top.
Giancarlo Zuin: page 502 bottom.
A. Ponzio/Overseas: page 505 bottom.

All black-and-white maps are by Livio Bourbon